W9-BHP-436

THE EXURBANITES

THE EXURBANITES

BY A. C. SPECTORSKY

WITH DRAWINGS BY ROBERT OSBORN

J. B. LIPPINCOTT COMPANY—PHILADELPHIA & NEW YORK

For Susan and Kathy

LIST OF CHAPTERS

I

WHAT IS AN EXURBANITE?

I would live all my life in nonchalance and insouciance
Were it not for making a living, which is rather a nouciance.
—OGDEN NASH

On a blazing hot summer night, in a lush and sylvan part of the world within sixty miles of New York City, an atmosphere prevailed which may cast some light on the present denizens of the area. It was midweek. Sundown had not brought the customary cooling breeze and most people were reluctant to go indoors to attempt sleep. The children had been permitted to stay up later than usual and were larking around in the moonlight, half-nude and sweaty and hysterically happy. Their parents were flopped in deck chairs and on tubular metal-and-plastic chaises, iced drinks in one hand and with the other dabbing at mosquitoes.

The wives were exhausted from the heat of the day; the husbands, facing the full force of it after having been air-conditioned since morning (except for quick dashes from train to office to lunch to office to train), were restless and uncomfortable with the unadmitted disappointment at the difference between their day-

1

light concept of their country lives and the reality of this night. In spite of the oppressive heat, there was an almost pulsing excitement in the still air.

Who were these people? How did they come to be where they were, generating in rural surroundings an atmosphere of the East Fifties?

It would be correct—but not complete—to call them commuters. But let's start at the beginning. Just what is a commuter, besides a rider of trains? Let's look at him.

The commuter is distinguished from other mortals by (perhaps most notably) his remarkable vigor. Under physical and psychic strains which might easily prove too much for the average urbanite or countryman, he not only survives but thrives.

The physical strains of his life start early each working day. On the average he rises an hour before his urban fellow workers, dresses and breakfasts more quickly, drives from half a mile to ten miles to a station, rides a train for at least a half hour—and only then copes with the city transportation which takes his non-commuting colleagues from home to office. In the evening the process is reversed, and he has barely climbed from his car at an hour when city people have already been happily relaxed for an hour or two. His dinner is usually correspondingly late and either his postprandial leisure or his sleep are accordingly curtailed. In the wintertime he may seldom see his home by daylight until the week end. He enjoys certain advantages in the summer, but he continues to pay heavily for them.

Every commuter suffers additional physical strains to varying degrees in the daily need to keep up his home and grounds, an endless and never completed series of major and minor chores only some of which his pride and finances allow him to delegate to paid help, which is generally scarce, incompetent, overpaid, and contrary. Furthermore, no matter how much he enjoys doing things himself (a subject to be dealt with at some length later) he doesn't invariably enjoy it to the same degree, and there are times when it's downright irksome—but there the chores are, always, waiting for him.

There are other physical attritions to which he is subject, frequently self-imposed under the correct, or mistaken, notion that they are fun. These include such week-end activities as outdoor sports and games for which his weekday sedentary life leaves him physically unfit and unprepared, and whose sole advantage is frequently merely that they render him as physically exhausted as his labors have left him mentally exhausted.

The psychic strains are even greater, and it is a wonder that the commuter is not a raving psychotic. Certainly, the manner of his life is schizoid in the extreme. For the commuter is usually a symbol-manipulator who lives like a thing-manipulator. He is a deskman—goods and products are his concerns only to the extent that he manipulates the symbols which stand for them. He is not only content to have it thus, he's proud and happy. Yet daily he steps from the train which has borne him home and into his non-working life, and there he strives to live like a thing-manipulator.

A frequent prescription for the tired urbanite is a complete change of scene and activity, preferably to rural surroundings in which physical activity may be substituted for mental effort. From a therapeutic viewpoint this may seem to bear some relation to the commuter's daily alternation from working life to home life, but the resemblance is deceiving; the alternate hot and cold plunges which are a drastic prescription resorted to for short periods in the treatment of certain afflictions offer a closer parallel —except that the commuter undergoes the shock of sudden change as a regular part of his life. Man's amazing adaptability has frequently been noted, but it is worth calling special attention to this extreme example, in which the human organism flourishes in a state of remarkably stable ambivalence.

At this point, the reader may object that generalization and abstraction have gone too far, that there are group and individual variations which require recognition. The objection is not only sustained, it's emphatically insisted on.

To the non-observant rider on any of dozens of commuter trains plying their ways between New York City and the myriad stations within a sixty-mile radius, it would not be apparent that two distinct subspecies of Homo sapiens were sharing their means of transportation in amicable silence. About one group much is known: these are the suburbanites, who daily travel from and to their jobs and their habitats, the suburbs. Superficially, suburbanites' lives bear a fairly close resemblance to those of the other group, but there are marked and critical differences. Furthermore, although the suburbanite's mode of life has been not only fairly thoroughly explored but lately even glorified, the second subspecies has not even been given a name of its own. This is a new group, a new class, which no sociologist, economist, anthropologist of the past foresaw, and only a few contemporary social anthropologists have even recognized. This group has its own folkways, its own anxieties and aspirations, its own frustrations and fulfillments. Individuals and isolated clusters of the subspecies exist in the environs of other large urban centers in the United States, but only about New York City are there enough of them concentrated in communities to give those communities a unique flavor.

So, let us, right now, give this group and its milieus a name. The name of the subspecies, then, is Exurbanite; its habitat, the Exurbs. The exurb is generally further from New York than the suburb on the same railway line. Its houses are more widely spaced and generally more various and more expensive. The town center tends to quaintness and class, rather than modernity and glass, and the further one lives from the station the better.

Exurbanites are almost exclusively gainfully employed in some facet of that vast and ill-defined activity known as communications. They divide, roughly, into two groups: those who have commercialized their talents, and those who exploit the results—and the word "exploit" as used here has no pejorative connotations. Exurbanites not only work in closely allied fields, they work in close proximity, rather than fanning out from the New York terminals to scattered parts of the city as suburbanites do. They tend to eat in the same restaurants (frequently on each other's expense accounts), they reflect the same tastes in garb, décor,

CERTAINLY THE MANNER OF HIS LIFE
IS SCHIZOID IN THE EXTREME.

and the arts (with minor but inflexible differences which are dictated by occupation) and they all do well and live better.

And why are they called exurbanites? Because they are "ex" in the sense of "out of," "away from"—and in no other, for they will always be urbanites at heart. These short-haul expatriates really never leave town, though they live in the counties of Fairfield, Rockland, Bucks, Westchester, or on the North Shore of Long Island. They are not urbanites, or suburbanites, or ruralites —and this is one of the roots of their special, king-sized constellation of problems.

The word "exurb" (and its derivatives "exurban" and "exurbanite") carries no connotation of something that has ceased to be, of something in the past; rather what is intended is a clarification of the something extra and special that has characterized the journey of the exurbanite, out and away from the city, in a wistful search for roots, for the realization of a dream, for a home. Instinctively he was aware that he could never be happy in the suburbs, even if the suburbs had not already been crowded. His personality, his way of life, his habits—all were (and are) somewhat flamboyant, and the word "suburbs" conjured up for him a picture of dull and demure domesticity utterly foreign to him. A generation earlier he might have sat on the terrace outside the Dome or the Select, and talked of what was going on, back in New York. But now he has largely lost his taste for rebellion and for the more exacting intellectual and artistic pursuits; and so, instead of the Dome, it is a living room in Westport or Katonah; instead of the Select, it is a patch of lawn near Doylestown or New City. But still his talk is the same: he still gossips about what is going on, back in New York.

For the exurbanite is a displaced New Yorker. He has moved from the city to the country. So, indeed, have hundreds of thousands of Americans, especially since the second World War; but for the exurbanite the case is different: for him the change is an exile. He will never quite completely permit himself to be absorbed into his new surroundings; he never will acclimate. He may join the Parent-Teacher Association in his new home, he may attend town meetings, he will almost surely try his hand at gardening or farming; but spiritually he will always be urban, an irreconcilable whose step, after walking a hundred country lanes, is still steadiest when it returns to the familiar crowded cross-walks of Madison Avenue. Resident in the country he may be, under any of several estimable devices, e.g., "The school system is better"; "It's great to get away from that carbon monoxide"; "I'm a new man since I got into the rhythm of the seasons," but the customs that were his in the city remain his in the country.

The exurbanite is well-to-do. So, again, are many Americans; but the exurbanite differs in that he is well-to-do no matter what his temporary economic status. Thus, he may be spectacularly unemployed, may be stealthily slipping around corners to pick up his unemployment insurance check, but he is still upper-bracket, still living at the absolute rock-bottom minimum standard of $12,000 a year. Unemployed, free lance, employed, or owner of his own business, he is always well-heeled.

The exurbanite, at his most typical, is an idea man—as we have called him, a symbol-manipulator. That is, he writes, edits, or publishes books, magazines, or newspapers; writes, directs, designs, costumes, or appears in radio, television, motion picture, or Broadway entertainments; or he is an artist, illustrator, photographer; or he composes popular songs, or commercial jingles; or he conceives, writes, lays out, or otherwise perpetrates the advertising programs which in turn support the magazines, newspapers, radio, and television media; or he sells the time or space for such advertising. He is, then, a singularly commercial merchant of dreams for the rest of the nation. And in recent years he has even penetrated to America's symbolic heart: the Madison Avenue Approach has invaded the White House, for the purpose of making politics palatable. There are, of course, other Americans who engage in these various pursuits; but the exurbanite exercises definitive control over them; and Exurbia is their capital.

These people, God save us all, set the styles, mold the fashions, and populate the dreams of the rest of the country. What they do will be done, a few weeks or months later, by their counter-

parts in Lake Forest and Santa Barbara and on the Main Line.
What they decree, via such esoteric channels as the "People Are
Talking About . . ." feature in Vogue, will all too often be picked
up and actually talked about, in Beverly Hills, Grosse Pointe, and
Sewickley. What they tell us to buy, by God, we buy. How they
tell us to act (even though they themselves would never dream
of acting so) is a blueprint for our behavior—speaking on a
national basis. When a foreign manufacturer has a luxury item—
like the Jaguar—that he wants the American people to accept, he
is fully aware that his purposes will be served and his job three-
quarters accomplished as soon as he can contrive to cajole the
exurbanite into buying it. (The job of selling is, of course, en-
trusted to other exurbanites.) The man from Schweppes whis-
pered first into an exurban ear. The man in the Hathaway shirt
is an exurbanite. But it goes further:

Here walks a man whose political opinions are shaped by what
he reads on the editorial page of Life. There goes a woman who
sneers at such-and-such a movie because she subscribes to The
New Yorker. Yonder totters an ancient whose tic is ascribable to
the fact that he cannot shake from his mind's ear the words,
"Don't Be Half-Safe," sung to the tune of "The Volga Boatmen."
That teen-ager insisted on scuttling her naturally fresh appearance
in dutiful response to some offhand remarks in Mademoiselle.
The pinched expression on this man's face is habitual since his
wife has been on the wonder diet touted by a woman's magazine
(in an article written by an exurban woman who was, and is, a
natural size-sixteen). On every hand the results are visible, tangible, often depressing, and frequently comic; manners and morals,
fads and foibles, furnishings and food; styles in clothes or in
housing, in games or in sex—even in the pets the ideal U. S.
family should take under its roof—all these are determined in
Exurbia.

The exurbanites may not have been the inventors, the dis-
coverers, although often they were; they may regard the fashions
they set with contempt and derision; but set them they most
certainly do. They are our nation's movers and shakers for ideas

GOODS AND PRODUCTS ARE HIS CONCERNS
ONLY TO THE EXTENT THAT HE MANIPULATES
THE SYMBOLS WHICH STAND FOR THEM.

and opinions, for what is fashionable and what is fun. And for what is dismal and disconcerting, too: for over there is a child whose sleep is richly disturbed by dreams that have as their starting-point—what? A comic-book? A television program? It doesn't matter: an exurbanite drew the pictures, or contrived the dialogue, or published the book, or directed the program. The dreams' origin was in Exurbia—and not only the child's dreams, but perhaps yours as well. The dreams may be of aspiration, or of terror, or of a new washing-machine. But in all likelihood they were first conceived on the 8:12.

It is indisputable that these people whose commodities are words, pictures, numbers, musical notes, are at the core of all, or almost all, that is thought and seen and heard and dreamed. Yet at the same time they are really far from it. They never participate. They set the stage, they dress the cast, they dim the lights and part the curtains on a nation's emotional experiences, but they are always backstage, never able fully to share in the reactions or the dreams of the audience. Even such a national emotional experience as war finds them busily engaged in manipulating the mass emotions—to sell war bonds, to inform and educate the troops, to buoy morale, to tell our allies what we are like, to divide and confuse our enemies, to assure and reassure those who stay at home, to record the history of the event—but seldom to participate in it. Thus they are cheated. But though many of them may be yearning, just for once, to be able to slip out and join the audience and sit back, relax, and become part of the crowd, at the same time they would scorn to do so. Being backstage is being in the know; hep; even hip. Being backstage is superior (and it pays well, too). To be in the audience is to be a square, to be the old lady from Dubuque, to be one of the cretins who crowd to watch radio or television quiz programs. To be in the audience is to be in the mass, the mass for whom the exurbanites manipulate mass communications.

There is, finally, one other gross clue by which the exurbanite may be identified, and it comes about in consequence of all his other distinguishing attributes: it is that he has created for him-

... WHOSE STEP, AFTER WALKING A HUNDRED COUNTRY LANES, IS STILL STEADIEST WHEN IT RETURNS TO THE FAMILIAR CROSSWALKS.

self problems, conflicts. Once again, it is obvious that every American has anxieties and conflicts; but in the case of the exurbanite, they are special and unique; they are self-contrived; they exist over and above the endemic malaises of the era; and, by their nature, they can never be resolved. These besetting ills are so uniquely characteristic that they may be lumped together under the label of the Exurban Syndrome. The most important of these conflicts deserves some random attention here, as the exurbanite is stepping forward to be introduced. This is the internal conflict set in motion by his quite natural desire to escape forever from the fantastic competition, the harassing frustrations, and the hideous insecurities of his daytime world in the communications industry, from what, in sum, he refers to as the Rat Race.

Every exurbanite—and there is no exception to this rule—believes firmly that he is escaping from the rat race, at least in part, at least for a time, by moving out of the city where the race is run and finding lodgment in Exurbia.

Most exurbanites—and there are very few exceptions to this rule—will assure you that by moving to the exurbs they have made a major step in the realization of their ambitions; they want nothing further, just more and better of the same. The average exurbanite has achieved, he will assure you in all seriousness, or is on the right path to achieving, his Dream, his Unlimited Dream.

How long it will take him to perceive how limited his dream is in fact varies from individual to individual. There are some who still, after ten or fifteen years of exurban life, insist with utmost vehemence that they are coursing down the one-way autobahn to happiness, that they would not change their way of life no matter what the Devil offered them. But the passion with which they deny that their dream is limited or tainted or corrupted suggests that they themselves may feel misgivings, that there are times when even happiness—or barbiturates, gin, or sheer fatigue —can't get them by that four a.m. spell of insomnia when a man faces himself with something akin to sober horror.

And, sure enough, sooner or later they give themselves away

by revealing their Secret Dream. Forgetful, they may reveal such a secret dream within the hour of insisting they have already scaled the summit of their loftiest ambition. Invariably—and there is no exception to *this* rule—their secret dream, if achieved, would take them still further away from New York, and in every case is designed to obliterate all memory of the rat race. Sadly, the secret dream is almost never realized (some say it never is).

But that Exurbia is a strictly Limited Dream most exurbanites come to realize, consciously or otherwise.

Thus far, we've looked at some of the stigmata by which an exurbanite may be recognized, and have only briefly glanced at the psychic organization—or disorganization—which lies beneath his commonly quite charming exterior. Later, we'll look deeper into those covert aspects of his personality which make him unique (and often uniquely miserable) and which render him particularly susceptible to the joys and torments of his limited and secret dreams. Right now, though, let's deal with tangibles and save the deep analysis until we've seen more of Exurbia, the scene of the limited dream.

2

WHAT AND WHERE IS EXURBIA, AND HOW IT GREW

If I ever adopt a coat of arms, it will show a ravenous draftsman sighting through a transit, over a shield marked "Soft Pickings."

—S. J. PERELMAN

MOST exurbanites (there are exceptions) live in a fan-shaped area twenty-five miles deep which reaches from the New York-New Jersey state line in the northwest around to the north shore of Long Island in the northeast. The exurbs begin, however, only after the suburbs peter out: spreading outward from New York City, roughly the first twenty-five miles is solid Suburbia; thereafter, for a belt extending another twenty-five miles, come the exurbs. Exurbia being a recent phenomenon, and a unique one, it may be interesting to explore the question of how the exurban way of life came to be first superimposed on and then to supersede earlier cultural patterns in certain areas, and then to ascertain why (in addition to fulfilling the minimum

14

logistic requirements for commuting) those areas were chosen by the pioneer exurbanites.

In other words, where are the exurbs and why? Let's see what we can learn from looking over the shoulder of a prospective exurbanite who locked himself in his office some few seasons ago in order to wrestle with the problem of where to move. He was a methodical man and he had also served a jolt with the army's corps of engineers, so he set about his labors scientifically. He had armed himself with a map of the countryside around New York City and with a compass. Sixty minutes was as much as he proposed to spend in the process of getting to his office. Sixty minutes, he told himself, equates to roughly fifty railroad miles: he inserted one foot of the compass at a point midway between Pennsylvania Station and Grand Central Station, took a deep breath, and inscribed a circle.

Within his circle, lay both the suburbs and the exurbs. What our specimen instinctively rejected, and what he instinctively included as within the realm of possibility, showed that he had the true stuff of an exurbanite in him.

He first glanced curiously at New Jersey. It is too much to say that he had previously been unaware that so much of New Jersey lies within a fifty-mile radius of New York City; he had, after all, friends who lived outside Peapack and Bernardsville, for instance, and he had occasionally driven through the section on his way to Princeton football games. But fundamentally, to him, New Jersey was the place from which, on the prevailing west wind over the Hudson, came a bad smell. Beyond it, though, was Bucks County, Pennsylvania, an exurb if ever there was one.

To the north were Rockland and Orange counties in New York. Both lie west of the Hudson. Both, he felt, warranted a look.

The Hudson, flowing south, cut across his map like a clock-hand pointing to twelve o'clock. On its east were Dutchess and Putnam counties and, directly south, Westchester County. The northern part of Westchester he hatched over with a pencil. Here were Katonah and Pawling, Chappaqua and Pleasantville. Good possibilities.

Southern Westchester—that is to say, Mamaroneck, Pelham, New Rochelle, Scarsdale, White Plains—all this is solid Suburbia. Our man ignored it completely.

But beyond southern Westchester, to the east, is Fairfield County, Connecticut. Here he was on firm ground. Here he had often week-ended; here lived many friends; here, he had heard, still other friends were planning to move. Fairfield County includes, as he considered it, towns like Westport, Weston, Darien, New Canaan, Greenwich, Redding Ridge, Bethel, Rowayton. A most promising territory.

If the Hudson River is, on a clock's face, the hand that points to noon, Long Island Sound is a hand pointing to two o'clock. And between two and three lies Long Island. On Long Island are Brooklyn and Queens which, to the exurbanite, are two adjoining plague spots. Beyond is Nassau County, a hotbed of real estate subdivisions, where, in the last decade, houses have been thrown up by the scores of thousands, architecturally as indistinguishable as English sparrows. It is said that when a good subdivider dies, he does not go to Heaven, he goes to Nassau County. It is almost exclusively suburban. But the extreme north shore of Nassau and adjoining Suffolk County are more approximately exurban. Our man did not rule them out.

Rockland County, then, and perhaps part of Orange; northern Westchester, and perhaps part of Putnam and Dutchess; Fairfield County in Connecticut; a thin slice of the North Shore of Long Island; all were good possibilities. To these he added, thanks to the engulfing wave of exurbanites to all available neighborhoods, a few isolated outposts of Exurbia in Mercer and Somerset counties in New Jersey where, *faute de mieux*, live a few pioneer exurbanites who tried to find themselves houseroom in the more acceptable exurbs, but discovered that real estate values had become, even for them, exorbitant. (Their beachheads, if experience affords a trustworthy yardstick, will grow.) Our man even considered a new and flourishing outpost in the environs of Princeton, inhabited by a strange admixture of comparatively young college faculty members (no full professors) and commuting exurbanites, many of whom divide their work between New York and Philadelphia; but that was as far as he would go.

Thanks to our methodical friend, we can now feel pretty sure about the geographical limits of the Exurbia of the 1940's and mid-1950's. But what was it that determined his procedure for so definitely finding a new habitat? Ignorant urbanites who have never felt the exurban itch used to attribute it to snobbery, to a desire to be different, exclusive, aloof. Nowadays, however, even the most calloused and insensitive know that this explanation is not only inadequate but also inaccurate. For it is not snobbery but conformity that plays a major part in magnetizing a prospective exurbanite to his future home although, ironically, he frequently alleges he is moving to escape from the stereotype of city life, a rationalization which is the more curious coming from a man whose work-area, whose clothes, whose restaurants stamp him as among the most uncompromisingly conventional of men.

But knowing where Exurbia is, and that the need to conform is one of the major drives which impelled its more recent residents to seek its increasingly crowded pastures, doesn't explain how and why it came to be and why it grew. What is it, after all, that makes an exurb acceptable to an exurbanite?

The growth of an exurb follows a fixed pattern and, to understand the latter-day recrudescence of these neighborhoods, it is useful to recall something of their past. They are alike in being physically attractive, for the most part, and for having been settled early in the country's history. Indeed, the exurbs are rich in historical tradition: the British landed in Westport (Fairfield County), Washington crossed the Hudson at Sneden's Landing (Rockland County), Bucks County in Pennsylvania was the scene of a dozen minor skirmishes of the Revolution; in northern Westchester (as today) Tories undercut the insurgents, and so on. An occasional statue or commemorative plaque, reverently disposed in these neighborhoods, attests to the brave days when; or marks where famous residents lived, or were born, or spent the night. But the original settlers have, largely, removed.

They left, either to join the various movements westward, or, enticed by city lights and the mushrooming growth of industrialism, to turn to the city. Those who remained have endowed the regions with a faint trace of native speech still to be discerned by the exurbanite with an acute ear, when he turns up at a local garage to have his valves ground, or when, at last resource, he seeks a baby-sitter at eight-thirty of a Saturday night.

Into the vacuum created when the original settlers departed,* there came, at the turn of the century, the immigrants, chiefly Italian and Polish. Some of these still farm the stony meadows; their descendants, with a glint in their eyes, have accepted the exurbanites as fair game, moved in on them, and, in the capacity of storekeepers or handymen, cheerfully ream them at every opportunity.

Meantime, in the age of the robber barons, there had come those who, sleek and fat, bought up huge tracts of the choicest countryside, imported flocks of sheep to crop the lawns to the proper length, and settled down to a splendiferous life of Veblenian fooferaw. Their gaudy history has been delightedly recorded elsewhere; here it suffices to say that to this era belongs the settlement of Tuxedo and Rumson, of Southport and Oyster Bay. Along both shores of the Sound and on either lip of the Hudson the forty- and fifty-, even the one-hundred-and-ten-room castles went up. These country demesnes, whose owners engaged in all the appropriate social customs, with the occasional exception of *droit du seigneur*, ranked with the nation's showiest. Some of them, indeed, are still extant, their present-day owners having successfully weathered the Sixteenth Amendment to the Constitution.† The pleasances have been whittled away to permit the incursions of pre-fab bungalows; the messuages have been rented

---

* Those who remained are occasionally of a fruity vintage. Thus, in Rockland County, there still exist descendants of the Jackson whites, spiritual first-cousins of the celebrated Jukes family.

* The black day when the Congress was constitutionally empowered "to lay and collect taxes on incomes, from whatever sources derived," was February 25, 1913. It is pertinent to note that Connecticut was one of the three states specifically to reject ratification.

to deserving, relatively indigent Old Dealers; but the owners still hang on, crusty and unreconstructed. These men, it should be noted, leaders in the city's financial and business community, blazed the commuting trail. At a time when commuting was still unheard of, when the exurbanite was still a mere gene in, as it might have been, Kansas, these men had to travel by train to and from the city: for their greater convenience, they contrived the private club car, still, in those innocent, taxless days, in fact a club. Lineal descendants of these club cars still roll, dignified appendages to the faster commuter trains.

The next notable change came in the 1920's and 1930's. Numerically, it was trivial; culturally, it was decisive. It was the advent and relatively brief residence of artists.

They were dedicated folk; they came to work, not to play. They came looking for a place where they would be able to put in a solid, undisturbed eight hours of concentration a day at easel or worktable. They had tired of the synthetic, non-creative Bohemians of Greenwich Village who, in their dirndls and corduroys, had already infested such hideaways as Woodstock so thickly that it was beginning to take on the appearance of Eighth Street and Sixth Avenue on a Saturday night. They were looking for three things: something inexpensive, something quiet and remote, but something not too far from New York City's galleries and museums. The suburbs were no answer; they discovered the exurbs. Men like Henry Varnum Poor settled in Rockland County; when Peter Blume announced to his Woodstock friends that he was moving to a place called Darien, most of them were hearing the name for the first time (and one or two of them, making a joke that at once became stale, murmured some variation on the theme of "stout Cortez").

On the heels of these pioneer artists came a few writers, then a trickle of stalwarts from the group that composed the Algonquin's Round Table. A handful of Broadway figures ventured timidly out into the country, just for the summer, blinked their eyes in the unaccustomed sunlight, and began tentatively casing cow-

barns, while visions of experimental summer theatres danced in
their heads. It was the first hint that a place in the country might
become fashionable in their set.

And now, in many cases driving out the pioneer artists and
writers, came the first appreciable wave of exurbanites—the com-
mercially successful artists and writers and editors. There was, in
those quaint days, no such thing as café society, but these people
would, when that amorphous group did come into existence, fall
naturally into it.

A poet, W. H. Auden, has called ours the Age of Anxiety, and
surely it is an age in which the figure of the psychoanalyst looms
large, even if perceived only dimly, sitting behind and just to one
side of a reclining figure. An essayist and critic, Louis Kronen-
berger, agreeing with Auden, went on to dub ours the Age of
Publicity. Certainly for the exurbs to have filled up, as they have,
nearly to the bursting-point, the publicist, in his various guises—
Broadway columnist, press agent, society chatterbox, vice-president
in charge of public relations—had to exercise his talents.

The exurbs would not have filled only because the suburbs
were overflowing and there were still people who wanted to move
out of the city for the sake of their children or for their own
peace of mind. The limelight had first to play on a few of the
city's darlings—the Broadway figures and the commercially successful artists and writers; the tattletales in the gossip columns
had first to tell of gay week ends around the swimming-pools of
the sleek, the witty, and the casually extramarital. The rest was
foreordained. Slowly at first, and latterly with a rush, all those who
are on the fringe of the arts decided that what was good enough
for artists would be even better for them—and besides, they de-
served it more, since they had more money, and since much of
their company's money was spent precisely in hiring these artists.

If the commercially successful artists and entertainers who
colonized Bucks, Rockland, and Fairfield counties, and the com-
mercially successful editors, writers, and publishers who colonized
northern Westchester and the North Shore of Long Island made
up the first wave of genuine exurbanites, the second wave—which

can be dated as taking place around 1938-40—consisted of those on the fringe of the commercial arts. In this wave were the more important executives of advertising, and the more important executives on the business side of the radio, newspaper, magazine, and book-publishing industries. Just after the second World War came the biggest influx of all: the junior executives, those who follow the market leaders, the up-and-coming eager beavers, men in their middle and late thirties, the ones who wanted to do the thing-to-do. And the thing-to-do, it had become abundantly clear, was to move to the country—and where else but the exurbs?

Typically, the move is not made all of a piece. There is an almost set pattern to the procedure by which the urban itch is transformed into the exurban reality, a period when the exurban-ite-to-be is in transition. His first exposure to Exurbia may have taken place years ago during visits which stirred in him no special feelings, unless they were those of annoyance at the inconvenience of the country, or the miseries of timetable slavery.

But there comes that first visit after the birth of the itch, and he's on his way. Usually, he arrives as a week-end guest during the summer, or as a late and unexpected entry for dinner as a result of two too many cocktails with an exurban colleague in the Biltmore bar. This time, he sees Exurbia with new eyes. He sniffs the air and almost paws the ground. He's equipped not with rose-colored glasses, but with 3-D and Technicolor wide-screen glasses, and the sounds of sparrows are stereophonically registered on his brain as a heavenly choir. Even his host's children seem tolerable—a sure sign that he's a goner.

His stations of the exurban cross now follow in order: summer renter, year-round renter, summer-cottage owner, year-round owner, old-time established year-round owner, acreage owner (as opposed to lot owner), and finally property owner, in which capacity, for "protection," he buys as many acres as he can afford —a word which is here used very loosely indeed. For by this time he has become cranky. There are too many, he says, goddam new-comers in this town.

And so they came, and so they still come, but it would be fair

to say that after the second World War the exurban migration
ceased to be a series of ever larger waves and became a flood.

Yet to establish the point requires the performance of more
than simple head counting. The problem is how to separate sheer,
mere commuters from exurbanites. After all, the trend out of
urban centers which is so notable a feature of national life is not
restricted to workers in the communications industry. During the
earlier years of exurban growth there were many city-dwellers who
were finding apartments hard to get, who were becoming dissatis-
fied with the New York City public school system and, at the
same time, were finding the rising cost of living a barrier to
putting their children in private schools. They, like city folk
everywhere, were getting sick of crowds and racket and traffic. And
those whose move from New York City was simply a local reflection of the national exodus were in some cases forced to move
into what we have arbitrarily labeled the exurbs, for the reason
that they could find no suitable home in the suburbs, or wanted
more rural surroundings.

But in recent years these people have virtually stopped emi-
grating to Exurbia because of the fantastic rise in real estate
values, for which the exurbanites are almost wholly responsible.
A desirable acre in Westport, for example, which might have
been bought for under $2,000 ten years ago, will fetch as high
as $10,000 today. This puts Westport property pretty much be-
yond the reach of that segment of the non-exurban middle class
which might otherwise find it an agreeable place to live.

So an approximately pure assay of exurban development may
be obtained by counting the number of commutation tickets sold
in selected years only in those towns which are key exurban
strongholds. When one does this, and bears in mind that a great
many exurbanites are not regular enough commuters to buy commutation tickets, and that many others commute by car, then one
can be presumed to have a true reflection (if not a head count)
of exurban growth.

Thus, back in 1935, no more than 318 people walked or were
driven to the platform of the Westport station to catch com-

muting trains. The number rose, slowly at first: 390 in 1938, 428
in 1939; then it jumped. It was 800 in 1949—the year of the big
wave. It was nearly 1,000 in 1951; by 1954 it had soared to more
than 1,200. All these figures are for the month of January, a
month regarded as typical by the fact-finders of the New York,
New Haven and Hartford Railroad.

What is true of Westport is true of nearly every station on the
New Haven's right of way from Port Chester, the last stop (outward bound) before the New York-Connecticut state line, to
Fairfield and Stratford, the last practicable exurban roosts (Stratford is 59.1 railroad miles from New York). Here are the totals,
in commutation tickets for those stations:

1935	1949	1954
4,292	8,787	11,427

an increase of nearly 250 percent in less than two decades.

And what is true on the New Haven is true on the New York
Central, which serves the communities of northern Westchester
and Putnam counties. Chappaqua's commuters were up from 306
in 1931 to 691 in 1949 to 904 in 1954. Bedford Hills, in the same
period, went from 177 to 243; Croton Falls from 22 to 98;
Brewster from 134 to 272.

The same can be said of commutation growth from those communities that are exurban on Long Island's North Shore; and of
the exurban communities whose hardy adopted sons and daughters, flying in the face of reason, undertake to commute from
Rockland County and Bucks County.

It may be wondered, at this point, why it seemed necessary in
assessing exurban development to resort to a commuter-ticket
count of selected stations when there are available from such
reliable sources as the Regional Plan Association exact figures on
population growth in commuting areas. The reason casts an interesting additional light on Exurbia. The fact is that population
growth far exceeds commuter growth in Exurbia because a siz-
able proportion of residents in Exurbia comprise the vast army
of those whose income is derived from selling goods and services

to exurbanites, who are, almost by definition, as incapable of making and doing for themselves as they are eager and able to pay for the things made and done.

A city family living in a four- or five-room apartment and owning one car can make use of only so much maid service and so much repair service for its radios, television set, iron, toaster, and car, and most home maintenance is taken care of by the landlord. But move the same family to Exurbia, and the servicing field day begins. It would be cruel to expose the extent of it when they first move, when they're in the stage of buying and building and remodeling. But even when they're established— and have grown more cautious about buying all the goods and services they're told they need—their dependence on help is stunning to behold.

Eight to ten rooms and a two-car garage is about average for an exurban family. In and surrounding these are, among other exurban appurtenances (and in addition to what the family had in the city): freezer, washer, ironer, drier, water pump, septic tank, electric garbage disposer, automatic heater, automatic hot water heater, all needing service; garden lawn and driveway to maintain; two cars, which average twenty miles a day each, to be kept in shape despite the beating they take on country roads and standing outdoors in all weather; outdoor furniture to scrape and paint annually and stow and exhume seasonally; house to keep painted, roof to repair, leaders and gutters to clear of leaves; weeds and poison ivy to spray; storm windows and screens to be seasonally alternated, painted, cleaned, repaired; storm damage to repair; children, sitters and maids to be taxied; a complete set of country clothes and gear for sport and leisure (in addition to a full city wardrobe) to be kept mended, cleaned, occasionally pressed; pets to be doctored; to say nothing of such outdoor gadgets as mowers (hand and power), trimmers, cultivators, electric worm-diggers, and other outdoor paraphernalia which constantly need paid servicing and frequently regular paid use. If the exurbanite fancies himself a home workshop wallah, there's his abuse of the unfamiliar toys to be dealt with; and if the family owns a boat . . . ! And by the way, anybody need a tree surgeon? Probably everybody, but certainly every exurbanite. He may not think so, and his trees may not think so, but the tree surgeon knows.

Purveyors of goods and services are not all newcomers, of course; perhaps more than half of them are recruited from the grown children of the natives who once farmed the lands exurbanites now live on. (Parenthetically, there are some services performed by exurbanites—in certain localities more exurban wives peddle real estate part-time than there are properties to sell.) It seems safer to measure the number of exurbanites by commuter-ticket count, and it's certainly the more conservative method.

So far, we've talked about Exurbia as though it were uniform in origin and background and present state of being throughout its geographic extent. This is far from the case. Exurbia, in fact, is like an ancient country before the days of its unification, when each duchy, fief, and earldom, each kingdom within a kingdom, had its individual manners and customs, even—despite a shared mother tongue—its own language habits.

This exurban differentiation has accelerated in the past ten years, for a reason which is not far to seek. For just as Exurbia appealed to would-be exurbanites, so like-minded and like-mannered people who planned to move to Exurbia selected like exurbs. Each new exurbanite who finally chose Westport over Rockland, or Bucks over northern Westchester, made the job of selection for those who followed him easier, for the mere presence of each contributed to defining the differences which are now so clearly apparent. Today, it's safe to say, most Westport exurbanites would feel strange and lonely in New City (Rockland), or New Hope (Bucks). And, most certainly, vice versa.

3

THE EXURBS:
FAIRFIELD, BUCKS, ROCKLAND

Next to drinking brandy before breakfast, the most fatal mistake a man can commit is to isolate himself in the country.

—S. J. PERELMAN

AMONG the exurbs, three—Fairfield, Bucks, Rockland—stand out as possessing more of what is uniquely exurban than any other places in the world. Yet the three present striking contrasts visually, atmospherically, in the attitudes and social organization of their inhabitants, and in these people's professional connections with New York City.

Fairfield is for the most part fairly flat, although as one proceeds eastward away from the city it opens up into slightly rolling country with an occasional sharp ridge presaging the hillier land which, beyond the county's boundary to the northeast, turns into the Berkshire foothills. And Fairfield has the Sound, and a consequent fringe of shore communities with boating exurbanites

26

in residence. By contrast, Bucks is inland-rural, in appearance evenly undulant as a sine curve; and Rockland perches and nestles on crags and steep hillsides, in tight canyon-like valleys, on brief plateaus with a view of the Hudson.

Architecturally and in interior décor, Fairfield hews a line whose terminals are, at one end, early American, and at the other Bauhaus modern. Bucks favors the Pennsylvania Dutch fashion, with an admixture of chi-chi Victorian and Japanese-y modern. Rockland is eclectic and individual, but a house-count and a living-room-count show a strong preference for self-consciously de-emphasized, we-just-happen-to-prefer-it Colonial.

To date, Fairfield, Bucks, and Rockland exurbanites have shown good taste in eschewing such newer styles as Flat-lot Split Level, and Noxious Ranch House, although suburban deployments of both, supported by flanking movements of Gas-station Modern, are rearing their ugly roofs in—you'll pardon the expression; it's a nasty one in Exurbia—housing developments. In Fairfield, these are being populated by youngsters who 'opes to be real exurbanites some day.

They probably won't be, though. Right now, they are for the most part employed at modest salaries in satellite jobs, which are only somewhat more than clerical, in the less-creative departments of the communications businesses. In the city, they compensate for this by being more undeviating in their adherence to the appearances of success in their cadre than the medium and big wheels they serve—and plot to replace. But in spending $10,000 they can't afford for a development house worth about half that, for the sake of an exurban address and a seat on the right train, they have already betrayed in a major way that lack of discernment which will preclude full exurban realization. To be a successful exurbanite (or just an exurbanite; there's no other kind) you have to be sensitive to what's acceptable, and there's no book to look it up in, nor anyone to tell you—though there are plenty who will judge instantly, with an inward sneer and a cool outward blandness which is murderously deceptive. The housing-development hopeful is a personally doomed variant of exurbanite,

but the increasing number of his warrens in Fairfield may indicate
that his foothold will keep growing with the years. So far, Bucks
and Rockland have suffered less from these incursions than other
exurbs, but they are subject to something perhaps even more
daunting: the encroachments of industry and the purely suburban
housing that goes with it.

And what of the exurbanites themselves? These days, Fairfielders are for the most part frankly committed to commercialism,
with emphasis on the commercializing of the arts. Compulsive
socializing is almost universal among them, with quantity a paramount objective. Rocklanders are different. The leaders and pace
setters are recruited from those who have done their creative best
in art, theatre, literature, music, and who have been fortunate
enough to find a lucrative market for their work. Rocklanders
are, for exurbanites, fiercely individualistic; it is part of their credo
to assert that they, unlike Fairfielders, moved out of the city to
get really away. Their socializing is selective, insistently informal,
stratified by cliques. Among exurbanites, Buckminsters are the
most nearly ruralized. They prefer to go broke and blistered by
trying to farm rather than strive for the junior-estate way of
life as practiced in Fairfield (at which they turn up their noses),
or the eccentric-recluse, country-gentleman manner of Rockland
(which they accept as suitable if you like it, but how can you?).

Much of the foregoing is explainable, in part, by circumstances
of work and travel. Fairfielders are in the main daily commuters
whose deskwork is done in New York in an office, or office building, and whose contact and personal public relations work is done
socially on the train and in the county. They must socialize to
keep their positions, if for no other reason. Rocklanders tend to
be seclusive and seemingly anti-social because they don't commute
regularly and do hard and serious work at home. Since they tend
to irregular hours and since much of their hardest creative thinking looks, to the outsider, like sitting around and twiddling, they
must protect themselves from uninvited dropper-inners and from
the temptations of procrastination. Buckminsters are so far from
their jobs, and their train schedules are so punishing, that many,

if not most, have a city pied-à-terre, whence they conduct a lot of their social lives, saving the time in the exurb for that ungrateful, taxing, expensive, dear farm.

The contrasts indicated so far serve to illustrate how different these three exurbs are from each other. Individual scrutiny will show how, from common roots and common motives, each developed its own distinguishing characteristics.

1

It is only fitting that, in any discussion of the exurbs, Fairfield County's name should lead the roll. To use a speech-habit of many of its inhabitants: A, it is the most famous; B, it is the fastest-growing; C, it is the richest in exurban manifestations. The fact is that Fairfield County is the archetype of exurbs. So rich is the complexity of its social life and so exotic are its communal customs, it is remarkable that very few exurbanites have withdrawn, overwhelmed, to brood in solitary silence somewhere in the woods north of Redding Ridge. There is a secessionist movement out that way, incidentally, but its adherents are for the most part non-commuting "geniuses" and its membership is small.

Since any tour of inspection will necessarily involve being severely jounced about, for the roads are formidably rutted by the incredible, the comic, and the melancholy, it would be prudent to delay the start of the journey long enough to stow away a few homely commonplace facts, as ballast.

Fairfield is one of Connecticut's eight counties, encompassing 633 square miles, bounded on the east by the Housatonic River, on the south by Long Island Sound, on the west by the surburbs of southern Westchester, and, in the north, fading vaguely off into a *terra incognita* of woods and farmland. Its population, concentrated along the shoreline, exceeds 560,000 (a thirty percent increase over 1940). The county is traversed by three roughly parallel highways; the Boston Post Road hugging the coast; the new, truck-infested Thruway; and, further inland, the Merritt Parkway. From these, ribs thrust out—state roads that bind the exurb together, Westport to Wilton and Weston, Fairfield to Easton and Redding Ridge, New Canaan and Silvermine to Darien and the non-exurban city of Norwalk.

Of course, the county is larger than the exurb. On entering Fairfield across New York's state line from Westchester, the first town is Greenwich, and here all is still suburban. It is wealthy, it is exclusive, it is even manorial, but it is still suburban. Here, real estate values soared early and held fast, and of the subsequent wave of exurbanites who came scrambling out of the metropolis, only the best-heeled could look for houseroom without blenching visibly.

The same, to a lesser extent, is true of the residential area around Stamford; although here, too, and especially in North Stamford Hills, there is a scattered complement of exurbanites.

The exurb proper does not begin until further east. The mink curtain may be said to fall just west of Darien, encompassing within its fold Noroton. A three-pronged base here also holds down a bastion of the old aristocracy of wealth: the Noroton Yacht Club, the Oxbridge Hunt Club, and the Wee Burn Golf Club. Sharing their rarefied atmosphere are the Tokeneke Club and a region of rock and tangled scrub along the shore, a residential section, known as Tokeneke. Here are a few modern mansions, many older and more ornate ones, some fabulous dwellings (including one that has a baronial hall decorated with trophies of the chase in Africa and housing a cathedral-sized organ), a few Italian villas, and several miles of private bridlepaths and semiprivate roads. But Tokeneke's lovely and rocky shoreline does not extend its exclusive sway very far: Tokeneke Creek joins Five Mile River, which borders the eastern side of Tokeneke, and immediately the atmosphere changes. For on the other side of that narrow river lies Rowayton, a delicious and crazy hodgepodge of boatyards, lobster fishermen, artists, writers, boating enthusiasts, and just plain local people.

Five Mile River, with Darien on one side and Rowayton on the other, is one of the loveliest small-craft harbors in the East. Fifty-thousand-dollar, twelve-meter racing yachts are berthed beside Bahamian ketches and old Friendship sloops. Fishermen, and local kids in outboards and sailing prams, weave in and out among yachts and houseboats flying the burgees of yacht clubs from Maine to Florida, or scoot under the clipper bow of a Chesapeake bugeye on which live the happily married and comparatively fundless offspring of two millionaire families.

Rowayton itself is all, all wrong, as anyone who lives there will tell you. The wonderful waterfront in the town proper is occupied almost entirely by stores; jerry-built Victorian is Rowayton's major architectural style. It has no class whatever. In fact, the town has no tangible status at all; it just happens to be one of the most engagingly cockeyed, delightful places in the exurb, as is attested by its real estate values, which have tripled and quadrupled in the past few years. Typical and revealing of the Rowayton scene is the fact that the Rand yachts in recent years have been berthed right opposite the drugstore, in such fashion that these one-hundred-foot-plus floating palaces dominate the mainstreet landscape—and that the local residents call each of them "London Terrace," not in malice or awe, but just out of homey good humor.

Eastward from Rowayton is the elegant Wee Burn beach, then Rowayton's own raffishly gay beach, then Roton Point (which once sported an amusement park); then Bell Island, a knobby bump packed solid with houses as close as they can be got to each other—and with two of the best beaches anywhere along the shore and, improbably enough, the atmosphere of a Mediterranean village; then Wilson Point Harbor, another yacht-filled marine playground; then Wilson Point itself, a newer and even richer Tokeneke; and on beyond the Norwalk Islands, Norwalk Harbor (half-commercial, half-pleasure), and so past Saugatuck Shores to Westport's Cedar Point Harbor, one of the prettiest and most difficult to sail into and out of in the area. Adjoining Cedar Point is Westport's Compo Beach, where swim the younger—that is to say, the non-pool-owning—exurbanites.

A few scant years ago, it would have been accurate to say that at this point, only a trifle more than halfway along Fairfield

County's shoreline, the further limits of the exurb were in sight, perhaps somewhere between Greens Farms and Southport. But exurbs are yeasty affairs: they keep expanding. Today, well inside the exurb is Southport, one of the most beautiful towns in all New England, one of the richest, one of the most rigidly Republican, where even the hamburger stand across from the Pequot Yacht Club has an air of entrenched and stodgy chic compared to which the Colony is brazen. Indeed, the exurban limits have pushed further, beyond Greenfield Hill and Fairfield, only to shrink back as they approach Bridgeport, which is not only irredeemably industrial but in addition elects with dismaying regularity a mayor who, even though he is far from being an actual Socialist, nonetheless runs with a Socialist label unmistakably appended to him. There are signs that Bridgeport itself may not halt the further enroachments of the exurb: for beyond Bridgeport is Stratford, which already claims half-a-hundred daily commuters, and where a Shakespearean repertory theatre, an American Stratford-on-Avon, has appeared, midwifed by the Theatre Guild's Lawrence Langner.

Nor, of course, does the exurb hug the coastline. It spills well over the Merritt Parkway, that handsome and lethal strip of road which is so perfectly and monotonously landscaped that drivers become hypnotized into maintaining the authorized fifty-five-miles-per-hour and pile into each other with appalling regularity. From Darien, the exurb pushes north across the parkway all the way to New Canaan; at Norwalk, an industrial and commercial center to which exurbanites go merely to shop (the supermarkets stock pheasant, grouse, woodcock), the exurb wanders through a hilly region to the north known as Silvermine, a bosky glen abounding in remodeled barns, houses cunningly constructed to simulate remodeled barns, garages turned into studios, studios built to look like carriage houses, and, of course, artists and writers as thick as daisies in a field. Beyond Silvermine are Wilton and Weston and Easton; and still further north are Georgetown, Redding, Redding Ridge, and Ridgefield, each with its quorum of exurbanites.

There have to be at least this many communities, and if things go as they have in the past ten years, there may have to be that many communities again—to absorb the newcomers. For the big inescapable fact about Fairfield as an exurb is its growth. Mention was made, in the preceding chapter, of one aspect of this growth, the county's swelling herd of commuters. Here are some statistics. Since 1935 the commuting population of Greenwich has doubled; Old Greenwich has tripled; Stamford has doubled; Noroton is up nearly five times, as is Darien; Norwalk has nearly doubled; Westport is up nearly four times; Greens Farms is up an astronomical twenty-four times; Fairfield up nearly five times; tony New Canaan, a slumbering village less than twenty years ago, is up nearly forty-two times; the exurbanites have crowded even as far north as Danbury, a hat-manufacturing town, multiplying its commuter population by twenty times. There are a few towns where the commuter head-count is down, but this may confidently be attributed to the fact of a near-by station having been accorded better commuter schedules, with consequent greater use of the station-wagon, or the jeep, or the Jaguar.

And there are further evidences of incredible growth. In 1937, New Canaan, which back in the 1870's had been forced, by reason of its few modest handicraft and small manufacturing shops, to build a railroad that would feed its products into the big city, was still somnolent; its First National Bank and Trust Company's deposits that year for the first time touched one million dollars. Today, they are well over thirteen millions. And Westport, which up until two years ago had only one bank, the Westport Bank and Trust Company, with assets which in 1944 were only $9,600,000, now boasts two banks, with assets of $24,200,000.

These bank deposits, comparably increased throughout the exurb, are wholly residential. Every exurbanite, after all, has become an exurbanite largely, he will tell you, to get away from clatter and rumble and crowd—everything which new industry brings in its trail. So he is dead set against new industry coming into his countryside. But when he resists the arrival of industry, he is posing for himself an insoluble dilemma: if there is no profit-making enterprise, from which to weed the coarse green banknotes to pay the taxes that will enable him to build new schools, new firehouses, new sewers, new roads, then where are they to come from? More people? But he loathes the idea of more people. Himself? But, as it is, he has to pay a Federal income tax, a New York State income tax (although he lives in Connecticut), and a constantly increasing local tax. Then what to do?

One answer, or rather one hopeful suggestion, has been to make sure that there will be no need to raise the local rates any further: keep the schools at their present size, buy more fire-extinguishers, and try to keep one's garbage at a sensible minimum. In other words: keep everybody else out, now that we're here. Perhaps no better insight into the mushrooming growth of Fairfield as an exurb can be attained than from considering the fashion in which the village fathers have gradually been chivvied around to the point where, grit their teeth and bite the bullet though they may, they have had to undertake some sort of "planning." The creeping socialism they have embraced is multiple-acre zoning. As it has been attempted in town after town throughout Fairfield, it works like this: Areas around the outskirts of the town are placed in zones in which, it is stipulated, no house may be built on a site less than two (or three, or four, or more) acres.

Well, sir, you should hear the howl from the long-time residents of the community, those who are referred to as clam-diggers, for example, or those who came to farm land hereabouts from Italy or Poland, fifty and sixty or more years ago. Their children have a habit of marrying as soon as they graduate from high school, and those children, once married, want to buy a quarter-acre and build a house and settle down to a winsome life, just like it talks about in, for example, *Woman's Day*, or *American Home*. These are the people described by the exurbanites as the townies. And they have some unexpected allies in those who were very, very rich back in the 1920's but who are now land-poor and would like nothing better than to parcel their land for sale as subdivisions. The latter citizens are adepts in talking about freedom of initiative, and how it is being undermined. The two groups together constitute a stubborn pocket of resistance to the exurbanites who, fearfully looking across the waters of Long Island Sound at what has happened and is still happening to their confreres of the North Shore, shudder with apprehension.

But enough of the merely quantitative aspects of Fairfield County's growth. It is the qualitative aspects that are eye-catching. Fairfield County is the richest county in the United States. Simple flat-footed statements like that require some sort of support. Here it is: Fairfield County is one of the country's few communities of which it can be boasted, on behalf of its inhabitants, that their gross income is in excess of one billion dollars. Furthermore, Fairfield County's buying income, per family, is $7,431, forty percent above the average for American metropolitan county areas, and highest in the country. And still furthermore, Fairfield County ranks first among metropolitan county areas for market quality, whatever that is.* Its index is 132, which puts it above oil-rich Amarillo by one point, and above all comparable areas by anywhere from five to eleven points. It is a shame to spike all those rumors about Texas, but, just in case there may be some home-grown chauvinists who would like to contend they can spend more than the exurbanites of Fairfield County here is the list:

1. Fairfield County	132	6. Cleveland	125
2. Amarillo	131	7. Toledo	125
3. Hartford	127	8. Indianapolis	124
4. Dallas	126	9. South Bend	123
5. Chicago	125	10. San Francisco-Oakland	123

Furthermore, even Standard Rate and Data Service rates the county tops in New England for something it calls "consumer

* All numbers and statistics in this paragraph are from a 1953 survey of buying power conducted by *Sales Management*.

spendable income per household." Returning to *Sales Management, they* say Fairfield County is the "most responsive" market, by which they mean "most responsive to the postponable purchase and to the quality line." Well, that's what they say.

But it goes still further. For these figures are all average figures. Now the word "average" does not mean the same as the word "median." That is to say, when it is cited that the average family in Fairfield County has an income of $7,431 every year, this does not mean that there are an equal number who earn more and who earn less than $7,431. What it means is that of all the families in the county, the mean extracted average earns that amount. And, in turn, that means there are a hell of a lot of families whose breadwinners pull down very handsome salaries and earnings indeed.

Specifically, 2,400 weekly newspaper subscribers in key exurban Fairfield County towns were queried and it was found that their median annual income was $12,323. Nearly sixty percent had incomes over $10,000 a year. Nearly forty percent had incomes over $15,000 a year. Twenty-four percent—nearly one fourth of these subscribers—could purr contentedly over incomes of more than $20,000 a year—at least, they could purr, were it not for their unique exurban spending problems. Whether the exurban population as a whole subscribes to these weekly newspapers is doubtful in the extreme, but it seems likely that an appreciable number of exurbanites *do* subscribe, and thus tilt upward the income figures which the survey discloses. Certainly it is true, however, that many exurbanites, dedicated New Yorkers in spirit, look down their noses at the local weekly newspaper and read it, if at all, on the sly, to look for their names, or at the classified ads alone. Just as certainly it is true that if only exurban incomes were under consideration, the figures would have to be higher. An informed guess would put twenty-four percent of the exurban population at well over $40,000 a year, which argues that Fairfield County's exurbanites are the wealthiest in the nation.

How do they spend their money?

Well, variously. In some cases, even as you and I. Being exurbanites, they hustle in to town, to see the latest play, or to hear the latest concert. They deal heavily in the metropolitan specialty shops and department stores: they average better than six charge accounts per family. There are bookstores, in this exurb, and these folk are highly literate: they buy books, some of which they may place in prominent positions on their coffee tables. They buy paintings, sometimes as investments; if they conceive it to be important to achieve status as hi-fi buffs they buy expensive and intricate equipment, and subsequently records. (Standard classics, yes; plus some modern and off-beat classical types like Poulenc; Friml, no. Show tunes by Porter, Coward, etc., yes; Victor Herbert, no. Jazz, yes—if it's "authentic"; Liberace, no. And, importantly, a heavy play to off-color records, those for example, dubbed off the master on which the recording artist fluffed and, in consequence, exchanged blue epithets with the boys in the band.) Or they get the hell out of their exurb, on business, or for pleasure, or for both. (If they can, they charge a vacation trip off as tax-deductible.) Every fourth one of them takes a holiday both summer and winter.

It would, however, be erroneous to say of Fairfield County's exurbanites that they spend money as did the loot-heavy monsters of Thorstein Veblen's day. They have it, they spend it, and in characteristically exotic ways; but these folk cannot be accused of spending it only for show. There seems to be, in fact, a kind of reverse cachet about spending money: status accrues to him whose frugality bespeaks a background of even greater wealth than present earned income. Here, where the attuned exurban eye is on the constant lookout for evidences of the phony, the *nouveau riche*, and the *nouveau venu*—and exurban wits are ever ready for bitchy humor at their expense—it's recognized as a sign of old-timer stability and indifference to fads to affect torn sneakers and patched corduroys and faded jeans; here, where so much is new, the old and sincerely beat-up has class.

Capitalizing on this spirit, the owners of Westport's Separate Shop, a specialty shop for women, spent months combing the antique markets of the eastern seaboard to mount and equip a

Victorian soda fountain. Opened in the spring of 1954 complete
with nickelodeon, waiters with handle-bar mustaches glued to
their upper lips, gas lights from Saratoga's Grand Union Hotel
(and equipped with electric bulbs), an 1880 soda fountain, and
an expensive variety of penny candies, this place, called The Ice
Cream Parlor, does, of course, a whopping business. It fits perfectly into every exurbanite's self-concept. Its fixtures might have
been selected on the basis of a mass exurban questionnaire. The
same sort of shop would do as well in any exurb; meantime the
Fairfield exurbanites willingly spend forty-five and fifty cents
apiece for Victorian sundaes.

There are three principal ways the Fairfield County exurbanites
spend money: booze, foreign cars, and regional stigmata.

Re booze: they get drunker more often, or at any rate drink
more, and more steadily, than other exurbanites, but confine
it to the home, mostly; there are not many saloons in the exurb
and those that do exist are patronized for the most part by
townies. In this exurb there is no counterpart of the elegant
city cocktail lounge for the simple reason that the need for it—
assignations, courtship, business drinking with important contacts
—doesn't exist; nor is there the counterpart of the "adopted"
neighborhood saloon, like Tim Costello's, where birds of a feather
can let their hair down without fear of having their drinking
habits, their trade talk, their friendships and quarrels observed by
outsiders. The Fairfield County exurbanite is, rather, a home-
body toper; his drinking is a matter of the automatic three
cocktails before dinner every night, and the automatic three-to-
six highballs most nights, and the automatic four or five cocktails
at parties every Friday, Saturday, and Sunday evening.

Re cars: Fairfield County's exurbanites lead the nation as
buyers of foreign cars. Not that they ignore the American brands,
but they are special and distinguished marks for vendors of
foreign makes. In fact, it takes a state to challenge the population of Fairfield County at buying these elite commodities; only
California buys more. The experience of those who sell Jaguars

to America is typical. They claim that, despite its price, their product has outstripped all foreign competitors in winning its way into American hearts. And they are swift to state that the national sale of Jaguars would never have come about had they not first been able to sell them to exurbanites, and especially to those exurbanites who live in Fairfield County.

In Fairfield County itself, of course, to read such information will bring only a politely stifled yawn and a wearily lifted eyebrow, and for two good reasons. Not only do residents there have merely to look at the roads or the parking-places to see the gleaming burnished foreign cars, but they can judge from another, more freakish circumstance. Their county newspaper—or, more accurately, the weekly magazine supplement tucked inside each of six of their weekly newspapers—the *Fairfield County Fair*, is unique in American journalism in that it prints a semi-regular department, "Sports Car Corner," given over to the ecstasies of foreign-car fans. And, after all, Fairfield County is headquarters for the Sports Car Club of America—its national office is right on the Post Road, halfway between Westport and Southport.

Re regional stigmata: here, rather pathetically, goes much of the exurbanite's extra cash, for it is by the purchase of these things, more than by any other method, that he achieves the status he believes he must have, the status which, if it does not fit the facts about the individual, at any rate fits the fancy in which he sees himself. These stigmata have been remarked before: *Life* (several of whose advertising and editorial hotshots of course live in the area) devoted a page or two to some of them: the post lanterns, the fireproofed hay, the split-rail fences, the antique bottle for the mantelpiece, the cobbler's bench for a coffee-table, the beagle, the huge green bottle that stands by the doorstep, the ship's model for another mantel, the hitching-post by the driveway. There are others: the driveway itself is, *de rigueur*, of bluestone; the barbecue is of fieldstone; and the tool shed is packed with the most expensive of do-it-yourself gadgets. Such stigmata may be carried to eye-bugging extremes, as in the radiant heating with which to warp the random-width floorboards of a living room, or the steam-pipes laid under the flagstone walk to melt off snow in the winter.

Your true exurbanite is gadget-happy. He is never so delighted as when he is combining his love for old things and his fascination with new ones. Hand-hewn oak pegs hold his Leica and Rolleiflex cases; he stores his electric worm-digger in a Hepplewhite chest.

And he will go to any lengths to create his mind's eye's perfect image of his surroundings. Once upon a time an exurbanite living in Weston began to brood on his dream-picture of himself. Something, he felt, was lacking. At length it came to him—the moment of piercing vision, he has confided to a friend, occurred around ten-thirty one morning when, in company with half-a-dozen other idea men of his advertising agency, he was sitting around a table in the conference room staring at a full-color picture of applesauce. That was what he needed—an apple orchard! That was what was required to complete his picture of himself. He needed an apple orchard to come home to, and he had just the field to grow it in, too; an apple orchard that would be filled with songbirds during the appropriate season, and carpeted with violets whenever violets sprang from the earth.

Excusing himself to the applesauce account executive, he left to set the wheels in motion: first, he bade his secretary have Research send him up everything they had on apples, the best varieties, where he could get them, how they were grown, where, under what circumstances, what was the yield per tree, what the market value per apple—the works. Then, having glanced at the works, he asked her to study them carefully, make him a digest, and recommend a choice. This she did. The next morning, he set more wheels in motion: he ordered a portable stump-puller ($465) for there were three stumps in his field, a jeep ($2,100), a gasoline-powered tree saw to cut up the stumps ($189.95), a five-horsepower riding tractor with full complement of attachments (plow, disc harrow, spike harrow, cultivator, seeder-fertilizer, gang mower, dump cart, lawn roller, sickle mower, rotary weed cutter, sprayer-compressor, insect fogger and, for foreseeable exigencies but not for this particular job, snowplow—all for about $4,000), and the services of a local youth to demonstrate each piece of equipment.

Within two week ends, this man had managed to break, or cause to break down, almost every one of his new gadgets. The expense of their repair was in the neighborhood of $250. Thereafter, he had recourse to another local youth who, with derisive skill, accomplished in a matter of hours what the exurbanite had taken four days and two evenings trying to do. His fee was $120. But our man's problems were not yet over. He had now the task of plowing his field and planting it. Another local youth (fee $85) took over. And so it went, right up to the planting of good-sized young trees, which would yield years sooner than less expensive seedlings, and including the laying down of the best sod around the trees—for who wants to wait for grass to grow?

The exurbanite, who gets full marks for perseverance, now is proud owner of an orchard of sixty-four apple trees (gross expense: $8,309.95), and it would be pleasant to be able to report that an ounce of humility had entered into his soul. But this man claims, to all his week-end visitors, that he pulled, plowed, planted, grafted, and nursed the whole project himself. A touching aspect of this is that if you required him to take a lie-detector test, he would advance willingly to the electrodes—and pass with flying colors. So far as he is concerned, he did do the whole job himself. And, as he gazes reflectively out over his orchard of a summer evening, while the fireflies pyramid over one tree after another, and the aphids busily suck the juice of one after another, he is content. (Incidentally, he was recently put in charge of copy for the applesauce account at his agency.)

An exurban attorney, himself something of an *avant*-Schweppes-man, once long ago commented, of Westport, that it was inhabited by people with the long, sensitive fingers of commercial artists. Others have made the same comment since, having adopted it as their own (an exurban trait) or arrived at it independently. It was true, in a sense, when he first made it, but since then the business accretion has taken place. Fairfield County—and in particular Westport and its halo of surrounding communities— has suffered a sea-change, into something rich and strange, and no longer particularly marked by long, sensitive fingers. The transformation was remarked in many trade journals; along Madison Avenue, everybody was vaguely aware of it; but it waited on a semi-retired adman to fix it in amber. This was John Orr Young, a Westporter of long standing, a commuting buff, and a sort of elder statesman of Exurbia.

Mr. Young some time ago sold out his founding interest in Young & Rubicam and is presently established as an advertising counselor. But the rhythm of his days having been fixed years ago, he hates to break it up. He likes commuting and continues to do it, though it is no longer necessary. He is a man of tidy habits, and he begrudges that hour which is not filled with rewarding accomplishment. As commuter, he is no snoozer, no bridgeplayer, no gabber, and at best an impatient newspaper-reader; he is happiest when he is working. He has written a book, while commuting, and his publishers gratefully rewarded the New Haven Railroad by emblazoning the book jacket with a photograph of the 8:12. His book behind him, Mr. Young looked around for other fruitful activities. Looking, he noticed, as others have before and since, how many of his Madison Avenue friends he saw around him; indeed, how many more there seemed to be, almost every morning. The rest of us would have seen fit to do no more than say, over the evening martini, "Saw that bum Perkins on the 6:02 tonight. Bet he's bought a place out here somewhere. God, the neighborhood's going off." But Mr. Young was made of sterner stuff than you or I. He decided to count.

He was interested in counting only admen and adwomen, or those directly involved in advertising. He let the velvet rope down far enough to admit television and radio executives, if they were in sales, or in advertising, or in promotion, or if they were gilt-edged producers. Public relations biggies qualified easily enough, as did artists (if they were able to cite the advertisements which they had drawn). Advertisers naturally were ushered to a favored section of his list. And he admitted also executives from the magazine and newspaper publishing dodge.

He counted idly, at first, and then with quickening excitement, sensing that he was on to something. He appointed eight or ten of his friends as captains, to cruise the aisles of the morning and evening commuter trains, checking their friends on his list. He recognized he was only human; that he was bound to err—probably most often on the side of omission. But at length he was ready. His list, the first list of exurbanites ever drawn up, constituting a proof by poll-count of what students of the new Exurbia had long suspected, was published in the *Westporter-Herald*, in late November, 1953.

Even though, on this list, there were only 375 names, he was justified in describing it as the "400 of Advertising." Agency presidents and board chairmen were a dime a dozen. Mere vice-presidents and account executives were the foot soldiers of this army. The list of accounts they serviced was, as Mr. Young pointed out, the list of products you have bought for your "kitchen, dining room, bath, living room, recreation or hobby room, clothes closets, basement, tool shed, garage, and out in the garden." His names were the *Debrett's*, the *Burke's Peerage*, the *Almanach de Gotha* of the advertising world. And they were residents of only six Fairfield County towns, Westport, Weston, Fairfield, Redding, Wilton, and Easton.

In printing his list, Mr. Young flung down the gauntlet: "Compare! Count 'em! Most and best per mile!" He urged his "ad friends" in Norwalk, Darien, Greenwich, Stamford, New Canaan, or such suburban backwashes as Bronxville or Scarsdale to answer his defi: could they name more talented exurbanites from their community? If they could, they have not been heard from. All is silence, from Darien, from Greenwich, from Scarsdale. Only from Detroit arose a clamor: their Adcraft Club's house organ claimed an edge, from just two Detroit suburbs, Birmingham and Bloomfield Hills. Mr. Young sniffs at their contention. "They've

THE DEGREE TO WHICH THE SELF-CONCEPT COINCIDES WITH REALITY IS ONE MEASURE OF NORMAL ADJUSTMENT AND SANITY.

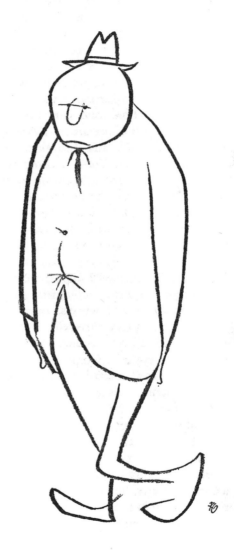

counted janitors," he says, "and stenographers and office-boys and youngsters who run the mimeograph machines. My list has on it nothing but talent."

And within a week, the *Westporter-Herald* had to print an additional eighty-one names of disgruntled exurbanites who resented having been left off Mr. Young's first list. Nor did that by any means complete the poll-count. Any knowledgeable exurbanite in the area can tell you the names of at least a dozen who were missed, a dozen whose positions on or near Madison Avenue are at least as glittering as many whom Mr. Young nailed. Skimming over his collection, one can find the publishers of *Fortune*, *Woman's Home Companion*, *Seventeen*, *Look*, *Harper's Bazaar*, *American Weekly*, and the president of Time, Inc. Lumped together under Mr. Young's category of "Miscellaneous" are no less than four retired advertising agency presidents. On this list, too, is Elmo Roper, the pollster. It is interesting to reflect on the commercial, political, and cultural conclusions Mr. Roper might arrive at if he were as indefatigable at polling his train mates as Mr. Young has been at counting them.

The pattern seems clear. Just as Fairfield County's original inhabitants, the Pequot Indians, were decimated and enslaved by the businesslike British colonists, so the original exurban settlers here, the artists and writers, have gradually been overwhelmed (and many of them enslaved) by the facile and charming idea-mongers of Madison Avenue. Money played a decisive role in this conquest of Fairfield County, and while there is much that can be ridiculed in this exurban way of life, the picture would not be true or complete without at least hinting at its other side.

Part of the truth is that these people who have hit a rich vein of gold in pursuing their occupation as commercial merchants of ideas have as great a degree of esthetic susceptibility to the virtues of material possessions as anyone else—and, in some cases, perhaps more. This exurb's millionaires may seem more millionairish, its artists more arty, but the exurbanites of Fairfield County can take rightful pride in their summer theatres and art galleries. Its public and private schools are, by national standards, excellent. It is a region of manicured lawns, lovely gardens, homes lived in and maintained with pride. It goes in for large and, relatively often, happy families. Its citizens feel they have a stake in the future. They are young, as populations go, and they do their best to stay that way.

If there is a snake in their garden, his head can be descried just over there, on the horizon of the future. The snake is the exurb's potential growth. As any Fairfield County exurbanite will tell you, from the lordly vantage point of three months' residence, there are too many newcomers. And, worse yet, there's still plenty of room for more. For Fairfield County has fifty percent more land area than Westchester County, and a population density only a little more than half as great.

As exurb, it is increasing in popularity, it is increasing in fame, and it does not seem to be decreasing in scarlet vitality. The archetype of exurbs, last to become fashionable, may well be the last to sink beneath the swells of a suburban sea.

In this regard, Fairfield, Bucks, and Rockland have a fear of the future in common. In Rockland, whose serenity is threatened by the new Thruway, there is a pervasive twilight-of-the-gods atmosphere. Rockland exurbanites are too mature, too *ennuyé*, and too world-weary to avail themselves of such standard means for blotting out the future as frivolously living it up in the present; they sign petitions and otherwise await the doom of their exurb with philosophic calm and go on about their business just as residents on the slope of a rumbling volcano must do. Bucks exurbanites are anxious because just to the south of them a steel mill—visible from some of the county's choicest high land—is bringing with it industrial housing and, in some ways more disturbing, housing which is lily-white, an unpleasant novelty in a community which is proud of its tradition of racial and religious equality. Change is imminent for all of them and the history of each is a history of change.

This is a fact which it is important to stress: Exurbia is not a stable phenomenon. Neither, of course, are cities, rural areas, or suburbs. But these latter change at a more stately rate, and enjoy long periods of comparative equilibrium. They can also look forward to continuing existence in a not too altered form—always excepting the possibilities of atomic destruction or act of God, in which case an attempt will be made to reconstruct them, if there's anyone left to do the job. But exurban history is so fast-paced and compressed as to be comparable to a stop-motion movie film, in which one sees within minutes a seed sprout, bud, flower, fade, and go to seed.

2

Of all the exurbs, Bucks is the one which—in outlining its history—shows most vividly the paradox of seeming bucolically stable while, in fact, having been in rapid flux since its exurban discovery (which is variously dated at 1900, and the early Thirties).

It was the earlier date when the artists discovered it. This was substantially in advance of the comparable discovery of Rockland or Fairfield; and it might be presumed that such seniority would predicate a far earlier onslaught on Bucks by the exurbanites. The county's inaccessibility saved it. William Lathrop came to New Hope in 1900 and settled there; on his heels arrived Edward Redfield and Daniel Garber and John Folinsbee and others, dozens of others, crowding into the valley of the Delaware and then, embarrassed by proximity, fanning out in all directions, as far west as Emmaus, as far north as Stroudsburg, rejoicing to find the stone-walled pig-houses they could convert into studios, delighting in the opportunities for quiet and concentration. Such opportunities would soon be threatened.

It was in the early 1930's that Bucks began to take on the high-patina sheen of glamor. A few names did it. They were mostly names from Broadway, and from the Algonquin's Round Table, hardy spirits who, seduced by the county's inaccessibility, determined to flee from those of their confreres who were already settling in and around Westport. They came to Bucks to avoid fashion; they brought fashion with them. As with a chain letter, the habit grew. The first settlers went for an automobile ride into unexplored territory somewhere west of the Hudson; as chance would have it, the road taken was Route 202 to Flemington and thence across the Delaware; one glimpse of those farmhouses with stone walls two feet thick, one phrase dropped by a real estate dealer about land up for grabs at $25 an acre, and the first sale had been consummated. Thereafter, that first purchaser dragooned friends down from New York for the week end, to help with house painting, or with clearing out poison ivy, or with knocking down inside partitions, and those friends became the second, third, and fourth purchasers. Then they in turn needed house guests, to give them a hand, and their house guests in turn toured the back roads, looking for likely properties. New links are added to this kind of chain with every passing summer.

The identity of the first glamorous purchaser has been mislaid, but according to one reliable account Dorothy Parker's house guests (she bought in 1936 and sold some ten years later) are responsible, directly or indirectly, for nearly sixty mortgages in various stages of amortization. Some of these celebrated folk, having bought, exploited their exurban hardships in order to help defray the costs of their lavish improvements. Thus, George S. Kaufman and Moss Hart wrote *George Washington Slept Here*, produced on Broadway in 1940, and S. J. Perelman snarled an occasional diatribe against the rural life in the pages of the *Saturday Evening Post*: in neither case was there any attempt to gloss over the difficulties, even the follies of their purchases, but the unmixed result was to bring more exurbanites, eager to grow gray as part-time farmers. Legends grew and flourished, especially about Hart's exurban retreat, bought in 1937 for $35,000 and sold in 1954 for $110,000. Kaufman later wrote:

"Only Moss could have planted thirty-five hundred new trees on his farm . . . and only Moss, in the midst of plenty, could have failed to find water at the end of three months and the digging of something like seventeen wells. Only Moss could have bought a hundred pigs to give his caretaker enough interest in the place to persuade him to stay on."

Of the trees, several people are said to have remarked: "It just goes to show what God could have done, if He'd had enough money." And, of course, each of the stories, each of the legends, only served to whet the appetites of other potential exurbanites, persuading them that they, too, should get lost in Bucks County at ruinous expense. The Spewacks came, found their farm too pleasant for work, and finally rented a bleak and cheerless office in Trenton. The links of the chain continue to be forged: a magazine advertising man invited an editor, the editor bought and invited a columnist, the columnist bought and invited an author, the author bought and invited an editor from *Life*; playwrights involved other playwrights; actors involved other actors; doctors involved other doctors; and at length advertising men eyed the area jealously and decided they could be farmers, too.

As exurb, Bucks County grew too crowded, land prices started to climb. Late arrivals were forced to spill over into Hunterdon County in New Jersey, on the other side of the river, where there weren't so many stone barns, but where at least they would be within driving distance of their friends. One enterprising citizen evolved a splendid technique: he bought old places and did just enough work on them so that a week-ending New Yorker would be able to see the possibilities. His delighted victims include a war correspondent, an editor of *Holiday* magazine, and a one-time motion picture scenarist from Hollywood. This last homestead had at one time belonged to a man who did considerable bootlegging, a fact which his neighbors discovered when they found that their cows, so far from having the head staggers, were reeling from the mash they had been eating at the foot of his property. The movie writer has since bought another farm, selling his first place to a television director, and so it goes, and so it goes.

But the exurbanites who have clustered in Bucks and near by differ from their fellows in exurbs to the north and east. Two considerations seem to have principally powered them into the journey so far from New York, motives which operated far less compellingly on the exurbanite bound for Westport or Sneden's Landing. Either the Bucks County exurbanite really wanted to get far,

far away from the rat race, so far away that he could effectively shut it out of his mind, or he was a man temporarily or permanently deluded into thinking he was a farmer. Both these motives deserve further examination, despite S. J. Perelman's remarks that "a farm is an irregular patch of nettles bounded by short-term notes, containing a fool and his wife who didn't know enough to stay in the city," and that "when, back in the mid-thirties, I left a cozy New York flat to exile myself in a stone pillbox in a swamp, I broke clean with the twentieth century."

First, as to getting far, far away from the rat race. Access to Bucks County is not simple for anyone from New York, no matter where in the county he is going and no matter how he chooses to get there. He has his choice of driving some seventy-five miles through heavy traffic over truck-infested super-highways in order to approach the last lap of ten or twenty or thirty more miles over dirt roads to his isolated hideaway, or of taking the Pennsylvania Railroad to Trenton and driving home, or of taking the Lehigh Valley Railroad to Flemington Junction or Easton before driving home, or of jouncing the whole distance by bus. Nor does the Lehigh Valley endear itself to its clients: its few trains run at improbable hours. There are even a few Bucks County exurbanites who say the hell with it and drive to Allentown to take a plane to New York—to be faced with the forty-five-minute drive in from LaGuardia. Despite these handicaps, there are more than a handful of daily commuters. True, their jobs are not, typically, of the nine-to-five kind; one may direct a radio soap-opera which requires his presence in town only from noon till four-thirty; another may lead an orchestra, working only from six till midnight; a third may have become entangled in a television newscast and be in town only for a couple of evening hours.

But, in addition to these, there is an appreciably large contingent of advertising agency executives and other slaves bound for office routine. One way or another, at one hour or another, they come to and from New York five days a week. Among these are the exurbanites who, when they get home, as like as not stretch a chain across their driveways. They are home, as in a burrow, and want no part of any human companionship until it is forced on them by the morrow. Over the week end, they remain secluded, declining to entertain or to be entertained. Some bear the scars of emotional traumas suffered by too much jostling around the turns of the rat race; some would be unable to face their jobs if they could not restore their tissues in rural peace; most of this type would blench at the prospect of becoming part of the febrile social life that obtains in, say, Weston or Darien.

Then there are the farmers. The ambivalence that overcomes the symbol-manipulator, goading him into becoming a thing-manipulator, is an important element in the make-up of many of the Bucks County farmer-exurbanites. Actually, there are many degrees of intensity of what might be termed the Bucks fever. For some, who may have been born and have grown up in Iowa or Kansas, the notion of some land on which they can grow vegetables is quite a natural component of the search for security in an insecure world, time, and walk of life. Thus, a television director will tell you he bought land because he wanted to farm, and it will not be an idle conversation-gambit. He knows something about farming from personal experience. He is not afraid of dirt, or stupid about making things grow from the dirt. But it happens that his impulse toward farming coincided with the eighth week of a term in his contract; that is, he had another week to sweat out before learning whether or not the option for another thirteen-week period was to be picked up by the client; he was thinking of what might happen, one of these days, when that option dropped with a clank.

At such a time, an acre of garden-produce would come in extremely handy; if the one acre of produce could be turned into ten, or twenty, or thirty, by God he might be able to show a profit on investment. So he bought. He may have bought sixty-five acres, dreaming of corn at $2.80 a bushel, with a hundred bushels to the acre. Such a low-register farmer has probably not actually done much work on his land. Typically, he may have sold forty of his sixty-five acres (for as much as he originally paid for the entire tract), or he may be renting his land out at five or ten dollars an acre to his neighbor who is a working dirt-farmer. But he still knows what he is talking about, when he engages in farm-type chitchat—the Bucks County substitute for gossip about the communications industry.

Some sort of visible evidence that the owner has a kinship with the working farmer constitutes, in its fashion, the regional stigmata of the Bucks County exurbanite. He keeps a couple of cows, or farms a half-acre of kitchen garden, or attends cattle-auctions with regularity. Budd Schulberg has pigs, no special breed, just pigs. It's farming country, and the exurbanites must keep their hands in. They purchase farm equipment. But here a marked difference must be pointed out. Where in Fairfield County a landowner will buy one expensive gadget after another—tractors, sickle bar mowers, stump-pullers, and so on—in Bucks the exurban-ites, being farm buffs or having actually had farming experience in their youth, make a habit of buying important farm equip-ment only when they know their near-by friends or neighbors will want to share its use. What in Fairfield may constitute status, in Bucks becomes a shared means toward status. Indeed, it is status not to buy unless to share, since that is the farmer's way.

Others, bitten more savagely by the farm-bug, pour fortunes into prize herds of cattle and, logically enough, are wiped out. There is an advertising wheel who is the classic example of this unfortunate type: he lost his home, barns, property, and hundreds of thousands of dollars on some Black Angus; it is a question whether ever again he will enjoy a steak dinner. Others, over whom the gods of chance minister in more kindly fashion, never get beyond the point of treating their acreage like an expensive toy. "I got a bang out of it," is the way a celebrated conductor of popular music explained to a friend he met on the commuters' train the fact that he had rented a bulldozer at $25 an hour for a ten-hour day. It turned out he had rented this behemoth to tuck up a culvert or two which had begun to show signs of slipping. "But," his friend objected, "a job like that shouldn't take more than a couple of hours!" "I know," answered the conductor, "but

I was having fun." His friend, puzzling as to what kind of bull-dozer could rent for $25 an hour—whenever he rented one, he could find what he wanted for eight or ten dollars—asked the conductor what he'd done all day with his monstrous toy. It turned out he had gleefully driven through his wood lot, grinding down second growth like matchwood, endangering his life with every succeeding foot of progress, and building roadways to nowhere.

There are, moreover, a few exurbanites who take their farming even more seriously still. These men, and they could live only in Bucks, seem actually to be more farmer than exurbanite. Whatever it is that takes them into New York has become secondary in their lives. For some of them, it would appear that their only reason to continue working is to supply their agents with a handsome ten percent. They really know their business, as farmers; what may have begun as a hobby is now an engrossing and nearly full-time occupation; they regard their trips to town as irksome chores, to be endured and completed as quickly as possible; the money they earn—and it is considerable—is sluiced into cattle-auctions; they handicap Guernsey cows as carefully as any Jamaica chalk-eater pores over *The Racing Form*.

One such exurbanite arises every morning, seven days a week, at five a.m. to supervise the milking of his $30,000 herd of dairy cattle; in addition, he has a hundred sheep and is cultivating a special clover, his own hybrid. His morning work is over by eleven; hastily he dresses and drives to Trenton to catch the 12:35. He is in a radio studio until late afternoon; he must hustle back to get home in time to supervise the evening milking. He is in bed by nine or ten. On Saturday and Sunday, days when his schedule mercifully does not require his presence in the radio studio, he takes care of his farm books. He is not happy, and can never be happy, unless he is working around the farm. If there is nothing else to do, he will mow a friend's meadow, getting so sunburned in the process that a dress shirt—sometimes necessary to his job in town—becomes torture. If his Sunday is free, he will go off somewhere to enter a stock-judging contest—and as like as not win it. This man is exceptional, perhaps, only in that he must go in to town every day. Others—Ezra Stone, for example, who maintains a herd of Ayreshires—find that their work takes them in to New York far more irregularly.

And this is another difference, setting Bucks apart from the other exurbs. Bucks is the only exurb where the non-commuting exurbanite outnumbers the commuter, and by as much, perhaps, as three-to-one. One side reaction of this fact is that the term "genius," so often derisively applied by the exurban commuter to the exurbanite who can work at home, is rarely if ever heard in Bucks.

It is, on the whole and by comparative standards, a happy, peaceful exurb. But even in Bucks County's happy-seeming farm atmosphere all is not well with the exurbanites, especially the older ones. At a recent gathering for pre-dinner cocktails at the Tow Path Inn three artist-farmers were among the guests of a local, genuine, pre-exurban, semi-millionaire gentleman farmer. As the group sat at outdoor tables beside the canal, fighting off mosquitoes and enjoying the sultry summer air, they all gave the appearance of being positively permeated with well-being. They would have a couple of drinks apiece, a good dinner, and would then go to the Bucks County Playhouse to see an excellent, professional cast perform a play which might make Broadway come fall.

Let's look beneath the surface calm of these three artists. Paul was a "natural" in his extreme youth. He'd come to New York, to the Village, from the Midwest. Within a year, he'd been taken to Paris as protégé of the editor-in-chief of a fashion magazine which specialized (and still does) in the newer manifestations of the finer, more fashionable arts. Paul had a great success that season. He met everybody important among the expatriates, including his fellow Midwesterners, Ernest Hemingway and Glenway Wescott. More importantly, he'd stayed on when his mentor went back to New York, and really learned to paint. Then he came back to New York, couldn't stand it; moved to Woodstock, couldn't stand it; tried the Florida Keys, couldn't stand them (too bleakly, bakingly quiet); tried Westport, couldn't take the pace; and finally settled in Bucks.

Paul liked Bucks. Here he could farm a little, and paint. Here he found people who were cultural sophisticates without being demonstrative about it, as in Westport; people who lived close to their land without being intellectually stunted, as in the Keys; people who were artists without being compulsively Bohemian, as in Woodstock; people who liked to be around artists without its affecting their temperament, as in the Village. But something happened to Paul's painting.

Being accustomed to express himself on canvas, he can't be very articulate about why he has stopped painting, but he puts it this way: "I haven't really stopped, I don't think. It's just that I can't finish a painting—nobody can, really."

Paul, in the last couple of years, has felt better and better about his exurban, typically Bucksian life. He farms more, paints less and less, drinks more, is more gregarious. An old and wise friend says of him that he must feel subconsciously that there was something specious and too easy about his early success, and something too comfortably unreal about exurban life. "He doesn't have the intellect to think it through, or the will to live to himself, as he used to," this man says. "It's so darn charming here in Bucks."

Take the second artist, Gregory. He sits blandly and graciously at the table on the flagged lower terrace of the inn and sips his drink and makes idle, pleasant, exurban talk. He's a successful commercial artist. He'll tell you that he has been for fifteen years. But there was a period of a year, when he first moved to Bucks, when he wasn't. This is how it came about. Gregory had been a serious artist since his late teens, and might have gone on doing the kind of serious non-commercial painting that was his whole life, and possibly achieved the rare fortune of making a living at it, but he wanted to get married. Love conquered all, as it is said to do, and Gregory turned to commercial art and, in less than due course, became a success.

Before long he moved his family from Greenwich Village to Greenwich, Connecticut. The more successful he got, the madder he got inside. One grim winter day, when he and his wife were in the midst of a long and aimless quarrel, his internal arrangements fell into a new pattern, much as the colored-glass shards in a kaleidoscope do when it's turned. In the ensuing weeks he did some personal bookkeeping and the finalized ledger showed him that he'd been spending his years doing the opposite of what he wanted most. Within another year he was divorced, and back in New York.

This was the period of his greatest commercial success. He drove himself constantly, lived frugally, became anti-social. He was working toward a goal: he wanted to amass enough money so that he could give up commercial art for just one year, during which he would be a serious painter again. What would happen after that year, he had no idea. But he would have that year, by God. And he did.

Gregory moved to an unheated one-room studio in New Hope. And he started to paint. "That was something," he says, now. "You see, I wanted to paint more than anything in the world, literally. Only I couldn't. I could paint too well, too slick, too easy, too fast. I could paint without thinking; I couldn't stop thinking about other things while I painted. I was soft and not used to living cheap and hard, like I used to. But that wasn't the trouble. It was this slickness. I tried painting with my left hand. I tried to teach my left hand, which wasn't so damn' trained, to paint the way I used to."

Gregory discovered, of course, that the slickness was not only in his right hand. Before his year was up, he'd bought a house outside the town and gone back to commercial art. He took up farming and became addicted to it: neither hand was too slick at it. He began to see people who lived around him. One night, at a party, he had more to drink than usual, and found himself telling his sympathetic hostess the story of his failure in attempting a return to serious painting, and how his marriage had been ruined by the corrupting power of commercialism. He told it haltingly, badly, with genuine feeling. He got a lot of sympathy. The next time he told it, he did it better and more easily. Now he can tell it very well, but he doesn't overdo it. He's an intelligent, sensitive, nice person. He's good company, in Bucks, even if he does drink quite a lot.

The third artist of the group is Konrad. His story is simpler. In the late Twenties and early Thirties his magazine covers were in steady demand at high prices. He made quite a lot of money and bought a big, beautiful house and farm near Doylestown. Someday, he assured everyone, he'd have enough money so that he could stop doing magazine covers and still have enough income to run his Bucks County farm as a farm, that is, at a modest profit. Then he would go back to art for art's sake, painting the way he wanted to and at his leisure.

What happened to Konrad was that the vogue for his covers passed before he was ready to quit. He tried to change his style and he accepted second-string assignments. He was near his goal and only needed another good year—well, two more good years. Of course, he could have sold the farm and the house—it was much bigger and grander than he needed—but he'd worked so hard for it that it seemed a shame to even consider parting with it now.

Today, Konrad is in chronic debt. He's closed off all but one small wing of his house. He drives a jalopy and he wears old clothes, not as an affectation, but because they're cheaper. He farms mightily, he secretly does leg art for pulp magazines, and he still talks about getting back to non-commercial painting. Everyone at the table likes him, pretends to take his ambition seriously, and knows his place is far more important to him than anything else in his past, present, or future.

It is limited and secret dreams like these—interesting, touching, not too disturbing—that give exurban Bucks some of its potent, socially sophisticated, deceptively hayseedy charm.

The breed is different in other ways, too. In Bucks, many of the creative folk live alone, women as well as men, radio writers like Ruth Borden, editors like Mary Leatherbee, novelists like Josephine Herbst. And where in every other exurb the typical house shelters a family of four or five or six or eight, in Bucks there are many couples either childless or whose children are grown and out in the world. The result is that far less of the exurban life is centered around the child.

Such variation in typical age-group and family-composition leads to other differences, as well. The week-end guest, as difficult to get rid of as crab grass, forces more dining out, especially in the summer, than is the case in other exurbs, and fortunately there are more and better places than elsewhere. Across the river in Lambertville, a radio actress runs an inn called River's Edge; the Black Bass Inn near New Hope, which in one form or another has been functioning since the early 1700's, has been equipped by its current owner with ironwork reputedly brought up from New Orleans; Tow Path Inn in New Hope grills your steaks in outdoor barbecues; River House, a onetime popular way-station for barge-captains, boasts a dining terrace overlooking the Delaware; Logan Inn, where the murals are by Moyer, used to have a corner on the Broadway trade, but the monopoly has been threatened by Monte Proser's Playhouse Inn, cheek-by-jowl with the Bucks County Playhouse, founded by the late Theron Bamberger, where actors disport in a former grist-mill. Besides the Playhouse, after dinner, there is St. John Terrell's Music Circus in Lambertville, another magnet for tourists and folk from Philadelphia and New York.

And if all these inns are too crowded, there are still the Washington Crossing Inn, at the spot where Washington crossed the Delaware, intent on snatching Trenton (and also at the spot where St. John Terrell crosses the Delaware every year, intent on snatching a little publicity); the Waterwheel Inn in Doylestown, and the Cutaloosa Inn not far outside. True to Bucks tradition, in most of these places one can gorge on country-smoked ham and shoofly pie, washed down with bottles of Goldtröpfchen. Devotees of the quaint may drive to Stockton, in New Jersey, and gape at the wishing-well of Colligan's Inn, where Rodgers and Hart got the inspiration for "There's a Small Hotel."

Week-end guests not only can eat well. They have been able to sense something else very rewarding, something on which the soul can feast, something that is in all probability a vestige of the bequest made to the area by the early Quakers: a toleration of others. Whatever the cause, it is almost tangible. Here, the natives speak of a man as being "from the city" and may mean either

New York or Philadelphia, but in neither event is there any connotation of enmity. The only rancor that one exurbanite has ever been able to sense on the part of the landed farmers has to do with their occasional resentment that the outlanders seem to want to buy only thick-walled stone farmhouses. By and large, farmer and exurbanite get along famously; and why not, where often the farmer rents the exurbanite's land at $10 an acre, sells his corn for $280 an acre, charges off $80 to seed and fertilizer and labor, and nets a profit of $190?

But it is more than money, it is something deep-rooted. Here in Bucks County is the Lighthouse Cemetery, founded in the earliest 1700's as a place where a man could be buried no matter what his skin color, his religion, or the manner of his death. In New Hope, as elsewhere in the county, Negroes lived next to whites, Jews bought houses next to gentiles, and no man concerned himself as to whether land values were rising or falling. (They were rising.) As social custom, this indifference to the color of a neighbor's skin and the dictates of a neighbor's conscience is traditional in Bucks County, and reaches back beyond the days when dozens of houses were stations on the Underground Railroad, helping to steer slaves to freedom.

And the tradition is one in which many of the exurbanites, in common with the other residents of the county, take considerable pride, just as they love their gently rolling hills and meadowlands, their woods and streams, their thick-walled farmhouses and their tiny towns made lovelier by the centuries. Most of the Bucks exurbanites have worked hard to make their faraway homes comfortable, and to fit themselves into a life of quiet and rural peace. The many obstacles have been surmounted; the inaccessibility itself is regarded as an important contribution to the charm of the county as exurb. It is likely that here in Bucks the limited dream is closer to being the secret dream, and closer to being realized, than in any other of New York City's exurbs—with the possible exception of Rockland, where the case is somewhat different, as we shall now see.

3

In fact, until comparatively recently, when there was first talk of opening a thoroughfare across the heart of the county, Rockland was perhaps the most genuinely happy exurb. Even now, although of all exurbs it faces most immediately the prospect of urban and suburban engulfment, there is a quiet, endearing, neurotically fatalistic charm to the exurban sadness over the imminence of change. These people, especially the founding members of the Rockland exurban community, were themselves in many cases the champions of change. In their youths they were the *avant-garde*. In microcosm, now, hid away in their exurb, they are like the last remnants of a dying civilization which led the world, reached a peak, and then stopped growing and developing, to become victims to the next wave of the future. This must be born in mind as we turn to a closer examination of that pie-shaped slab of hilly, wooded real estate known as Rockland County.

Today, there hangs over it a hush of brooding expectancy. The people who live there—exurbanites and others—are not quite sure what is going to happen, and not quite sure whether they are for or against whatever it is that may happen. They don't know whether the hush is autumnal, betokening the death of one of the pleasantest exurban retreats that ever a fortunate few found and cherished, or something ominous, a prelude to a cataclysm that may make of their secluded fastness a booming, blaring, traffic-laden, semi-metropolitan suburb. About all that can be said of them with assurance is that they are facing the future in the tradition of Rocklanders, that is, in a state of disagreement with each other, in a condition of individuality that is unlike, and proudly so, any other exurban neighborhood in the environs of New York.

Change, when it comes to a backwater, to a forgotten area like Rockland County, is a mixed blessing. It may spell progress or it may spell the horrors. To the exurbanite who is no regular commuter, and who loves his house tucked away in sylvan privacy, change is something that is going to come bustling up to him, elbowing him, pushing him around, surrounding him with billboards and hot-dog stands and carbon monoxide. His next-door neighbor may love his house as dearly, but have to commute to New York five days a week; and for him, who has had to contend with the inadequacies of the New Jersey & New York Railroad Company, or pray that a winter's fall of snow will not frustrate his car-pool, change can be a very beguiling thing. For many Rockland County villagers, change is an unmitigated nuisance, and they have been about with petitions, urging that change go away, nor bother to come again another day. Their pastors have rung their church bells in protest against it. Their politicians, however, on a modest, village level, have minimized the protests. And their bankers see nothing but profitable benefit accruing from change. If it seems strange that the advent of one big new thoroughfare could arouse so much pro and con throughout the area, two things should be remembered: Rockland County's triangle is small—only some twenty miles on a side—so that the repercussions of the Thruway are felt on every hand; and, in any event, Rockland, with many of the county's villages strung like beads along Route 9-W and with many of the county's exurbanites as thick as weeds along South Mountain Road, has always been especially road-conscious.

And change has already come. The county's population has swollen: from 75,000 in 1940, to 90,000 in 1950, to well over 100,000 in 1954. A significant part of this increase has been exurban, but more recently it has been suburban, with rashes of ranch-type houses breaking out and spreading, apparently unchecked. It may be that Rockland is the fastest growing area in the metropolitan district, and it may be that it will continue to grow, even faster. Industry, apparently undismayed by relative difficulty of access, is thrusting its steel-and-cement fingers into these rural valleys. There can be no doubt that real estate values in the county will soar. But what of the exurb's special character?

What of its individual flavor? What of its relaxed and leisurely way of life?

These things have all been shaped by the county's geography and, to a rather lesser extent, by its history. The one is rough and rocky, affording magnificent prospects in every direction; the other is venerable and rocky, and has left its mark all over, in the form of houses two centuries old and names of families still older and still today active in county life.

One side of Rockland's triangle runs along the Hudson River, falling steeply down from high bluffs. This side begins at Palisades, some twelve miles north of the George Washington Bridge, and reaches north, unfolding one stunning view after another, past Piermont and the Nyacks, past High Tor, with its revolving beacon light, past Tomkins Cove, where wartime freighters are berthed by their dozens, on north to Iona Island, in the shadow of Bear Mountain. Along this side live most of the county's residents; along this side, too, are remnants of the county's former industrial life—old mines and ironworks, the shell of the once celebrated brick-making center at Haverstraw, the shadow of the once extensive shipbuilding center at Nyack.

The county's southwestern leg is the New York-New Jersey state line, extending from Palisades up and out past Suffern to Sloatsburg. Here, too, villages are clustered: Tappan, Orangeburg, Shanks Village, Pearl River, Nanuet, west to Suffern and, just over the county line in Orange, the wealthy enclave of Tuxedo Park.

The third side, the county's northwestern leg, cuts back across hilly and forested country from Sloatsburg through the Palisades Interstate Park in the Ramapo Mountains, and on, back to the Hudson, at Bear Mountain.

Exactly central is the county's seat, New City, which is still little more than a white courthouse and a cluster of stores and filling-stations. New City is flanked by Congers and Spring Valley.

And where, in all this, is the exurb?

It is not easy to locate. In fact, and this is one of the charms of Rockland County, the county itself is pretty easy to lose. Pre-

suming that you take dead aim on Rockland County from New
York City, you will drive up the West Side Highway to the
George Washington Bridge, cross it, and, unless you are keeping
a sharp lookout, miss Rockland entirely and end up somewhere
in New Jersey. Route 9-W is a sharp right, just as you get off
the bridge. Nod once, or even blink, and you are past it, and must
beat a complicated course back along winding (and lovely)
country roads.

Once on 9-W, your troubles are still not over, if you are searching out an exurban retreat. You will drive north past various highway eyesores, past the brand-new Prentice-Hall publishing plant,
past what was once the extensive Dwight Morrow estate, past
what was once the excellent FM experimental station of the late
Major Armstrong, up and around the shoulder of a hill to the first
breath-taking panoramic view of the Hudson, down again along
a steep, wooded grade, until you are fetched up by a stop light.
When it is green again, on you will go and, none the wiser, you
will have gone right by a small but flourishing exurb, without
ever having seen it, without having noticed anything more arrest-
ing than a onetime church that has been converted into an
antique store. This store, and a flagpole on a minuscule patch of
village green, and a general store and post office hidden behind
some trees to your left, constitute the village of Palisades. And
the exurb? It was on your right, hidden behind the trees. You
must turn round and drive back, to find the roads that lead to it.
Its name is Sneden's Landing, but it is called Sneden's, or, merely,
the Landing. This pleasant parochial snobbism is everywhere to be
noticed in Rockland County.

The Landing is a clutch of small, mostly old houses that cling
and cluster thickly along Landing Road, which winds steeply
down from 9-W to the river. They are on top of each other; they
are all about each other; their backs are on the road or they are
off, hidden at the end of curling driveways that may seem like
tunnels through the branches of the locust trees. And despite
their haphazard, helter-skelter disposition up and down the bank,
and among the trees, few of them have, or need, any owner's or

renter's name on the roadway, to guide the questing guest. For the Landing is so ingrown that one may stop anywhere, inquire at any house, and be given precise directions as to how to reach one's goal. The directions are precise, in the sense that one will be told exactly where to drive, around which curves and along which driveways; yet at the same time they may be puzzling. One who is looking for the Smiths, for example, may be told that they live in the Browns' house, just down there, and the third to the left. The Browns, one will learn later, have not lived in this house for seven years, and there have been four families in succession living in the house since then, but to Landing residents it will still be the Browns' house, even though most or all will know the Smiths live there now. Or the house may bear a raffish name, or a quaint: Stone House, Château Hash, the Pirate's Lair, the Dingdong, and so on. According to exegetes of local myth and ritual, these names were clapped on these houses by pre-Revolutionary river pirates; it is a harmless conceit, and one that pleases Sneden's exurbanites.

Certainly many of the houses are very old. In one or two of them lived the original Molly Sneden herself, owner and operator of a ferry across the Hudson back in the eighteenth century, when this break in the stretch of Palisades was an important ferry-landing, a link in the shipping of the produce of Dutch farmers into New York. Mistress Sneden played a counter-Revolutionary role: she was a Tory, given to hiding runaway redcoats, and only very unwillingly putting her ferry at the disposal of Washington and his troops. With the decline of the county's industry and agriculture, the ferry's importance declined, and at length disappeared. Her name, however, was handed down through the generations; it can be found twice on the plaque memorializing those who fought and died in the first World War, and which is on the tiny village green, just off 9-W.

As an exurb, Sneden's has its origin back in the days a few years after that war. The owner of much of the choicest land, a woman descended via various merchants and officers from the Captain James Lawrence who won fame in every history book by saying, "Don't give up the ship!", had married a sculptor, François

Tonetti, and to her house on spring and summer week ends came artist friends from New York. There were several small cottages and small houses already standing on the land. It was only a matter of time before these were being loaned, then rented for the summer, then rented for the year, then—as Exurbia began to flourish—for indefinite periods. Lustrous theatre names followed the artistic names and subsequently, as is ever the case in an exurban evolution, the more commercial folk from radio and the big slick magazines found their way into this seclusion. For a time, Mrs. Tonetti ruled with a firm but pleasant hand; her word was law, and her disapproving eyebrow sufficient to still a considerable tendency toward all-night parties that was beginning to generate. Such festivities, in as cramped and jumbled an exurb as Sneden's, can be trying. If the slumbrous night is pierced too often by the studied squeals of toothsome young actresses fleeing the embraces of their caprizant week-end hosts, the entire exurban population will begin to mutter and shift uneasily from foot to foot. Those living on the lower levels of the parterre are uneasily aware that their neighbors above and behind them can practically spit down their chimneys. Unless each householder keeps a firm grip on himself, things are likely to degenerate into Macdougall Alley, only with mosquitoes. Then Mrs. Tonetti died, some time ago, and her land was divided among her four children, who subsequently sold small parcels to near and dear friends, who in turn built still further.

Sale, resale, and lease have all contributed to the process by which the exurb has gradually come out from under the relatively staid aegis of Mrs. Tonetti, but in self-protection, this exurb remains comparatively quiet and circumspect. In the first place, many of its residents, by the nature of their work, require periods of absolute privacy, peace, and quiet, for the exacting concentration of finishing a book, or a magazine article, or getting up in a part, or writing a television play the deadline for which was, as usual, two weeks ago. Such being the case, privacy is, by and large, respected.

Some of the newer houses, a few of them designed by the

architect son-in-law of Mrs. Tonetti, are comfortable, conservative adaptations of traditional styles; others, more recently built by other architects who have settled in Sneden's, are equally comfortable but of modern design, combining fieldstone and glass to take advantage of their perches along the bluff.

One may search in vain for any of the stigmata that distinguish other exurbs. Here, as elsewhere in Rockland County, the fetish is non-conformity, individuality, originality. The houses are unpretentious, and bear the owner's stamp. Few are living here for show, and those few who do are in uncomfortable territory. For those who do not care about éclat, Sneden's has proven a pleasant retreat and, since it is limited by its geography in its further growth, it has seemed possible that it would always remain so. It is difficult for one who has once lived in Sneden's to throw off memories of it, and the hold of placid twilights, looking out over his river.

The exurbanites in Sneden's have much in common with those who live further beyond in Rockland County, on South Mountain Road, and yet the two communities have very little to do with each other. It is another aspect of the live-and-let-live atmosphere that pervades the county. As with the Landing, it is very easy for the searcher to bypass the Road completely. As you proceed on up 9-W past Piermont, past Grandview, past Tallman Mountain State Park, past various roadhouses, through various infinitesimal villages, you will come presently to another splendid view of the Hudson spread out beneath you, winding past green-shouldered hills into the distance. Bemused, you will in all likelihood ignore the sharp turnoff to the left which you must make to reach New City. Nor, indeed, should you go so far as New City. A road, not particularly well marked, bearing to the right, will lead you away from New City and, if you are sufficiently alert to take it, you will find yourself on South Mountain Road. Here you will gradually realize, you are in another exurb. Your principal clue will be postboxes, for on South Mountain Road (*the* Road) householders are less shy than their counterparts in Sneden's Landing.

The names on the postboxes include some old Rockland County names, like Conklin and Blauvelt, Eberling and Sloat; but there are others, too, and to list them one would have to plead guilty to a form of name-dropping, one which an exurbanite has described as Sardi's Tic, for the majority of names are familiar in show biz. The road itself has been cut along the southern flank of some hills, and reaches from High Tor on the east to a highway that threads through Mount Ivy and Spring Valley on the west.

Above the road, cut into the hillside, are some exurban homes; others are below the road, along the banks of Wolf Creek. As exurb, it has some striking points of similarity to Sneden's: the first artists arrived thirty-odd years ago; the trail blazer was also the wife of a sculptor, Mrs. Mary Mowbray-Clark, whose example was followed shortly by some friends from Greenwich Village, vestigial remnants of the twilight of the Gaelic revival. On their heels came the theatrical people and more recently, in the familiar pattern, the magazine, book-publishing, and television types. Years ago, this group was more tightly knit: Henry Varnum Poor, the painter, and his wife, Bessie Breuer, and the Maxwell Andersons constituted the core of a social unit in which feuds were at times protracted; but affairs have become more casual and informal since the war. To account for this, there is, in the first place, the influx of latter-day exurbanites. There is more room for new building along the Road, more room for the newcomer than in Sneden's, and Poor has had a hand in building some of these newer houses. A few of the houses strive for magnificence, as must befit a cinema mogul. There seems to be a trend toward modern design, as must befit a forward-looking exurbanite. But, by and large, the houses lend a feeling of relaxation and content, without pretentiousness. And the ingrown atmosphere of years ago is gradually dissipating.

There's an atmosphere of mutually respecting gentleness in the air, even when there is devastating commentary just beneath the surface. An example of the kind of murderous gemütlichkeit which one may encounter among sophisticated Roaders may be of value in illustrating this. It happened not long ago that a visitor to a Rockland couple inquired about a friend, another Rocklander, who had been having domestic difficulties, and whom the visitor had not seen for a couple of years. In reply to the inquiry, the visitor's host said, "Oh, haven't you heard? He's remarried."

"Oh? Is he happy?"

"Probably. It's nobody we know. Very pretty, though. He's sending her to an analyst and he bought her a mink coat. . . ."

The visitor turned to his hostess. "Do you know her? Ever see her?"

"Yes," she replied. "She came in the other day on the way to the city. 'You must help me,' she said, 'I'm on my way to my analyst's and I haven't dreamed anything. Lend me a dream, please do.' You know, I always dream. And this child, you know. She doesn't need analysis at all. In a few years here, of course. But not now. It was very sweet and touching. And, of course, original. That's important, isn't it?"

But the truly noteworthy aspect of life along this road, as of life at Sneden's and as of life among the exurbanites wherever they may be scattered through the county (there are isolated outposts of Exurbia in the Nyacks, around Suffern, at Stony Point, and in the countryside near Spring Valley) is the lack of any effort at homogeneity. Unlike Fairfield County, whose social life has a smooth and inclusive pattern and routine, or Bucks, with its dining out and its playhouse, in Rockland County the joint, the communal, the organized is *vieux jeu*. Thus, despite the concentration of theatre folk, of writers, actors, directors, no attempt at a summer theatre has ever succeeded, and the few desultory efforts have invariably died of inanition. Even such an enterprise as a regular poker game soon becomes sporadic and casual. Perhaps it is the demands of these exurbanites' careers, which may, at long-distance whim, deposit them overnight in Beverly Hills for six months or six years; perhaps it is the nature of their temperaments, which demands of them individuality. But for many of the Rockland County exurbanites, showing up at a first-night on Broadway is perhaps their principal concession to conformity.

For many of them commuting is an unnecessary nuisance, and this is just as well, for commuting from Rockland is a trial. There are trains, there are cars, there are—for a few adventurous spirits among the newer and younger exurbanites—planes, and, presumably, there are pogo-sticks. It is a question which is the easiest.

Most of the exurbanites who have to commute seem to resign themselves to car-pools. And some have made their car-pooling a fruitful experience. One such pool, comprising a deodorant manufacturer, an advertising executive, a public relations tycoon, a radio station representative, and a *Life* magazine advertising man, used their time in planning a setup where they and their friends could have a joint swimming-pool, tennis courts, soft-ball diamond, and ice-skating rink. They ended up by forming the Nyack Field Club, after purchasing an estate from Oom the Omnipotent. Two hundred families, having plunked down initiation fees of $250 and $400, are the club's membership.

Older readers may remember Oom. More prosaically Pierre Bernard, he arrived from England in the mid-Twenties, set himself up as psyche-soother to the lazy rich, preached yoga, convinced himself, left for India to return with the title of Doctor, and, because of his talent for catching the interest of female Vanderbilts, landed spang in the more lurid pages of the Sunday supplements where he occasionally makes a nostalgic reappearance. The word that always fitted into a headline, along with "Oom," was "orgy," but the charge was a hummer. All Oom was up to was an attempt to keep his ladies on the move, generally by group dancing. "Life is motion," he said, "keep busy." He himself kept busy: he was for a time president of one county bank and director of several others. The reaction of the community is symptomatic of the native Rocklander's relaxed acceptance of the most outlandish capers. The tolerance extended to Oom was greatest at a time when he was under most flamboyant attack in the metropolitan tabloids.

This tolerance is traditional, in Rockland, and goes far to explain why the first trail-blazing artists were not subjected to the
usual criticism of "free-love" or "communism."

Rockland has its quota of curious divergencies from the norm,
both past and present. It was in Haverstraw that Robert Owen
launched a Socialist community, back in the 1820's. The county
was full of stops on the Underground Railroad for runaway
slaves, in the years just before the Civil War; many of them ran
no further, finding the hills of Rockland so tolerant that they
could settle down with the descendants of some of the ladies
who had, a couple of generations earlier, done much for the
morale of Washington's Revolutionary troops. This mating has
produced a small group of communities far back in the wooded
hills. Its folk are collectively called the Jackson whites. It took
the draft, during the second World War, to disturb their withdrawal from modern civilization. Of mixed Indian, white, and
Negro blood, they continue to live in the Ramapos, presumably
undisturbed even by television, engaging in a little peaceful
poaching every now and then, occasionally sloping down to
Exurbia to try their hand at an odd job or two, but never at so
much as three. More recently, the county has given houseroom
to Alexandra Tolstoy's Reed Farm, home-from-home for a slew
of White Russians, and even occasionally finds jobs for her
charges.

Privately, the native Rocklander may think the whole caboodle,
artists, exurbanites, Jackson whites, and White Russians, belong
properly in the Rockland State Hospital, but publicly the friction
is slight.

The reactions to the Thruway, noted earlier, are still being
manifested. The governor, back in 1950, addressed a group of
Nyack citizens at the corner of Burd Street and Broadway. If,
he intoned, he were investing in real estate, he would buy in
Rockland County. This sweetmeat tossed the citizenry was not
enough to calm their concern. Rockland exurbanites have always
delighted in the charm of Nyack, and of South Nyack, where
they have done much of their shopping; some of the houses,

curlicued and turreted in full Victorian fashion, have been favorites for exurbanites who incline to the quaint. And gradually it was borne in on them that the new highway's interchanges, off the Tappan Bridge, were practically going to obliterate South Nyack. To the west, strenuous complaints from Suffern and Spring Valley caused some re-routing. To the south, exurbanites in Grand View, in Piermont, and in Sneden's strove to resist a link connecting the bridge entrance at South Nyack with the New Jersey Turnpike. It is here that church bells were rung, summoning the rebellious to the signing of petitions.

"It will place Rockland and Westchester counties five minutes apart," says the president of the Suffern National Bank and Trust Company. But the exurbanites don't want to be only five minutes from Westchester.

"It takes Rockland out of the hinterlands and puts us overnight in an urban area," says the bank president, reflecting on the sum of his assets. But it was to get out of the urban area and into the hinterlands that the exurbanites came here.

"We will rival Bergen County in New Jersey and Queens County in New York," proclaims the president of the First National Bank of Spring Valley. And the exurbanites shudder.

"While new building records are being created monthly, in Rockland County, it is nothing to what will happen shortly," said the bank president. "Two large builders from Long Island were here today and each arranged to build a hundred and fifty houses in Ramapo. We are swamped with applications from small industries which want to settle here." The exurbanites, for their part, are building storm-cellars.

It is still too early to tell what will become of Rockland County as an exurb. It may persist, stubbornly, or it may go down fighting vainly against the onrush of what is called progress. The exurbanites in Nyack have already seen the writing on the wall, just as the wall has already felt the impact of the house-wrecker's giant iron ball. For Sneden's and for Grand View, it may be different; their jealously guarded preserve may still persevere, sheltered by the trees. Up on South Mountain the case is more gloomy.

Here, the exurbanites own, each of them, considerable acreage. The exurb is not zoned in any formal sense, but the owners have verbally agreed, amongst themselves, that they will not sell. But the bulldozers have been at work, just a few miles away.

You get the impression, if you sit with a South Mountain Road exurbanite on his terrace overlooking Wolf Creek, while the grapes slowly swell under their broad leaves, and the bees buzz companionably about your ankles, and the stream purls and murmurs, that maybe you are sitting in on a re-enactment of the third act of *The Cherry Orchard.* The benign atmosphere is threatened; there is something hostile abroad. Here, where so many plays have been written, so many songs and symphonies, here where it has been so idyllic for so long, where so many pots of preserves have been put up, so many gardens grown, so many artsy-craftsy curtains handloomed, there is an autumnal sadness.

If you bend an ear attentively, you may be able to hear a distant sound, as if from the sky, the sound of a violin string breaking, dying away, melancholy. Silence ensues, broken not by the stroke of an axe on the trees in the distant cherry orchard but by the sound of a distant bulldozer, busily at its work of road grading, by the sound of a jackhammer, by the sound of a dozen, two-dozen, six-dozen ranch houses and split levels being reared overnight. Ruefully, the South Mountain Roader contemplates his future. Soon, he feels, the first of his neighbors will have had a bellyful and will decide to move, selling his twenty acres. And on them will spring up, like Jason's adversaries from the teeth of the dragon, a fearful crop of suburban homes. He sighs, thinking of the very real delights of his life in this pleasant, withdrawn exurb.

Fairfield, Bucks, Rockland. Three prime exurbs on the threshold of change, three that present contrasts but face a common danger, each in its own way. Meanwhile, though, they thrive.

At a Fairfield party you will meet trade celebrities, that is, people who have fame within the communications industry even though they may be unknown outside it. Mingling with them will be public celebrities from television and the theatre. A leaven of advertising folk and commercial artists will provide a kind of participating audience, a Greek-letter chorus. It will be gay and loud and childish and everyone will become convivially drunk. Before the evening is over, chances are you'll see at least one husband (probably the businessman square whose wife is a celebrity) decide to throw off the shackles of dull care by cavorting and camping with a lampshade on his head. Everyone will be polite about it and only his wife will die inside. And there will be jokes, the best and funniest and dirtiest jokes, but above all the newest ones, the jokes that will be told (stag only) in Suburbia a month later.

Go to a party in Bucks. Meet the nation's top magazine editors. Hear the latest poop on how to get the government to help you build a lake—several Bucks exurbanites have done it, farmers all. Here it's more decorous than in Fairfield, the jokes are cleaner, the drinking is at a steadier and less frenetic pace. Total alcohol consumed will be about the same, but in Bucks there will be less likelihood of encountering the man or woman who drinks too much too fast, passes out or gets sick or both, and then either has to be taken home (by a furious spouse) or put in the spare room to sleep it off. That, by the way, is almost a standard production at the larger Fairfield parties.

Go to a party—that rarer thing—in Rockland. Nobody tells jokes. Sharp and witty conversation and character assassination by epigram have taken their place. Jokes are considered immature and as distasteful as trade jargon—which is a requirement for communication on the inside level in Fairfield. In Rockland, the following subjects are not considered fit topics for conversation: national politics; individual earnings, property costs and assessments; sexual anomalies and adventures, psychoanalysis—except as these apply to anyone not present; the currently-on-view products of those present; the taking seriously of best sellers. In Rockland they've had it, long, long ago. Nor will you meet celebrities at Rockland parties, except for those Rocklanders who are what they refer to, with an amused gesture of hooking two fingers of each hand so you can see that the word is in quotes, as "real" celebrities, i.e., people who have made a reputation for their work and not for themselves via appearances in mass entertainment media. But the chances are good that you will meet next year's shining light of the Alfred A. Knopf list, or of the off-Broadway theatre, or of a one-man show in a Fifty-seventh Street gallery. For Rocklanders have an uncanny way of anticipating taste and trend, and of being through with a person, an idea, a creative work, before the rest of Exurbia takes it up and creates a fad which will penetrate later still into the brighter echelons of the rest of America.

In Fairfield, first-name dropping is so prevalent that Martha can only mean Martha Raye. In Rockland it's probably Graham, just as Tennessee is a playwright and Truman is not an ex-president. In Bucks, Martha's last name is probably Washington, and is the appellation not of a historic character but of a new hybrid, early-blooming zinnia.

Let's postulate, to illustrate some of the foregoing, the existence-to-be of Saturday night parties in Fairfield, Bucks, and Rockland. (Something wrong here already, as the sharper eyes will have discerned: Rockland parties may be on a Saturday night, but they obviously don't have to be and since it's conventional to have parties on Saturday night it's preferable not to. On the other hand, it's provincial to do things merely because they aren't conventional. Additionally, a Saturday night party is not only conventional, it's also traditional—and tradition is fine. So we're on fairly safe ground after all.) And let's see how their membership is recruited.

FAIRFIELD

(Preliminary phone call from a man high up at 485 Madison Avenue to one a few floors higher at 30 Rockefeller Plaza)

DAVE: Hi, boy, how's it going at the word factory?
DICK: Okay, Dad. How's *with* you?
DAVE: Listen, lad. You wired in on plans for Saturday?
DICK: Well, I heard something was cooking by you guys, but I

haven't touched base with Bets yet. You know, kids and stuff. . . .

DAVE: Well, look. It's going to be a real ball. Tell Bets if she gets a sitter I'll give her five gold stars for her toothbrush chart.

DICK: Will do. *(He'd like to chuckle at that crack about the gold stars but he won't—he'll use it down the hall in five minutes.)*

DAVE: Oh, and Reechahrd . . . don't forget, we were together, strictly biznaz, Wednesday night, in case it comes up.

DICK: Don't worry, boy. I'm writing a How-Not-To, "The Power of Negative Thinking." Your bride's a mind reader. Nice gal, though. Believe me, you're lucky to have her. By the way: is we or is we ain't going to get an escalator into that contract? I mean, is it going to be a marriage or a divorce, or what? I can't play footsie with it much longer; the client's got the needle in me.

DAVE: Tell you what, meet me in the bar car and we'll make talk.

DICK: Oke, boy. You hold the seats, I'll get the drinks. And I'll remember to cover for you on that Wednesday night deal. . . .

DAVE: Thanks, son. And don't worry about that contract; you've got a built-in salesman here, to wit, little me.

DICK: Good boy. So don't go goofing off early and forget.

DAVE: You bombing me? Don't worry. . . . Gotta go now, Coast's on the other pipe.

DICK: Well, take care.

DAVE: Have fun.

BUCKS

(Excerpt from a call from a lady working with her hat on in the Graybar Building to another lady in her studio near Doylestown)

MARIE: I hate to bother you in the middle of the day like this, Helene, I know you're working.

HELENE: Oh, Marie. It's a pleasure to be interrupted by somebody besides the children, bless them, and the man that's taking so unconscionably long with the retaining wall, damn him. How is it in the city?

MARIE: Hot.

HELENE: Here, too.

MARIE: Well, it *is* summer, as they say. Now there's an intelligent remark. So well put, too. . . . By the way, dear, I called to ask if you and Harvey would come by Saturday evening for a drink. It's not a party, just a few people you know. I'm asking you now because I won't be down until Friday.

HELENE: Why, I think we'd love to if Harv doesn't have to stay with Pride o'Bourne. Isn't that a silly name for a mere cow? Last year she dropped her calf on the Fourth of July. . . .

MARIE: Downright inconsiderate, I call it. But do come, please. And come early enough so I can show you the way we laid out the herb garden.

ROCKLAND

(Fragment of a preliminary chat between two ladies of South Mountain Road who have met at the market in New City)

VANESSA: Well, Astrid?

ASTRID: Oh, hello, Vanessa.

VANESSA: How's the play going?

ASTRID: Oh, Jed's half out of his mind. He always is at the end.

VANESSA: I'm sorry . . . but of course I know I needn't be. I meant I was hoping you and he might come over tomorrow night. It might help him to have to talk to people, and I promise it will be very small.

ASTRID: Well, I don't know, I don't know. . . .

VANESSA: I shan't urge you, of course. Tennessee will be there, and Carson, and George has asked that young man that makes those little iron tactiles that you roll on the floor, you know. *(Astrid doesn't know, but she will. In a month all Rockland will know and in three months the young man and his little iron abstractions will have a spread in* Life. *By that time the young man will be invited to Westport, not the Road.)*

ASTRID: Well, dear, it's good of you, but as I say, I don't

know. Buzz and his wife *were* coming to dinner, and maybe Bill . . .

VANESSA: Sloane?

ASTRID: Mauldin.

VANESSA: Well, I suppose I could ask you to bring them, but . . .

ASTRID: Of course. It's silly to try; everyone would be annoyed at the thought except George and his amusement upsets Jed. I'll see if I can postpone them, shall I? I know Jed wants to see George very much.

And so it goes.

4

THE EXURBS: THE NORTH SHORE, NORTHERN WESTCHESTER AND ELSEWHERE

There are only the pursued, the pursuing, the busy and the tired.

—F. SCOTT FITZGERALD

In the past twenty years, the United States has been most fickle in its selection of types for hero-worship. It is difficult to realize, in the light of the present, that Bankers and Business Executives once were heroes, in the Twenties.

—JOHN P. MARQUAND

ALTHOUGH the exurbs on the North Shore of Long Island and in the northern part of Westchester differ from each other in many respects, they are alike in several basic ways. First, they are far older, as exurbs, than Fairfield, Bucks, or Rockland. Second, they are more select and snobbish. Third, their exurbanites are more frequently second generation, that is, they are children of commuting parents and, though born out of town, are "exurban" to the core. Finally, there is an imposing contingent of businessmen exurbanites among their populations, especially along the North Shore, where this type predominates. (Calling a banker, a stockbroker, or any other businessman an exurbanite may seem like a contradiction, but it is not. Not all businessmen qualify as exurbanites, of course, but some do, specifically those symbol-manipulating ones whose social customs and inner conflicts hew to the exurban pattern as already described.)

But there is one critical difference between the other exurbs we've discussed and those of the North Shore and northern Westchester. This is that their exurbanites have striven to conform to what they found when they arrived; they wanted not only to live like the people already there, but to be like them, too, whereas in the other exurbs the exurbanites changed the local ways or superimposed their own.

These two exurbs are also different in that both have exurbanite, as opposed to native, traditions, generations old, to which the present exurbanites adhere to a degree, and which markedly influence their lives. On the North Shore there is the F. Scott Fitzgerald and Veblenianly-motivated-millionaire tradition, fast fading but still powerful. In northern Westchester, the tradition is one of complex local politics. (Additionally, northern Westchester exurbanites are perhaps the most active in school and civic affairs.) With these traditions in mind, let's take a closer look at these places of refuge from the rat race, and at the history which plays so much more important a role in their contemporary life than do the histories of the other exurbs.

1

In the galaxy of exurbs, there has been one super-nova, one star which flared suddenly to garish brilliance, blazed for nearly a decade, and thereafter subsided to its present steady glow. At its most incandescent, it was really something. If you were to take a child prodigy, endow him with an inclination toward juvenile delinquency, and supply him with the wealth of Croesus, his subsequent activity might be remindful of how things were in this exurb back in the bad old days. The North Shore was the first fashionable exurb. Its nights were riotous and its days hung over.

Things have quieted down considerably in the last quarter century. The suburbs have steadily and implacably nibbled away at the big estates which were, in one way or another, the theatres for the Jazz Age extravaganzas. These days, the exurb is being crowded back against the waters of the Sound, or squeezed further east, out along the island's northern edge. Today, to someone who remembers the gaudy éclat of the Jazz Age on the North Shore's gold coast, the place seems staid and middle-aged, even dowdy; and it is a fact that the children born there, the first generation of exurban babies, have grown, gone away to college, come back to find jobs in Wall Street or on Madison Avenue, and taken their fathers' places in the same old rolling stock of the Long Island Rail Road.

And yet it grows, and keeps on growing. Its expansion is in two directions: inward, into the spaces once filled by the land holdings of the richest men of their era, and outward, out past the county line dividing Nassau from Suffolk, out past Northport and Smithtown and Stony Brook, all the way to Port Jefferson and even beyond. With time, the limits of the exurb will be pushed still further. And simultaneously the vacuums left in the exclusive incorporated villages of the township of Oyster Bay will gradually fill as the millionaires depart. Already they are partially filled. Villages where once the number of taxpayers did not exceed fifty can already count five times that number. Into the once select neighborhoods are flocking the recently well-heeled of the communications industry, but with a difference. Where in other exurbs the house is sold to him who can afford to pay the price, in the residential villages of the North Shore the new exurbanite is likely to be a man whose father was in the Social Register, or whose wife's family has always been, or who, at the very least, would like one day to see his name added to the roll. On the

North Shore, Exurbia adds one more facet to all its others: social prestige.

To the auslander, there has always been a certain amount of puzzlement about the North Shore. He would like to know what all the shouting is about. As it seems to him, there is an island, and on its western end are two boroughs of New York City (Brooklyn and Queens), which consist first of commercial and industrial slums and then of rows and rows of dreary subdivision houses, built in the 1920's and 1930's; and beyond them stretch circles and crescents of still more subdivision homes, built in the 1940's and 1950's; and beyond them are a few scattered and unimpressive towns separated from each other by potato farms and cauliflower farms and duck farms; and so it goes, all the way to Peconic Bay, with, to either side, an occasional clam-digging bed. The whole island, as the tourist sees it, is shaped like a whale complete with its two flukes, traversed by some excellent parkways and occasionally splotched green by a state park or a golf course. Where is the exurb, where a neighborhood that could attract the rich and the glamorous? Where is the North Shore, anyway?

The North Shore is not obviously there for any passing tourist to gawk at. The rich men who first bought up and made fashionable the residential area along the bays and inlets and harbors of Long Island Sound were careful to see to that. Out of deference to the quick, as well as to the ghostly, rich, the network of parkways laid down in the 1930's only skirts the fringes of the exurbs. The cars that jam the Northern State Parkway or the Grand Central Parkway cannot be heard in the exurban estates of the North Shore; no carbon monoxide floats from the Jericho Turnpike or the North Hempstead Turnpike to offend the nostrils of the North Shore exurbanite, as he stands on his lawn overlooking the Sound. Nassau County, once largely farmland, has been crammed to the bursting point with middle-class suburbanites: 300,000 of them in 1930 had become 400,000 in 1940 and now they number more than 700,000; but along the highly restricted North Shore, while the exurban population has also increased, the rate has not been nearly so vulgarly rapid as it has in the real estate developments in the middle of the island.

The North Shore is different, and not merely because it is richer. Even its geology is different. Whereas the great bulk of Long Island sits on Pleistocene gravel, sand and clay, the North Shore hugs its knees atop two-hundred-foot bluffs of cretaceous semi-consolidated sediments including some schist, and while the residents of the rest of the island may not know the difference and may not care a rap for the schist, the inhabitants of the North Shore know that it does make their physical surroundings different. The only wooded rolling hills on the entire island are here, along the North Shore. Bluffs look out over the Sound and the inlets and harbors are carved handsomely and accommodatingly for the myriads of small craft in which, each summer, the North Shore takes to the water.

When first the very, very rich became interested in this shoreline, much of it was wild and some of it was still Indian reservation. They came to buy in the early years of the century, and they bought with a casual and sweeping unconcern. The Morgans bought two islands, East Island and West Island, just up from Hempstead Bay. They built a private causeway to join the two islands and another to join one of the islands to the mainland; they hired ex-marines to patrol their plums and keep off intruders from either land or sea; the *Corsair* swung at anchor off Matinicock Point, and to see her people flocked from all over the island. South of the Morgans, in Glen Cove, Charles Pratt picked up one thousand choice acres with some of his Standard Oil money. He, too, hired private police to patrol his wooded roads, and he built a half-dozen mansions to house his relatives. To the west, on one promontory of Sands Point, Hearst erected a castle that had been shipped, case by case, from Wales. To the east, near Oyster Bay, one of the Woolworth family tossed together a $3,500,000 week-end stopover. Henry Carnegie Phipps' house was valued at a mere $1,000,000, but, at Lloyd Neck, Marshall Field spent a reputed $15,000,000 for château and gardens. His former wife's two-thousand-acre estate at Huntington was worth

rather less. Chrysler, Hutton, Whitney, Brady, Aldrich, Guest—
one after another the castles and châteaux went up, sufficient to
rival the valley of the Loire. When Clarence Mackay married
Anna Case, the entire Philharmonic Symphony was materialized
in the shrubbery, as in a Hollywood musical, to accompany the
ceremony.

Before long, the locals, sniffing a good thing, began slapping
some horrendous taxes on these huge estates. When a man is
presented with a tax bill of $2,256,000, he begins to think. The
Morgans, the Mackays, the Harvey Gibsons, the George Bakers,
and a few others (a very few others) finally clubbed together
to incorporate their own village, Lattington, so that they as incor-
porators would be in a position to keep the taxes down. Naturally
enough, these folk were not disposed to let the *jacquerie* come
mousing around. While they held sway, there were no roads,
much less turnpikes or parkways, to permit the populace too close
a view. The only thing that could ever catch up with them—the
tables of mortality—eventually did. They had left tribes of children behind them, and almost to a man these children saw no
point in shouldering the responsibilities of huge estates, or in
paying the taxes on them, or in trying to find the servants to
staff them. The estates have not all disappeared, but a great
many of them have. One by one they have been converted to
other uses. Several have been turned over to educational institu-
tions; several have been sold to religious orders. Where once the
characteristic sound was of coupons being clipped, now there is
only the click of beads or the rustle of pages. Still other big estates
have been sold for real estate developments. A strenuous effort
was made to keep such developments above the subdivision level
and most of the North Shore is zoned at a minimum of two acres.
Typically, the houses in such developments cost anywhere from
$40,000 to $60,000—which makes them a nice goal for the successful young exurbanite on his way up the ladder.

But long before the huge estates had been sold or broken up,
the first writers had begun to pioneer in the area. F. Scott Fitzgerald and Ring Lardner were living in Great Neck in the early

1920's, eyeing their wealthier neighbors from a disrespectful distance. Fitzgerald was, of course, particularly interested in the life of the North Shore. *The Great Gatsby* is the fruit of his acute vision, a novel which is still the definitive work on the mores of Long Island's gold coast in the days of the Jazz Age. As he listed the guests who came to Jay Gatsby's parties, Fitzgerald was making note, for the first time in American letters, of the emergence of what was to become café society, the combination of Social Register names, theatrical celebrities, *nouveau riche*, and underworld figures, of gamblers and comedians and movie magnates and polo players and chorus girls, the combination whose residence still today sets the North Shore apart, lending it its peculiar exurban distinction.

In this period, the region's characteristic stamp was set. If it was set by the very rich and the socially registered, it was also of a kind to attract a special breed of exurbanite, one either born to or with a native predilection for a rather greater social snobbery than other exurbanites. The pattern set was, at least in emphasis, quite different from that of other exurbs. Here on the North Shore, club life is of far greater importance than elsewhere. Every dinghy owner would like to become eligible for a yacht club membership; every yacht club member, deep down inside and although he may deny it vigorously, would like to be put up and accepted into the fellowship of Seawanhaka-Corinthian. Seawanhaka-Corinthian is on Centre Island, sheltered by Plum Point, and the prospect from its clubhouse porch across Oyster Bay Harbor is of nothing but the very best-groomed estates.

Country clubs are more numerous and, again, more vital in the life of this exurb. Among these, Piping Rock carries the most cachet, with Cedar Creek perhaps running it a close second. These two clubs have beaches which are proximate, off Fox Point. At Piping Rock, during the Little Season (June and September) the club is busy with parties for debutantes, some the daughters of older, king-sized exurbanites. Membership restrictions are effectively enforced. All these clubs are in the township of Oyster Bay, but the same traditions, to a greater or lesser extent, obtain for the clubs that dot the countryside beyond the Nassau-Suffolk county line, in Huntington or beyond, in Northport, Smithtown, and Stony Brook.

Emphasis on country club life and yacht club life has led, in this exurb, to the habit of dining out. There are quite proper inns, devoted to eating alone, and then there are also country restaurants with excellent kitchens where, after dinner, if a couple is so minded, they may obtain the use of a room upstairs. But the better restaurants decline to augment their income in such a fashion. In Locust Valley, there is Camanari's, the old Weeks Hotel of grandfather's day, where Jenny Jerome, Winston Churchill's mother, used to go for Sunday dinner. Near Jericho there is the Beau Séjour, and Villa Victor is outside Syosset on Route 25-A. But hereabouts the caravansary of best repute is Rothmann's Inn at East Norwich, like the exurb, two generations old. Here, of a Saturday night, the place is jammed with crew haircuts and tans from the tennis court or the waters of the Sound. Here, of a Sunday noon, the old and respected Meadowbrook Hunt is wont to stop by, after a hard run, for a stirrup-cup, or a hunt breakfast.

The Meadowbrook Hunt is the North Shore's oldest; it may meet at Piping Rock, or at the Whitney place in Wheatley, or at Sir Ashley Sparks' home near Syosset. It is the most social and the best-heeled. Seventy-five or a hundred huntsmen may turn up in blacks or pinks, on a Sunday morning, during the season. Further out, there is the Oaks Hunt, and still further the Smithtown Hunt, for the North Shore is the horsiest of the exurbs. Half the members of the Turf and Field Club at Belmont come from the North Shore. And those people so minded can, if acceptable, join the Buckram Beagles, and go running up and down hill in all kinds of weather to their hearts' content. When the exurb was still in its super-nova stage, the horsy set had another distraction: polo. But it got to the point where a man had to take his choice between paying his taxes or maintaining his string of ponies, so polo has been withdrawn, more and more, to the playing-fields of Aiken.

This cannot represent too great a loss for the more recent exurban arrivals, few of whom can have the funds, the energy, or the idleness to warrant their becoming regular polo-players. Your exurbanite is made of milder stuff. In the Twenties, when Guest, Hitchcock, Harriman, Sanford, and Bostwick were big names, later to be joined, in the Thirties, by Iglehart and von Stade and the others, the exurbanites, while they might hold still to watch a chukker or two, were more likely to have their interest caught by the tales of the bloody croquet games being played on the Sands Point sward of Herbert Bayard Swope by such muscled athletes as Harpo Marx and Alexander Woollcott. Swope was one of the early publishers to settle on the North Shore. Among many others, Harold Guinzburg, Nelson Doubleday, and Stanley Young joined up later on. (Sometimes a publisher, like Swope, manages to combine publishing and horses. Such a one is Alicia Patterson, whose *Newsday* has grown in ten years to a circulation of some 250,000, most of it in Nassau County. She won a Pulitzer Prize for a series her paper ran on the need for new hospitals in Nassau County only a year after her husband, Harry Guggenheim, had won the Kentucky Derby with Dark Star.)

The interest of new exurbanites in moving out to the North Shore coincided with the period of the breaking up of the big estates. The monstrous castles stood on great tracts of land in which a monastery, for example, might be little interested. On the other hand, the exurban arivals were decidedly interested in such land, most of which was on or near the Sound. They were far more interested in picking up ten or twenty acres on J. P. Morgan's East Island than they were in settling in Great Neck, which was rapidly becoming, like Greenwich across the water, heavily suburban. And so it has come about that the exurbanites have built their moderately impressive homes at decent intervals in the neighborhood of the old châteaux. Morgan's East Island, on which the big house now belongs to the Roman Catholic Sisters of St. John the Baptist, has afforded a roost for nearly a dozen exurbanites. Hurdling Bayville, which is a colony of summer cottages, and coming to the village of Centre Island, there is

another exurbanite gathering which includes the editors of both
Vogue and *Harper's Bazaar*, Carmel Snow and Edna Woolman
Chase (whose daughter Ilka, now married to a Dr. Brown, also
lives here).

If Fairfield County features publishers of large national magazines, the North Shore can counter with the loftiest executives
from the home offices of the motion picture industry, and with
some from the highest level of radio and television, like the chairman of the board of CBS, whose place is on Whitney Lake, near
Manhasset, and NBC's Pat Weaver, who lives at Sands Point.

Lately, the pressure for still more building has continued in the
more restricted areas of Oyster Bay township. Real estate agents,
thanks to the growing exurbanite demand, have sold land around
Syosset and especially around Brookville. To the north, the more
languid rich are growing impatient with the speed with which the
exurbanites are moving in on them. They realize it is better than
having more Levittowns on the island, but they take the position
that Brookville is one of the exclusive incorporated villages of
Oyster Bay, and don't look too kindly on an influx that may well
include some people whom they would find socially unacceptable.
Regretfully, they are beginning to write Brookville off. They are
beginning to call it Brookvile. And as an indication of how land
values are appreciating around what has become a most popular
exurban colony, an educator who bought one hundred acres for
$150,000 a couple of years ago has to keep brushing realtors away
like flies. They are offering her $500,000 for the same acreage.

On the North Shore, as in Westchester, there are also the
second generation exurbanites, now grown and back from the
wars. Youngsters graduate from Yale, go to see their uncles who
are account executives, and are given jobs running the mimeograph
machine. Come Christmas, as one cynical network executive put
it, "Someone gives them a stop-watch and they become TV
producers. It seems to be as good training as any other." They are
then prepared to don their Brooks Brothers pink shirts and black
knitted silk ties, and take their places at the Syosset platform of
the Long Island Rail Road as full-fledged, second generation
exurbanites. Of course, it's not that simple. There are, among the

second generation exurbanites of the North Shore, a whopping contingent who are as thoroughly trained in their work and as serious about it as anyone else.

So far, we have talked of the North Shore as though it were one homogeneous community whose parts were only geographically removed from each other. Actually, each community, in its growth and present state of being, differs from its fellows, although exurban Nassau, as we've seen, is pretty evenly stereotyped, as is exurban Suffolk. On the North Shore, differences are rather by counties than by townships. Syosset's commuting population is rapidly becoming one of the island's largest, from 151 in 1930, to 514 in 1950, to 923 in 1953. The population of the township of Oyster Bay has gone, over the same period, from 37,000 in 1930 to 43,000 in 1940, to better than 67,000 in 1950. And it is this township which includes most of the communities of the North Shore west of Suffolk County.

In Suffolk County, the growth has been even more rapid, principally because of the various restrictions (chiefly anti-Semitic) that have controlled Oyster Bay's growth. Not one town on the Port Jefferson line but showed an increase in the period 1930-1950, according to the Long Island Rail Road's figures; not one town whose real estate agents will not insist there has been even greater growth since. Port Jefferson, which is some forty miles from Manhattan, is nothing like so far away as, say, Stratford, on the New Haven's tracks, but is at least six times as far if the LIRR's indignities are heaped on the scale; yet in 1950 there were 157 commuters prepared to suffer those indignities to get to New York.

As to differences within the exurb: exurban Suffolk is not so closely tied to the Social Register as is North Shore Nassau. Life is more casual. The exurbanites who have moved out here, to handsome houses on Asharoken Beach or on the wooded bluffs around Northport, are likely to take their sailing or their fishing more seriously. The Surfcasters' Club, which includes many exurbanites among its members, maintains a watch around the clock, no matter how foul the weather, so that the membership can be informed when the tommy cods are running, when the flounders or blackfish, when the porgies or mackerel or bluefish, when the snappers or big striped bass. As in nearly every other exurb, there are hordes of children in the towns along Suffolk's North Shore, and their parents have seen to it that the schools are as well-staffed and physically as handsome as possible. Parents in Suffolk are justifiably proud of their public school system; it is far better than the public schools of Nassau's North Shore, where the parents can usually afford to send their kids away to private schools or to the Friends Academy in near-by Locust Valley, and so do not insist on a first-rate public school system.

In exurban Suffolk, fathers and mothers both turn out for the PTA meetings and the fathers in addition cheerfully spend hours of their free time on behalf of the schools, raising money at White Elephant sales, painting, decorating, building.

Not satisfied with trying to forget their rat-race symbol-manipulation by such thing-manipulation on behalf of the schools, many husbands are gluttons for more of the same around their homes. Along Asharoken Beach, for example, where the early settlers included John Golden, Olin Downes, and Rube Goldberg, and where the typical stigmata are the blue spruce and the azalea bush, there was in the last couple of years a fever of outdoor barbecue building. Building a barbecue can get out of hand. One man who started out to construct a simple backyard stone barbecue went on to lay down a patio, enclose part of the patio, build a game room off the enclosure, landscape the whole thing, undertake a sunken garden and a swimming-pool as part of the landscaping, and finally build two cabanas near the swimming-pool. Something that he figured would cost maybe $1,000 ended by setting him back closer to $25,000.

The differences between Nassau and Suffolk are far less apparent at night, especially in summer. North Shore exurbanites are not addicted to quiet evenings at home. On Saturday nights, the yacht clubs and the country clubs are alive, and the young women dress more carefully and less informally than in, say, Bucks County, or Rockland. Their gowns are evening clothes that are feminine and dressy and, their wearers confidently trust, alluring. Nor are they always intended to allure merely the wearers' own husbands. The North Shore remembers the period of its greatest zing, back in the Jazz Age, and such habits are not likely to disappear.

This is another instance in which exurbanites, typically, are victims of nostalgic feelings about things they never did. Having been, in most cases, precocious children, they were sensitive in their formative years to the goings on of their elders, antics and posturings which they took more seriously—observing them wistfully from without—than the people who were exhibiting them. *The Sun Also Rises, Jurgen, This Side of Paradise,* and similar fiction of the Twenties were read by today's exurbanites when they were a little too young. Today, resident on the North Shore and committed to the daily round of business and family life, they strive (not consciously) to make true what was probably never entirely true, to generate in their lives some of the sad-gay excitements of that impulsive, self-destructive behavior which had a charm of a kind, but which was extensively glamorized when the present generation of exurbanites was absorbing, at puberty, ideas and attitudes more suitable to their elders recently returned from the first World War.

F. Scott Fitzgerald recalled, in one of his autobiographical essays, how he had shocked a young acquaintance, a Wall Street businessman, by suggesting a cocktail before lunch. That was in 1920. Today, the refusal of a cocktail might shock a North Shore exurbanite of comparable age. But this is by no means to suggest that all, or indeed any but an older minority of the exurbanites living on the North Shore participate in dubious social activity. Nor do the younger majority approve of it, or find it amusing. But they know it goes on. Typically, however, without them. They are far too busy enjoying their small boats, or fishing, or occupied with their growing young, or trying to improve their already handsome homes.

2

In northern Westchester, life is taken more seriously and the rat race is displaced after hours not so much by giddy goings on, but

by an exurban form of rat race which involves the contestants in
a vortex of local politics, PTA activity, and genteel socializing,
not all of it entirely voluntary.

An example of the latter which made exurban history for one
family will serve to illustrate. The occasion was a dance given to
raise money for the Republican fund. Present, by invitation, were
the cream of the exurban population, among them some secret
Democrats who felt it expedient to swallow their convictions in
the name of sociability and continued acceptance in the community—not to mention continued gainful employment. During
the festivities, one exurban wife (political affiliation unknown)
expressed the boredom she shared with her immediate group, and
suggested in bell-like tones that the proceedings could be considerably enlivened by putting Wallace on the bandstand. It
happened that this comment was made during one of those spells
of complete silence which sometimes overtake a group gathering.
Everyone heard it and everyone but her husband smiled. He was
appalled, but quickly realized that everyone else had taken it for
granted that she meant DeWitt Wallace, of *Reader's Digest*, and
not the former Vice-President resident in this exurb.

To understand something of how and why this exurb came to
be the way it is, one must have some familiarity with its history
and geography, and especially with its unique political organization. A good starting-place is the narrow waist of Westchester
County, from the Hudson River to the corner where Connecticut's
Fairfield County angles sharply in, across which stretches a belt
of reservoirs and cemeteries, a strip of indeterminate depth a few
miles to the north of White Plains that has been dubbed by one
county planning expert the Kensico Barrier. It forms, very approximately, the dividing line between the suburbs and the exurbs.
South of the barrier live more than eighty percent of Westchester's six hundred and fifty thousand people. These are the folk
who have made the name of Westchester synonymous all over
the United States with a suburban area. From them Helen
Hokinson might have drawn (and probably did) the inspiration
for the bulk of her *New Yorker* cartoons. The area's population

is not exclusively suburban: around Purchase and Harrison, for example, there probably live a few exurbanites, and another few, aiming originally for Fairfield County, may have got no further than Rye. But spiritually and characteristically southern Westchester is solid suburb.

North of the barrier there are lovely lakes, farms, rolling meadows, woodland, and some stretches of countryside still quite wild, not to mention state parks and reservations. These are powerful enticements to exurbanites fleeing the rat race. And quite apart from the natural beauties of the northern county, there is snob value, a potent magnet on one group of potential exurbanites. In the first place, the very rich had bought up great tracts of land to the north, all the way to the slanting northern boundary of the county and beyond, into Putnam County, around Brewster and Mahopac; they had treated their purchases variously, sometimes farming them in gentlemanly fashion, sometimes erecting on them châteaux of unredeemed incongruity. The most celebrated of these estates, the thirty-five-hundred-acre demesne of the Rockefellers at Pocantico Hills, has gone on a diet, what with taxes and the servant problem, and has slimmed down considerably; and many of the others have been cut up, parceled out among the children of large nineteenth-century families, and eventually digested in relatively modest gulps of fifty, one hundred, and one hundred and fifty acres by the richer exurbanites. But there are still some of these manors hidden away in the woods, especially to the north of Bedford Village.

In addition to the precedent established by the rich, there was, for the exurbanites, a second lure, like a Royal Coachman twitched above a trout stream. This was the advent to northern Westchester, in the early 1930's, of some personable, even glamorous Broadway figures. Non-farming playwrights, disenchanted by the moo of a cow in Bucks County and repelled from Fairfield County by the too continuous tinkle of ice in cocktail shakers, had bought places all the way from Pleasantville to Bedford Village, where Tallulah Bankhead was an early squatter. There is status in owning land that marches with Miss Bankhead's.

And so the exurbanites squeezed through the Kensico Barrier and, liking what they found, fanned outward.

Merely because it lies beyond the barrier, it should not be assumed that all of northern Westchester is an exurb. To regard an address in Ossining as prideful is a consideration limited to restricted circles, whose members in any event regard it as only a temporary address. Further up along the Hudson is Peekskill, conceivably important for commerce, but no exurban hideaway. Indeed, a great swatch of the northwestern part of the county is given over to colonies of summer cottages. The northward course of the exurbanites has taken them rather away from the Hudson. The townships where they have settled have names that are not overly familiar, for reasons that will be explained in a moment; but their capture by the exurbanites was gradual. Mount Pleasant was overrun, and New Castle thereafter invested, after which Bedford and Yorktown and Pound Ridge were attacked and beachheads established in Lewisboro, North Salem, and Somers. The occupation has been, in the main, to the north and east; it has followed, broadly, the lines laid down by the New York Central and especially by its Harlem Valley Division; the principal enclaves were in order, Pleasantville, Armonk, Chappaqua, Mount Kisco, Bedford Hills, Bedford Village, Pound Ridge, Yorktown Heights, and Goldens Bridge.

It is important to note that the towns, villages, and places here listed are not particularly important, except as stations along a railroad or highway, for the exurbanites were diligent in search of the rural, and almost never bought or built houses in the center of the town, the village, or the place. It is also important to note, unless we are to be hopelessly bogged down in confusion, that these place-names coincide only occasionally with the names of the townships listed earlier. There is a reason for this, a good, sound, political reason. North of the barrier there are eleven townships; in the same area there are two dozen or more police districts, and God knows how many school districts and fire districts. Over each police district there are separately elected or appointed officials; over each school district separately elected or appointed officials; over each fire district, mercifully, volunteer fire departments. It is quite possible for a family to live in a township that has two, three, or more different police, school, or fire districts lopping off one or other of its *arrondissements*. It is even possible for a family to live so strategically situated that its volunteer fire department will be housed in one place, its school board in a second, and its local police in a third. The word "place" is used advisedly. When it comes to describing an entity like Chappaqua, for example, the word "town" cannot be used, nor can the word "village," nor, strictly speaking, can the word "hamlet." Chappaqua is, from the standpoint of incorporation or organization, non-existent. It is only a place. On this rich confusion feasts an old Republican machine which has raised gerrymandering to a topiary art, and which stays on top thanks partly to a device known as permanent personal registration (by which a countryman registers once and may move away or die, but his name remains forever enrolled, to be faithfully voted, so say the envious Democrats, whenever necessary), and which has, by reason of the chaos, a wonderfully high number of the faithful to feed at the public trough, either through election or through appointment.

These northern townships help to keep the county respectably Republican, something which it has been, with a few exceptions, since the formation of the Republican party. Back in those days, northern Westchester was considered radical. There was talk of how the unionization of labor might be a good thing, the free land policy was argued, women's suffrage was openly espoused, Quakers in the area shuttled many a slave along the Underground Railroad, and one of the region's principal citizens was Horace Greeley, a maverick who had prematurely supported Lincoln and whose New York *Tribune* was an upstart crusading journal.* This radicalism seems to have been a hangover of the

* Greeley lived in Chappaqua and, after the New York Central thrust a spur into the Harlem Valley back in 1847, was one of history's first commuters. His house still stands, but is no longer a residence. It has become a combination shrine-tearoom-gift shoppe.

days that followed on the American Revolution. Colonel Frederick Philipse, the third Lord of the Manor of Philipseburg and an ardent Tory, held the region firmly under his thumb during the Revolution: the British may never have marched in force north of the Croton hills, but, on the other hand, they never needed to, for they would have found few rebels to disperse. But after the Revolution, when the lobsterbacks had been driven off, Philipse's lands were carved up and sold to loyal colonials by the Commissioners of Forfeitures. Nothing is left to keep green the memory of his extensive holdings save a railroad station in a county park on the Hudson, just south of the barrier.

Other exurbs are Republican—in fact, all exurbs seem to be Republican—but none is more determinedly Republican than northern Westchester. Here the egghead sticks out like a furuncle. This is the countryside dominated by the ten daily newspapers owned by or associated with the Macy interests. There are one or two independent weekly newspapers of liberal Democratic persuasion, notably Mount Pleasant's *The Townsman*, but they are lonely voices. Once, a tiny group of exurbanites rented a store on Chappaqua's main street and put up signs proclaiming that here was the headquarters of the Independent Voters for Roosevelt. A prominent real estate agent stopped by, stared, stepped in, and spat on the floor. The occurrence occasioned no particular astonishment.

Such an atmosphere has unquestionably exerted a powerful influence on the exurbanites who have settled here. Some among the first to arrive found the atmosphere completely congenial. They were not vice-presidents, associate editors, assistants to the publishers; they were presidents, editors-in-chief, publishers, men who were near or at the summit of their particular peak of the communications industry. Long-time residents in some northern Westchester communities have commented, about these early arrivals, that they brought in their train a following of second echelon dependents.

A spectacular example of this phenomenon is, of course, the personnel of the *Reader's Digest*, which is edited and published in the area, and most of whose many senior, roving, and associate editors have settled at a discreet distance from Editor DeWitt Wallace's home outside of Mount Kisco. But the same trend operates in connection with enterprises of the communications industry housed well outside the exurb. Thus, the president of a company manufacturing cigarettes buys a model farm in the area; before long, cigarette account executives, or advertising agency wheels who would like to become cigarette account executives, consider the neighborhood and, for one reason or another, also buy a farm, more modest perhaps, not a model perhaps, but a farm, a talking-point. After which, exurbanites on the way up the ladder, copy writers, art directors, get the same religion. It is an aspect of the conformity so dear to the heart of most exurbanites, and as soon as they are settled the political aspect of this conformity takes charge of their opinions.

The tendency of city people who have always registered and voted Democratic to switch their allegiance once they buy a house outside the city has been recognized by politicians for a long time, and faithfully reported by political writers in the newspapers, usually around election time. No attempt will be made here to discuss this shift except insofar as it applies to the exurbanites in the northern Westchester area.

There seem to be two causes for the change of heart. The first has already been mentioned: conformity. Conformity is a far more imperious influence in this exurb than in the city. In the city a man may melt into the mass, disappear in the subway to emerge in a district wholly removed from Madison Avenue, not only geographically but spiritually and intellectually; the compulsions to consort in the evening with the same people one sees at work are not so dictatorial. Just as the average New York apartment dweller gives his next-door neighbor across the hall or on the floor above no more than a frosty glance and a perfunctory good-morning, so the New Yorker in the communications industry may be, in his off-hours, a hot-music devotee and spend his evenings in Harlem or at Eddie Condon's in the Village or huddled by the loudspeaker of his hellbox.

But in the exurb his choice is straitened. He will encounter his upper-echelon associates twice a day on the train and as like as not at cocktail parties or week-end social gatherings. He must take on the protective coloration of like political opinions in order to survive without undue discomfort. He may, if he is stubborn and independently minded, vote the straight Democratic ticket once he is in the privacy of the voting-booth, but his influence in the community in persuading others to do likewise is necessarily extinguished. He joins no Democratic committees, canvasses no voters, attends no Democratic rallies, and contributes Democratic dollars only by stealth. Contending, as he must, with so many other strains that flow from his removal from the city to northern Westchester, it is no wonder that his politics, which in any event probably never exacted strong allegiance, are changed. Or, if his political and social convictions are important to him, and had on the whole moved him to associate himself with the Democratic party in New York, he may quite honestly feel that he can accomplish more good for his fellows by working within the Republican structure in northern Westchester than by announcing himself or showing himself to be a Democrat—a gesture of independence which not only may hurt him, but which he reasons will weaken his effectiveness as a mover of opinion, which every exurbanite dearly believes he is.

The other cause for the shift is more subtle. It is associated with a vague feeling that one will get along better in the community if one registers Republican. This has little to do with one's relationships with other exurbanites but rather with one's relationships with the natives of the township. It is, actually, another aspect of conformity, of doing in Rome as the Romans do. One northern Westchester exurbanite explained it this way: "The election officials are mostly Republican, and they get to know it if you register Democratic. One of them may be the township or village tax assessor. He might take it into his head to assess my property at its full value, one of these days. Why ask for trouble?"

Currently, there are signs that the shift may be tapering off.

Especially in the southern foot of the exurb, enough new arrivals are renting, buying, and building to be able to create, within the larger community, their own distinct groups, and thereby encourage more and more exurbanites into a mood of independence. Near Pleasantville, for instance, one large estate was bought by a group of like-minded people many of whom were eggheads. They put up homes in the $35,000 category, some of them modern, one of them a Frank Lloyd Wright design. They were, predominantly, Democrats in New York, and they remained Democrats in the exurb. As this is written, they are having their troubles and are being referred to as a non-co-operating co-op.

The dominant tone of northern Westchester is, however, of staid and almost stuffy wealth. In the countryside around Mount Kisco, Pound Ridge and Bedford Village, upper-level exurbanites have bought big farms, have often enclosed them with split-rail fences, are likely to have purchased herds of Black Angus to dispose over the landscape, and in many cases may have hired enthusiastic young Cornell graduates to run the whole shebang. These exurbanites are distinctly gentlemen farmers, and not to be counted in the callus-handed company of the dedicated Bucks County exurbanites. For a while, the northern Westchester farms were expensive and handsome toys, pleasant backgrounds against which the exurbanites could pose, like Men of Distinction. They delighted in showing week-end guests through the barns and stables. They delighted, also, in using their farms as a handy method of keeping their considerable income taxes down to a respectable level until, come a black day, the crosspatches at the Bureau of Internal Revenue decreed that losses flowing from one given business enterprise could not be applied against profitable income from another, wholly separate, enterprise. Since then, the Cornell-graduate farm-managers have been urged to show how well they can manage.

It will have been noticed that little has been said of northern Westchester's social life. It is, in the main, less noteworthy than that of the other exurbs, although it does entail considerable organized, away-from-home activity. For the horsy there are the

Goldens Bridge Hounds, a hunt that meets in the countryside
north of Katonah. For golfers, there is the Bedford Golf and
Tennis Club, which is comfortably posh, and there are two or
three country clubs—all restricted—within easy driving distance of
Chappaqua and Mount Kisco. The Mount Kisco Country Club
is the scene of New Castle's two big annual social affairs, the
Junior League Dance and the Episcopal Church's Black Tie
Dance, to which latter everybody who has a black tie comes, while
all restrictions are for one night ignored. There is also the Whip-
poorwill Golf Club near Chappaqua, supported principally by
Reader's Digest's overflowing staff of editors and the free-lance
writers who supply the magazine's planted articles; it has been
dogged by misfortunes, nearly going bankrupt, once burning down;
but, rebuilt, it still offers a bar where a perfectly respectable sixty-
cent drink can be bought for $1.25.

Except for these foci of organized social life, however, northern
Westchester's after-hours and week-end entertainment centers
pretty much in the home, especially for the newer crop of exurbanites which came to the region in 1949 and thereafter. An impelling
reason for this is that the type of younger city person who
chooses northern Westchester as the scene for his emergence as an
exurbanite is generally more genuinely concerned (as opposed to
guiltily anxious) about his children than those who select other
exurbs. And where there are many young children whose parents
consider their upbringing and welfare as of engrossing and paramount importance, rather than as just a duty which can be
deputized to maids and baby-sitters, the hours of relaxation tend
to be spent on home grounds.

Actually, while the newer crop of exurbanites conforms in general to pioneer exurbanite patterns, it shows some marked contrasts. Mention has been made of the fact that the newer northern
Westchesterites migrated from the city earlier in their lives than
the old-timers. In this connection, the United States Census
figures of 1950 are revealing. The township of New Castle, for
example, which embraces much of the residential area around
Mount Kisco and Chappaqua, reported that 18.5 percent of its

population was from five to fourteen years old—that is to say, of primary and secondary school age. In only one of the exurb's townships was this percentage higher, and that was in Somers, north of the Croton Reservoir, where exurbanites are also thickly sprinkled. The age group from twenty-five to forty-four, which embraces most of the big ninth wave of exurbanites, had its largest complement, 34.2 percent, in Pound Ridge; New Castle's comparable citizenry represented 32.4 percent of the population. There were slim pickings among the next generation: Pound Ridge reported only 8.6 percent of its population in the fifty-five to sixty-four age group, New Castle only 8.2 percent, in the face of, for example, Pelham's 14 percent.

It would seem clear from these statistics that the reason most frequently offered for moving out of town, when one is catechized by confirmed New Yorkers about a contemplated move to Exurbia, namely, the children, is valid for the 1949-50 wave of northern Westchester exurbanites. In this exurb we can see a striking example of how the good and valid reason—better, less crowded, and cheaper schooling—can be self-defeating when too many people of the same kind get the same idea at the same time.

That the 1949-50 wave of northern Westchester exurbanites were concerned about schooling their young is borne out by the composition of the various committees formed to accomplish this or that for a given school.

In Pleasantville, for example, a committee was formed to explore all the questions attendant on obtaining the services of a full-time psychologist for the local primary school. The older residents of Pleasantville said that in their day no full-time psychologist was necessary, or even desirable. Since the older residents include the town fathers, which is to say the town politicians charged with debating and deciding how high the taxes will go that support the school system and such scholastic fripperies as a full-time psychologist, it was necessary to select the members of the committee with great care. They were charged with such tasks as determining who would be the best available psychologist, how much he would cost, how much was paid for an analogous psychologist in comparable communities within or without the area, how much of a hike in the school tax his salary would represent, how best such a hike could be put over, and how best to contend with local politics to insure the hiring of such a man.

The committee numbered ten. There was the promotion manager of *Fortune*, an advertising counselor, the music arranger on the Milton Berle television show, and the composer of the music for an old pop tune called "The Music Goes Round and Round." There were also six housewives. They spent an incalculable number of man- and woman-hours, and they eventually got their psychologist, part-time.

The population of New Castle's Central School District Number Four, which, faithful to the chaos of northern Westchester, serves families around Chappaqua and part of Mount Kisco as well, rose from 3,700 in 1940 to 4,900 in 1950; the number of pupils in the same period rose from 829 to 1,248. The one old school was insufficient and a new school had to be built. A new school, of course, involved a radical increase in the school tax rate, and the pain this caused older residents whose children were grown and in college already was grievous indeed. What was required was the formation of a committee of the most talented and distinguished of the new exurban population. Impressive brochures were produced under the direction of an exurbanite who earned much of his income by doing commercial art for *Collier's*; the editor of *Fortune* chaired the committee, and after a whirlwind public relations campaign Chappaqua had a new secondary school.

But no sooner had that fight been won than the whole thing had to be done over again. For in four years the population of the school district had shot up even higher, to 6,000, and the number of young to be schooled was more than 1,500. Besides, the pupils were all getting older. What was needed, by 1952, was a brand-new high school. The new secondary school was already operating at 111 percent of capacity, with more than thirty children to a class where twenty-seven was the recommended maximum. Looking into the future, the apprehensive exurbanites envisioned a population by 1965 of about 9,000, with a consequent host of 2,230 children to be educated. A spot survey showed that only by the narrowest of squeaks was a majority—fifty-one percent —of the district's residents in favor of a new high school. Once again, an intensive public relations campaign was indicated. The school building committee included some familiar exurban names; on it were the wives of people such as *Fortune*'s treasurer, *The New Yorker*'s fiction editor, and a BBD&O art director. It testifies to the communal enterprise of the new exurban population that all difficulties were overcome. The necessary bond issue was approved. Land for the new high school was bought from a one-time exurbanite whose job in the communications industry has removed him from the exurb. (He did all right, too: $30,000 for twenty-seven acres.)

It is not only in the educational field that exurban crowding has brought troubles to the people of northern Westchester. Closely tied to the school situation is the tax rate, which is going forward like a kite. Hereabouts, taxes are based on the assessed value of the property owned and the assessed value is about one third of the real value. One hardship is worked on the old-time, non-exurban population of a place like Chappaqua: assessments tend to be higher the closer a property is to the center of the hamlet. Reflecting former values, a house within walking distance of the shopping center is assessed higher than the home that is ten minutes' drive distant. But it is precisely these latter homes that are more attractive to the new exurban purchasers. Thus a man with a house and land worth $75,000 on today's real market will be given an assessment of about $25,000, and have to pay only around $600 school tax. If he has a large family his stake in insuring an educational program for the district comparable to the best private school facilities becomes obvious. And it also explains why a great many exurbanites have moved away from New York. It even explains how some exurban parents can decide they can afford large families. The notion of six children going to school at a cost of $600 in school tax is beguiling.

Real estate agents in Chappaqua, Mount Kisco and Pound

Ridge report that a sure way for them to get listings for their port-folios is to call up the parents of the children in the graduating class of the local high schools. They phone such parents in February or March, and ask them if they are planning to sell. An appreciable proportion report, each year, that they are, but never nearly enough to allow for the continuing waves of newcomers.

For, just as northern Westchester is finding it hard to keep up with its increasing school needs, so it is finding itself increasingly crowded. For some, this spells prosperity. For a man who had spent a pleasant summer working at the Mount Kisco summer theatre ten years ago, and who returned for a visit last summer, it spelled the end of the peace and quiet he had fondly recalled. The fact is that northern Westchester, that staid, old, dignified exurb, is coming into its second youth. In Chappaqua, Cadman's Drug Store, a center for the ice-cream-soda set, got so crowded as the years went by that its owner reluctantly decided to rip out the soda counter in an effort to keep the number of customers within bounds. But because use of his telephone is free, his store is still a hotbed of teen-agers making dates.

The town's old hardware store, moved to a central location, refurbished, renamed the Country Store, equipped with a cracker-barrel containing free Nabisco cookies, and girt about with a neat white picket fence, has doubled its gross in the last four years, and does an especially heavy business in do-it-yourself gadgets dur-ing the Christmas season. In Mount Kisco the citizens are pre-paring for an expected qualitative leap, from rural town to smart exurban shopping center. Bedford Village and Pound Ridge, once sleepy hamlets geared only for the sale of groceries and Sunday newspapers, are likewise shiny with a new exurban prosperity.

The *Reader's Digest*, long ago forced to move, first, from its $25-a-month headquarters over Pendleton Dudley's garage in Pleasantville, to a floor in a Pleasantville bank building, and, finally, after other moves to larger and larger quarters, to a million-dollar edifice outside Chappaqua, continues to expand, if not physically then in terms of its press-run, both in English and in foreign languages. From twice as many editors as the magazine contains articles in a given month, it is now approaching thrice as many, and there seems no reason to believe that the end is in sight.

Additionally, northern Westchester had created a Frankenstein's monster in the shape of its magnificent parkway system. As long as the area was traversed by only a few winding, two-lane, soft-shouldered roads, motorists were few and came, perhaps, only to revel in the spectacular beauties of autumn or spring. But then came the Saw Mill River Parkway and the Taconic State Parkway. Now any car-owner from Manhattan can be in the heart of northern Westchester in an hour or a little more, and can see for himself how seductive life is in an exurb. To the established residents, it seems not so much that any Manhattan motorist can inspect their countryside as that every Manhattan motorist not only can but does, frequently leaving the detritus of his picnics behind him.

In the face of the continuing invasion, in one township and incorporated village after another, steps are being taken. Land is being rezoned. Residential areas are being upgraded everywhere—up to one acre, up to two acres, up, in some places, to four and even five acres. Where choice residential properties begin at $1,000 an acre, such upgrading will unquestionably have the effect of permitting only the wealthier Manhattan executives to buy.

This has already, as in Fairfield County, created tensions between the new exurban population and those native to the region. The population of the area is becoming stratified: a few, necessary, low-income laborers, then a big leap to the forty-year-old exurbanite at the $20,000-a-year level (minimum), then another big leap to the owners of estates, whose income is largely from investments. The white-collar professional with a modest income is harder and harder put to find a decent place to live. Fine physical plants for education are all very well, but where are the teachers to live? There is a comparatively undesirable stretch of residential area along the New York Central's right of way between Pleasantville and Mount Kisco, on low ground, where, these days, there is much building of homes that cost from $20,000 to $30,000; elsewhere prospects are bleak.

It may seem that northern Westchester, as exurb, is approaching its saturation point, thanks to the zoning regulations. Actually, however, the future would appear to hold a quite different answer. It may turn out that northern Westchester's character will undergo a revolution of extensive implications: that even before it has matured as exurb, the region will become a suburb.

Meanwhile, the residents of northern Westchester can rejoice in their forested hills and lakes and guard them as jealously as they know how, hoping that not too many more like themselves will follow from the city. They can plunge into the activities that mean pleasant surroundings and sound schooling for their children, conscious that they could not find or create any better, in any other exurb. They can be proud, too, of their other civic accomplishments, for it is true of northern Westchester that much of its socializing is organized around benign and altruistic group efforts on behalf of those in the county who are less fortunate. This is one reason for the wholesome quality of much of this exurb's social life. It presents a marked contrast to the goings on in its sister exurb in age and social status, the North Shore.

But in both—as in all other exurbs—there is a unity of feeling and of interests among the exurbanites. Except for a few disgruntled souls, they wouldn't swap their exurb for any other.

And this is odder than it may seem on the surface. One might be tempted to say that obviously the reasons which impel people of the same sort to seek each other's company would obtain in keeping them together in their chosen exurbs. This is true, to a degree. But we must not forget that, however delightful an exurb may be for those who have helped to make it what it is—whether the North Shore, northern Westchester, Fairfield, Bucks, or Rockland—there is always the lurking secret dream, the emerging awareness of the limited dream, and the daily frustrations of the rat race. This potent combination could prove lethal to the happiest community. It will be examined in detail in succeeding chapters; but it seems fitting to end this section with a tribute to these people, these exurbanites, who cleave so loyally and, on the whole, so happily, to the exurbs they've created.

3

As to the chances of exurbs springing up elsewhere over the country, the prospect is less than sanguine. There is no question that there are plenty of men and women living in the environs of cities other than New York who have all the earmarks of the exurbanite. After all, symbols are manipulated on a branch office basis in many other places. A few magazines are published elsewhere, a few publishing houses are fixed in Boston, or Philadelphia, or Chicago, and advertising agencies thrive in many cities.

The citizens of Dallas enjoy a lively legitimate theatre, and actors can find work in St. Louis, and San Francisco. There are a few network shows on radio and television that originate from Detroit, Chicago, Philadelphia, and San Francisco. Los Angeles has Hollywood and Beverly Hills and Bel Air—where the exurbanite has developed into an entirely different subspecies, worthy of an entirely separate inquiry. Washington, too, has its quota of exurbanites. In all these places, and perhaps in a few others, there work and live men and women whose tasks, whose habits, and whose particular way of life correspond almost exactly with those of the New York exurbanite.

But there is a difference. In no case (except for Hollywood), and not even including Carmel, are they concentrated in sufficient numbers to lend the rich flavor to a residential neighborhood requisite to make of it a true exurb. To meet the physical requirements of an exurb is not an insuperable task: all that is required is beauty, and there are, scattered throughout the country, a myriad of places more beautiful than Bucks, Rockland, Fairfield, Westchester, or Long Island. The historical background is not required and in any event it is present in a number of lovelier habitats.

Moreover, artists have chosen other places to live and work and

make popular than the five exurbs of New York City. Nor has
fashion ignored such places as Lake Forest, or Santa Barbara, or
Warrenton-Middleburg, or the Main Line, or the Peninsula—
and all these are residential neighborhoods reasonably proximate
to a metropolis. But the genuine exurb must have a considerable
quota of exurbanites, or it fails. It need not have exurbanites as a
majority of its residential population, or even of its commuting
population, but it must have enough to cast the distinctive, febrile
glow. And there are simply not enough of the breed in large
enough clusters outside cities other than New York to count.
Nor are there likely to be, so long as New York remains the center
of excitement, the symbol of symbols, the aspiring confluence of
all glamorous ambitions, the nexus of competition, the heart of
the communications world. Which it is and will remain for the
foreseeable future.

With the single exception, as has been said, of Hollywood.

Hollywood lacks the historical background, no artists having
settled there in earlier days to lend the neighborhood tone. And
some will assert that the place, far from being physically handsome, is an affront to the senses. But when all this has been said,

there can still be no question that exurbanites have settled there thickly.

Recently, there have come to Hollywood new hordes of writers, actors and musicians as television depends more and more on Hollywood names, on TV films, on celebrities. The advertising agency executives trooped faithfully out afterward, along with the package producers, talent agents, transcription company personnel, and the gossip columnists and nightclub circuit riders. This entire hegira came straight from the rectangle of Manhattan which is the heartland of the communications industry, and superficially it would seem to make of the area a prime exurb, especially when to the physical colonization has been added some of the aspects of an exurb: the characteristic stigmata (such as smoked glasses, the open shirt-collar for men during business hours, the mink coat over slacks for women during daylight hours even in July, and so on), and the characteristic snobbisms: for a time the Bel Air Fire Department had an unlisted phone number, the better to avert the possibility of being disturbed by the peasants who live merely in Beverly Hills.

Despite all this, however, Hollywood cannot qualify as a true

exurb, and the reason has to do with the attitude its more typically exurban inhabitants have toward their temporary home. The key word here is "temporary." The exurbanite resident in Hollywood can never come to believe that he is here to stay—and this is true even if he has been breathing the mimosaceous miasma for upward of twenty years. Hollywood is not even a limited dream.

When first impressed into service in the galleys of Hollywood, the male in the communications business typically arrives alone. On some level of his consciousness he carries the conviction that life here is a little improper. He not only plans to conduct a personal survey solo, but, in the same fashion that he would be reluctant to squire his family into a bagnio, he bids them stay back east until he has had time to case the joint. Later he may arrange for their arrival and even buy for them a house that has all the appearances of permanence. His sojourn may last while his children graduate from the Hollywood High School and even from U.C.L.A. or Southern California. But he can never rid himself of the sense of transience.

This apprehension is borne in on him in a dozen ways, as it is even on native-born Hollywood proto-exurbanites: the chattering teletype from the home office in New York, which—whether he is in motion pictures, radio, television, or simple advertising—demands him at noon, and may detain him till eight at night; the knowledge that it is New York critics whose assessment of his product is most important; the awareness that in New York sit men of his own age, temperament, and taste who are scornfully derisive of his life and mores, and that *The New Yorker* has a division of news breaks devoted to "Life in Hollywood." There is, for most, the conviction that only the decisions made in New York will be of importance to his future security, his future paycheck, his future success, and so on. All of which being the case, he can seldom form even a limited dream from his life in Hollywood. His dream is, almost invariably, of New York.

This is true of most advertising men, who realize that power is vested in New York; it is true of a majority of motion picture scenarists, who know that the legitimate theatre of Broadway, despite its chronic invalidism, is strength counterposed to Holly-wood's weakness. For the same reason it holds for the actors and actresses and directors, and for comparable reasons it is true of the handsomely paid folk of radio and television.

Naturally, there are individual exceptions. Hollywood abounds in pseudo-creative people who are making big dough there and who luxuriate in its climate and sensuous delights. Others are so specialized in training and experience that only the cinema capital provides them a livelihood. For still others, the sybaritic oppor-tunities offered by near-by vacation places afford ample reason for staying put. And there is a handful of truly creative people who, though exurban to the core in their attitudes, find a reasonable degree of fulfillment in their work and a high degree of good family living in Hollywood's modern houses. But these are so few as to be insufficient to create for themselves a genuine exurb. They are exiles among the wahoos.

Not far from Chicago (but very far as commuting standards in that area go—some fifty-five miles) there are people who think of their habitat, Woodstock, Illinois, as an exurb. The town is quaint enough to have been used as background for films taken for "Hawkins Falls," a TV soaper. The commuting residents who work in ad agencies live far from the station, an exurban character-istic. Their nesting-places are known as Bull Valley, Greenwood, and Westwood. Here they go in for larger farms than in Bucks, and finer homes than in Westport, but in other ways their emula-tion of Exurbia is more exact: it has been said that among them extramarital sex is so ordinary that people raise their eyebrows at marital relations, an obvious exaggeration which may have at its core a nasty nugget of truth. But all this does not make an exurb.

Examples could be multiplied from the environs of cities all across the country, but of each it may be said that there aren't now nor are there likely to be enough exurban types to create their own kind of community, which is, in some ways, perhaps a good thing.

5

ON WHEELS

The pleasure of travel . . . only exists as a matter of fact in retrospect and seldom in the present, at the instant when it is being experienced.

—JORIS-KARL HUYSMANS

Now that we've met the exurbanite and toured his habitat, we are ready to consider that one most compelling factor in the shaping of his daily schedule; his means of getting to and from work. Unless he drives, in which case his office hours control his travels, he must adjust his life to the timetables of Exurbia's railroads. Thus, he finds himself enlisted in a well-disciplined army, whether he likes it or not. Before inspecting him on his train, it will be useful to get an approximate picture of the corps in which he and his fellow commuters daily take their places.

There are today roughly 360,000 people commuting into New York City.* This total represents an increase of over 60,000 since

* For the statistical information in the first part of this chapter I am indebted to the Regional Plan Association, whose most recent study of New York's commuters is dated July, 1951.

112

1930, a surprisingly small gain when you consider that there are half again as many suburban (and exurban) families as there were in 1930. Further, at the time (1950) when the last careful estimate was made of all railroad commuters, there was evident an actual and significant decline: from 270,000 in 1930 to 227,000 in 1950. Most of the decrease has been ascribed to the fact that many commuters from Queens transferred their allegiance from the Long Island Rail Road to the urban subway system, for which none will blame them; but an important cause has also been resentment of the steady rise in the price of commutation tickets. Sullen commuters have reverted to the wartime practice of car-pools, and in sufficient numbers to cause both the New York Central and the New York, New Haven and Hartford railroads to wonder what should be done. Thus far, comparatively few improvements have been made, but recourse, in the best public relations tradition, has been had to surveys. Surveys of the commuter are afoot, and while things are in that gelatinous stage, it can be freely predicted that commuters will not appreciably return to travel by rail.

Executives of the New Haven, at least, must be aware that some of their clients got their backs well up. A couple of years ago, a hike in commutation rates was in the wind: the Interstate Commerce Commission, it was announced, was being petitioned for a small increase—thirty-three-and-one-third percent. This would have meant, for Fairfield County commuters, an increased charge per capita of from $90 to $150 a year.

The commuters closed ranks, and the exurbanites among them, old hands at surveys, prospectuses, and presentations, promptly came up with some numbers of their own. Such a hike, they contended, would rob Fairfield County merchants of $200,000 from Greenwich, $110,000 from New Canaan, $120,000 from Westport, $55,000 from Wilton, $170,000 from Stamford, $150,000 from Darien, $30,000 from Danbury, and $230,000 from Fairfield and Southport. There are a lot of zeroes in these numbers; in a presentation they were impressive. Fortunately, in addition, the New Haven was about to engage in a big proxy fight, testing whether the existing board of directors or any board of directors so conceived and so dedicated can long endure. It seemed expedient to withdraw the petition for the rate increase. Too late: a Fairfield County Commuters' Association had already been formed and, having tasted sweet victory so promptly, engaged to become a permanent addition to the landscape.

To the least crusty New Haven director, the whole thing must have smacked of socialism, perhaps even of communism, but it all depends on whose ox is gored. John Orr Young, founder of Young & Rubicam, long-time commuter, blessed the enterprise. The Commuters' Association, he wrote, affords an "instance of how to get things done in a typical American community," and Mr. Young's choice of the word "typical" to describe Fairfield County must deserve the homage of all advertising men.

The point is that the most respectable, the most conservative of men will, as commuters, take the position that, if one is getting back a little of one's own against the railroad, much is permitted that would never be otherwise sanctioned. In the holiday season, even wealthy exurbanites have been known to trade off their commutation tickets to friends, or seek to obtain those of friends who are about to go on vacation. Such antagonisms, cheerful enough, are directed with greater or lesser intensity toward all the railroads used by commuters to New York City: the Pennsylvania, the New Jersey Central, the Delaware, Lackawanna, and Western, the Erie, the New York, Susquehanna, and Western, the New York Central, the Lehigh Valley, the Reading, the New Haven, and the Long Island.

About the last two, it may be said that their commuting exurbanites are proud of their railroads. The Fairfielders feel superior because theirs is the best equipped and most punctual commuter line; the Long Islanders are illogically but understandably full of pride because theirs is the worst by far; so bad, in fact, that it seems to them it must reflect credit on them for having courage to subject themselves to it regularly.

The Long Island Rail Road has been riddled by authorities, by experts, by men far better qualified to deal with its vagaries than the present writer, but a word or two demands inclusion. Patrons of the LIRR take as ordinary, hardships and indignities which cause the occasional railroad traveler to the North Shore to marvel. It must have been about the LIRR that the line, "It's a hell of a way to run a railroad," was first uttered. Quite apart from its rolling stock (overheated or completely unheated in winter, only capriciously air-conditioned in summer) and its corduroy road-beds, there is the question of its schedules. It is not proposed to take the railroad to task here for occasionally permitting one of its trains to arrive a trifle late. But when trains fail to show up at all, there should be a reasonable explanation for their behavior.

A musician with the Symphony of the Air who, while Toscanini was still its *régisseur*, was required to be prompt for rehearsals or else, several times came to the Northport station for a train around noon, waited until after traintime, asked the station agent what the hell, and was informed that the train just wasn't running "that day." He got into the habit of having his wife wait outside, in the car, until it was clear that the train would not appear, and then asking her to drive him to town.

Then there is the seventh circle of hell known as changing at Jamaica. People who have not done this will be skeptical. Standard operating procedure, for someone taking a train to the North Shore, is to get on his train in the Pennsylvania Station, be carried to Jamaica, get out, walk across the platform, wait until a train pulls in, walk through this train to the next platform, walk across that platform, climb into the next train that heaves into position on this third track, and sit down, wondering whether the directions he received from the trainman back in his first train were correct.

This would be all right if the LIRR operated only two or three branches or divisions. But it operates eight. A passenger is at the mercy of directions mumbled by a harassed and busy trainman. What this can mean can be illustrated like this: Suppose you want to go to Sea Cliff, on the North Shore. You will have to change at Jamaica. At Jamaica the trainman will mutter something about going through a train and getting on the next but one on the third track. If you ask him to repeat the instructions he

will do so, in a pained voice. You follow his directions and sit
down in a vintage coach. When the trainman on this train comes
to pick up your ticket he tells you that you are on the train bound
for Seaford, a pleasant suburban community on the South Shore.
You have your choice of going on to Rockville Centre, getting
out, and taking a bus across the island to Sea Cliff (if one should
happen along), or of getting off at the first station and waiting for
a train going back to Jamaica from the other direction. This sort
of thing happens to at least two middle-aged shoppers every day,
if not every train.

Coming in to Jamaica from the outlying exurbs is no better.
The LIRR has worked it out so that five trains of eight cars
apiece arrive at the Jamaica platform from which one train of
ten cars is expected to transport their occupants to Manhattan.

Faced with such snarls, the exurbanite has been at pains to
work out superior methods of commuting. Some drive their cars
to the farthest outlying subway station in Queens, and proceed
from there. Others club together and hire launches to transport
them from a convenient harbor of the North Shore to a landing
at the foot of East Twenty-first Street; pleasant, if the weather
holds, but at best uncertain. A seaplane is quicker, easier, and less
trouble than the LIRR. And if the LIRR's commutation rates
keep on going up as they have been doing in the last dozen or so
years, a seaplane may not be too much more expensive.

And now let us consider the transformations which exurbanites
have begun to work in the long-established practices of ordinary
commuters. These can be seen even before the morning train's
whistle has been heard coming around the bend. The first of
them has to do with the car in which the exurbanite is driven to
the station. To the ordinary commuter, a car is what his wife
drives him to the station in. But to the exurbanite, a car must
be something more, it must testify to his sensitivity in under-
standing what is expected of him. There are variations here, shadings, almost ineffable but nevertheless important distinctions: in
one exurban enclave, the pecking order in car ownership gives
top place to the Jaguar, in another to the Italian sports car, in

another to a rehabilitated Pierce Arrow. Throughout Exurbia, there is cachet in arriving at the station in a jeep, for that presumes that the Cadillac is being used to take the children to school.

The ordinary commuter may not notice these things, but the exurbanite does. For him they are critical. His eye is recording and his brain automatically cataloguing such matters of status at all times, even when the orange juice and coffee are still a hot ball in his stomach, even while he is giving his wife a dutiful kiss good-bye, or striving to park his station car within reasonable walking distance of the station, an increasingly difficult feat in most exurbs.

Now the exurbanite buys his *Herald Tribune* or *Times* or *Wall Street Journal,* and moves out on the platform. Before the train arrives, there will be time to remark on another exurban innovation to commuter ritual, the deferential salutation.

It comes about because of class distinction. It is incorrect to suppose that exurban class distinctions are so widely marked as, say, those between the enlisted man and the commissioned officer. On an exurban station platform, all are admissible to the officers' club, but, nevertheless, there are second lieutenants and full four-star generals, and the former must take care not to jostle. This is true even if the one is a copy writer for one agency and the other executive vice-president of another agency; it is true even if the one is not in the advertising business at all. For the average exurbanite can never be sure: he may be writing lyrics for Tin Pan Alley today, but who knows whether tomorrow he may not be employing his talent on behalf of some agency, writing commercial jingles for television cartoons? Today's featured player on Broadway must face the time when his hit show will close, and he will be forced (a mortgage is a mortgage) to become tomorrow's contract player for the glory of soap, cheese, beer, or cigarettes.

Not all the commuting trains have dining cars in the morning, but they are a popular feature. One exurbanite recently moved to a new exurb served by a train so equipped. After a few mornings spent getting his bearings, he observed that there was one group

of commuters who always managed to be first in the dining car.
He noticed that each morning they stood beside the same crack
in the concrete of the platform and he took to standing as close
to them as he could without actually intruding on their conversation. Then came the morning when no one stood by the crack.
There was the usual group, but they were a few yards further down
the platform. The exurbanite, somewhat daunted, nevertheless
took up his stand over the crack. Here came the train, here came
the dining car—and there it went, past him, to come to rest a
few yards further down the platform. The commuters, still chatting pleasantly, climbed aboard.

The freshman exurbanite went up to the others and spoke to
them. How had they known about the dining car? What had
happened to the crack? They stared at him a trifle coolly, then
one explained. It seemed that it was common knowledge that on
every other Thursday, Pete, a substitute engineer, was in the cab,
and Pete always brought his train to a stop a few yards further on.

If the 200-proof exurbanite displays just the right combination
of affability and deference to those exurbanites who, in his intricate scheme of status, rank him, he is equally careful in the
face he turns to those he deems his inferiors. Tocqueville, who
wrote, a century ago, so much that is shrewd and penetrating
about Americans, has a paragraph that fits the plight of the
middle-flight exurbanite with his ever-changing obligation, now
to bow, now to snub: "It is not easy clearly to distinguish at a
glance those who respectively belong to [the different ranks].
Secret hostilities then arise in the community; one set of men
endeavor by innumerable artifices to penetrate, or to appear to
penetrate, among those who are above them; another set are constantly in arms against these usurpers of their rights; or rather the
same individual does both at once, and while he seeks to raise himself into a higher circle, he is always on the defensive against the
intrusion of those below him."

It takes an act of God to break down these class distinctions.
On a Monday morning, everything is as usual; on a Monday night,
there is a great fall of snow, or a cold rain that freezes and knocks

out power lines. The next morning, there are four-star generals and ensigns, all barriers down, topping each other with exchanges of calamity; but once again, come Wednesday, the gates are barred.

Deference to the real or prospective boss is so important among the eager-beaver exurbanites as to leave them little time for the usual amenities. By way of example, there is the treatment accorded to women. On the New York Central's commuting train down the Harlem Valley there are still seats aplenty at Chappaqua, and the courtly, old-world grace with which women are permitted to climb on board first would delight the most captious. By the time the train arrives at Pleasantville, however, seats are scarcer and only the most attractive or the most decrepit women are given any priority. Come White Plains and women are thrust aside; every man is for himself.

Up to now, it has been assumed that the train for which all are waiting, as they stand self-consciously on the platform, is the most popular of the morning. Actually, most exurbs have three, and some have four or even more. Typically, there is the train a few minutes after seven-thirty, for the slave who must be in his office by nine o'clock, and no fooling. Within fifteen minutes after eight, the train which is generally the most crowded pulls in, and the plushy junior executives climb aboard. These are the men (and women) who either have to or like to feel that they should get to the office by nine-thirty. The train that leaves a few minutes before nine, and which will deposit its riders in New York City so that they may reach their office by ten, is generally referred to as the bankers' train, a slander on those much-slandered businessmen, who are more often at their desks an hour earlier. There is, in addition, a train from most exurbs a few minutes after nine; it is scheduled to arrive in the city after ten. Its riders are the unemployed, the self-employed, entertainment talent, the wives who have shopping to do, and those with hangovers. It is usually the second most crowded of the morning.

But no matter what the train, most exurbanites have slipped smoothly into the behavior patterns established for them by ordi-

nary commuters, once they are on the train. Indeed, even before
the train stops at the platform to pick them up, they have begun
to divide into clearly differentiated categories. That group over
there, the one whose members had been chatting together with the
mutual derision which indicates all believe each shares the same
status level; now that the train slows to stop, they part company,
and go in different directions. Two are headed for the smoker, the
place of which in the train's length, of course, they know. One
is an eager beaver: he is heading for the very first car of the train,
so that he may escape the crowd at Grand Central, and be the
more swiftly at his office for the ten o'clock coffee break. The
fourth, a young surgeon, heads for the fifth car, for he knows
that when the train stops at 125th Street, his stop because it is
nearer his hospital, the fifth car will land him right at that station's
flight of exit stairs. Already, two of the four are beginning to
tense up, as they approach the rat race.

There are, of course, thousands of exurban commuters who are
unaware of the extreme modes of behavior cited and to come.
They are nice, happy people who enjoy as best they can the
period spent on the platforms of their stations and on the trains.
They are, like all commuters, cautious about making new train
acquaintances, since they have to ride the same train every day
and dread the possibility of acquiring as permanent seat companion a dreadful bore, but otherwise they are open and friendly
and seem innocent of caste distinctions. Nor do they spend all
their travel and waiting time in promoting.

These good people are, in fact, unusually cheery for the start
of a working day. And if some of them are merely putting up a
front, and others are only being cheerfully friendly to keep
thoughts of the day ahead in abeyance, such is not the case
with all, by far. There are only three sorts of occasions on which
they are usually surly or vocally unpleasant. First are the eves and
mornings after such holidays as Christmas, New Year's, the
Fourth of July, Thanksgiving, and Labor Day—times when the
hard-pressed railroads never seem able to mass enough rolling

stock to take care of the crowds, when trains run late, when ancient cars are exhumed for commuters while the newer ones are reserved for longer hauls. Second is that period each spring when the summer residents move out to the exurbs, to crowd the trains and occupy favorite seats. Third are those times when a square (either a new exurbanite or a city visitor) has the effrontery to sit down alone on one of the facing pairs of seats reserved for cardplayers, a *gaffe* few true commuters will commit even if it means standing all the way.

With this caution in mind, let's get aboard. Once on the train, the differentiated categories become more marked, and even the casual student can distinguish the varieties. They number five: reader, sleeper, talker, worker, and cardplayer. By and large, they are self-explanatory: the reader wants to read his morning newspaper without interruption; the sleeper wants to sleep behind his morning newspaper without interruption; the talker wants to gab; the worker wants to impress himself and his boss, if possible, with the diligence with which he has already tackled a briefcase full of papers; and the cardplayer wants what every cardplayer wants. These categories have been remarked by other observers of the commuter and would not rate mention here, except for two considerations. One is the change which the exurbanite has wrought within these five categories. The other has to do with shadings.

First, as to the exurbanite's influence. As far as the cardplayer is concerned, the difference is one largely of degree. Cardplayers have shuffled, dealt, and played in New York commuters' trains since whist, through auction, and on down to point-count contract. What the exurbanite has done is to lend the games to the rest of the car. More extroverted than the ordinary commuter, the exurbanite makes sure you know he has made, or lost, the redoubled slam. Even before the cards have appeared he wants you to know he is with you, and what he is about. His early morning gladness reverberates throughout the smoking car. "I have a seat!" he cries to his partners, or "I have a fourth!"

The reader and the sleeper have stayed about as they always were. Exurbanites, unless hungover, are less likely to fall into the category of sleepers in any event.

To the talkers, a few exurbanites have added a new dimension. This came about when the wags among them realized that there were not many talkers among ordinary commuters. Working in pairs, they did a bit, sometimes in dialect, sometimes straight. The routine was calculated to outrage the ordinary commuter. One of the earliest pairs to function so, a free-lance commercial artist and a *Life* photographer who travel down from Chappaqua on the New York Central, were each, as it happened, expert at a kind of proto-German dialect. In loud voices they carried on a lurid conversation about their deals in black-market watches, the sky-high profits they had cleared, the simplicity with which any European could flummox customs officials on this side, the ease with which they could effect favorable trades in Europe, giving American Hershey bars for Swiss watches and (here their voices would drop a bit, and take on lubricity) women.

Another new kind of talker is the relatively independent egghead exurbanite. He talks, again with a friend of like persuasion, to scandalize the Republicans who form the overwhelming majority of ordinary commuters and exurbanites alike. This talker can function only if he is either self-employed or securely successful as a free lance. His usual gambit is to take his sermon from the respectably Republican *Herald Tribune*, but shape it for his own Democratic ends. But his is a lonely voice in the solid ranks of Republicans. Those who were there state there has never been a trip like the one the 8:12 from Westport made the morning after the Eisenhower landslide. They practically built bonfires in the aisle. The most commonly heard remark was: "First time in my life I voted for a winner!"

The ordinary commuter-worker is usually simply a man interested in his profession to the exclusion of all else. Some of this breed still ride the trains; some are exurbanites who find this hour the day's best for uninterrupted work they can't get done in their offices. A Pleasantville diagnostician who commutes to the city, married to a woman who also commutes, bids her good-bye as the train pulls in, and retires to a non-smoking car where he can bury himself in medical literature. His hours to and from New York, he says, are perhaps the most valuable of his day. He is one of those who demand silence, even to the point of his having written a kidding-on-the-square letter to the New York Central, urging that cars be set aside for non-talkers, just as cars are presently set aside for smokers. There are many who would second his motion.

But there is another kind of exurban train-worker and his clan increases. He uses the fifty or sixty or seventy minutes to make deals, to get in solid, to impress. Free-lance artist's representatives use the time to peddle their flesh to agency art directors, actor's agents gab with television producers, a copy writer can confer with an account executive, an agency veepee can make a pitch to a prospective client. Some of the smaller fry contend that only on the train can they get to see their company's big brass. Appointments are literally set up for conferences on the train.

And there is another side to the new kind of work done. A network vice-president used daily to ride to town with an underling from his own department. Presently the vice-president got a promotion. There was a logical man to replace him, as head of department, and then there was his daily shadow. The logical man got the job—for a decent interval. Then the shadow took over. This little drama had been played out before the eyes of at least two dozen knowledgeable fellow exurbanites. One of them commented, of the shadow who got the vice-presidency: "Don't get the idea that he'll goof off. He's a good man. He just made sure it would happen, that's all." Making sure occupies the time of many exurbanites.

This extension of the business day to the train is, however, limited to the New Haven and, to a lesser extent, to the New York Central's Harlem Valley Division. It is one of the clues that would enable the experienced observer to tell exactly where he was, without reference to landmarks outside. There are others.

For example, the card game played on the New York Central's Putnam Division is more likely to be pinochle than bridge. None of the exurbanites who commute from Mercer County in New Jersey play cards; any card playing on the Pennsylvania or the Reading began back in Trenton, or in Philadelphia. Even on the same line, different trains will have appreciable differences. Those who take the trains which go only as far as Greenwich or Stamford are inclined to believe that the Westporters all bring out bottles of booze as soon as they get on their evening train and that the ride is one long bacchanalia, repeated five times a week. This is not strictly true. But it is true that the Greenwich-Stamford group inclines more to the stuffy and the sedentary, and that the Darien-Westport contingent is younger, louder, and more easily imagined as the life of a Deke house party.

This tendency on the part of exurbanites to fantasize about their counterparts who live elsewhere, or travel elsewhere, reaches its zenith in respect to the private club cars. Nearly every railroad feeding into New York leases one or more club cars to private associations, groups of men formed strictly for the purpose, and the myths about these cars abound.

It is believed that the subscribers to the club car have sufficient reason for drawing the blinds down over the car's windows. Proponents of this myth hint that the subscribers: a) get blind drunk, b) are serviced by party-girls, c) engage in a running, morning-and-night poker game for which chips are unnecessary, but large, coarse Treasury notes are, and, d) can't stand the sight of lesser mortals. It is believed members pay $500 (or $1,000, or take your choice) for the privilege of belonging. The facts are considerably more prosaic.

The oldest of the private club-car associations—they used to be clubs but for tax purposes were revamped into associations of subscribers—is the Special Car Associates, which leases cars from the New Haven for a bit more than $12,500 a year, tax included. Most of the subscribers get on or off at Greenwich. The association dates back to the 1880's, and evolved, according to tradition, from the fact that a handful of friends used to play a daily game of poker in the baggage car, sitting on boxes, before a steadily growing audience of kibitzers. When the kibitzers got so numerous that it was a question of them or the baggage, the private club car was born.

The Special Car Associates are limited, by their bylaws, to a membership of 250; this is actually many more than can be accommodated in their three multiple-unit, self-propelled, air-conditioned, fluorescent-lighted, stainless steel, custom-decorated cars, which seat sixty each. Actual membership is at present about 235. But all subscribers do not ride every day. One subscriber has maintained good standing by paying his annual subscription every year for the past twenty years—although he has spent most of them in Paris. Annual turnover of members is well under ten percent, and most of the vacancies arise for actuarial reasons. Subscribers are drawn chiefly from the financial and business community; there are, in addition, a few men who have scaled the summits of the exurbanites' mountain range of aspiration, the very top brass of the bigger ad agencies.

The private club car that goes to New Canaan is similar, and costs the same amount. The one to Southport, however, is merely a standard club car with no frills. It costs only $8,800 a year. On the New York Central, there is a club car to Brewster ($6,049 a year), another to Harmon (same bruise), and a third to Pawling ($10,050 a year). This last boasts a porter and, at present, sixty-seven members. On the Long Island, one goes to Oyster Bay ($6,000 a year), one to Port Jefferson ($6,960 a year), one to Patchogue and Speonk (same fee), and a fourth to Rockaway ($6,000 a year). All the club-car associations have been in existence for many years and none has taken out a liquor license —and, as one secretary said, "Nor will we, as long as I have anything to say about it"—although coffee in the morning and tea in the afternoon is not uncommon. The fee to subscribers ranges from $150 to $200 a year, over and above, of course, the usual train fare. As like as not, the private club car is coupled into the train just behind the engine, affording subscribers the opportunity to duck into the station ahead of hoi polloi, and be in the office in plenty of time to scowl at those unfortunates who come scuttling in five minutes later.

The journey over, there is still an opportunity for the double-dyed exurbanite to show his mettle. The ordinary commuter simply hustles into Grand Central's huge main room, bucks the crowd, and makes his way wherever he's going. But the exurbanite with the inside dope is cannier. If by luck his train has pulled up on Track Sixteen, he does not head toward the station, but in the opposite direction. Presently he comes to a flight of iron stairs. Up these he climbs, comes to a door, opens it, and passes through. He is on Forty-eighth Street, just east of Park Avenue. The door which he closed behind him is thoroughly ordinary. All it has on it is the apparently cryptic legend, F. E. He will use the same door that evening, to get back down to his train.

If, as occasionally happens, he finds the door locked, he is not upset, for he has a key that will unlock it. Uncounted moons ago, some enterprising exurbanite with a friend strategically placed in the hierarchy of the New Haven or the New York Central got hold of a key to this door. Since then, in an endless chain, others have been struck off, each a lineal descendant of that first key. The key imparts to its owner a sense of being chosen.

Comparably, if the exurbanite has come from Chappaqua or Pleasantville, and has in consequence alighted from his train on the lower level, does he walk up a ramp or a flight of stairs like some peasant? Not he. He walks to the end of the platform, takes a sharp right, and finds himself confronting a bank of four elevators, which have been nicknamed the Cardiac Special. He rides to Vanderbilt Avenue and Forty-third Street in style.

At the day's end, the exurbanite has an even greater choice of trains to take him home. If he is very wealthy, or if he is un-employed, there will be a train leaving for his exurb around four-thirty. At five leave the trains to which, typically, are coupled the private club cars. The most crowded trains are those that leave between five-thirty and six; at this hour, as he sits in his window-seat, he can look to left or right and see trains just like his, with exurbanites and ordinary commuters in serried ranks, row on row, each reading his newspaper (at night it is either the *World-Telegram* or the *Journal-American*; the *Post* gets practically no play). If, in exurban spirit, he has paused at the Biltmore bar and gotten lost, there will be a train around seven, which will give him ample time to think up a story for his wife.

Once upon a time, an exurbanite will tell you, a man bound for the 5:12 got lost in the Biltmore bar, missed the 5:12, ordered another drink, missed the 5:32 narrowly, ordered another drink, easily missed the 6:02, ordered another drink, and then missed the 7:02. By this time he had found a complaisant young lady who, fearful that he might catch cold, took him home and bundled him up tenderly, keeping him warm under a comforter. When he arrived home the next night he marched straight up to his wife, looked her straight in the eye, and announced. "Darling, I cannot tell a lie. Las: night I got drunk and spent the night with a blonde." Frostily she glared at him. "Don't give me any of that," she snapped. "How much did you lose?"

But if the exurbanite is fortunate enough to have so managed his life that he lives in one of the exurbs at which stop the New Haven's preferred exurban trains, he need never pause at the Biltmore bar. These trains include bar cars.

Once, long ago as the thirsty count time, the New York Central had a bar car, but not now. The Reading boasts a bar car, but it is rarely jammed. Some of the New Haven's trains in the late afternoon on the Danbury or the New Canaan branches include dining cars on which—or, rather, on the outer platforms of which—mothers may have to stand, clutching the hands of their hungry young, for fifty miles or more, until the home stations of the thirsty, whisky-drinking males seated at the dinner tables have been reached and passed. The New Haven's first bar car of the day is a decorous rolling saloon, catering to the wealthily sedate and the wistful unemployed. The New Haven's last bar car of the night is given over to those so sodden or so weary that they rarely lift more than one drink to their lips.

It is left to the bar cars between five and seven to maintain the tradition of hard drinking. Here the clientele is solidly exurban. Here the young hucksters throng to look back on their day with loathing and to get a good start on their evening. There are only fourteen cars on the train that leaves about six and they are all pretty full, but the bar car is always full to overflowing. Nor is the entire car given over to the bar. Approximately one half of its length is filled with normal train seats, in which sit normal train sitters, gripping their one normal highball. But around them the air beats and pulsates with the jabber of the bandarlog, the throng of exurbanites who have jammed the half of the car in which the bar has been set up, the mob of men and women who believe that their best interests will be served if they can manage to stay within six feet of the main source of supply.

On a recent, and not atypical, midweek evening, the first arrival in the 6:02's bar car clocked in at 5:29. Unfortunately, the two barmen had not quite finished setting up. They were still lining up the crates of Schweppes and Heublein martinis, of Canadian Club and Old Grand Dad, of Ballantine and White Rock and Canada Dry. They ranged the glasses, and behind them the paper cups, for they knew the glasses would be snatched up rapidly. The tubs of ice were placed at arm's length. At 5:40 came two more young, hardy, thirsty exurbanites. At 5:41 arrived a hard-bitten female copy writer, clutching a dollar bill at the ready, and sat down across from the service bar. By 5:42 the car was beginning to fill up, and the men were loosening their ties.

The first order was given and filled at 5:45; it was for two double-scotches. By this time the queue in front of the service bar numbered ten, and the bar itself was thickly invested.

At six there were forty people in the car, and their cries for booze filled the air. By the time the train began to pull out all the glasses were gone, and drinks were being served in paper cups. The drinkers themselves, gasping in the fetid air, had begun to overflow into the cars in front of and in back of the bar car. The barkeep, McGrath, and Woody, who tends the service bar, had no rest.

The management of the New Haven refuses to divulge how high soar the very considerable grosses per month of the 6:02's bar car, and for a reason which must be decried as silly. It is the claim of the New Haven's public relations officers that they get so many complaints from long-suffering wives as to indicate that the less publicity attending the extent of the drinking on the 6:02 the better. When pressed as to how many complaints in fact they received in, say, a month, these hardies mumbled something about how they have heard about two letters since "last January."

The true reaction of most exurban wives to the 6:02's bar car is quite different. They regard it, and entirely correctly, as the single most potent factor in getting their husbands past the Biltmore bar, and home to a relatively prompt dinner.

Commuters are still homeward-bound on trains that may leave at late as eleven-thirty (those who hustled away from the theatre) and twelve-fifteen (those who tarried for a drink). On these late trains, the likelihood is that there will be a clutch of drunken exurbanites. In fact, the police of peaceful Pleasantville are likely to have their busiest moments when they meet the late trains, and it becomes the policeman's lot to drive the lushes home. One CBS executive, of exalted status, was not so fortunate. He took dead aim on his Fairfield County objective, but fell asleep and overshot the mark, landing in Bridgeport where he found he would have a forty-minute wait before a train passed through in the opposite direction. He called his wife, apologized for her vain wait at the station, and asked her to meet him on his way back. Thirty-five of those waiting minutes he spent in a pub, climbed aboard the train, fell asleep, and landed back again in New York, where he said the hell with it, and took a room at the Biltmore. He has since moved back to the city.

There are, of course, exurban commuters for whom the journey to and from New York is nothing but a chore, a humdrum occasion drained of any emotional content, affecting them no more than the nuisance of having to shave every morning before breakfast. Just as certainly, however, for a possible majority, these trips are freighted with emotion: apprehension and tension in the morning, delicious and occasionally even abandoned relief in the late afternoon or early evening. The tensions are so tangible, as they prepare to come to grips with their day (one exurbanite remembers how an exurban acquaintance used to beseech him to accompany him from train platform to near-by saloon, and stand with him while he drank one or two boilermakers before reporting to his office), the joyous end-of-day letdown is so universal, that one might conclude their days at work are wretched in the extreme. This is not invariably the case. There are many happy toilers in the communications world and even those who are miserable have their happy moments on the job. But evidence suggests that for the majority their working days are a foretaste of a special exurban hell.

6

AT WORK,

or

THE HIGHER THE FEWER

If I am not for myself, who will be for me?
If I am for myself only, what am I?
If not now—when?

—TALMUDIC SAYING

There is nothing so degrading as the constant anxiety
about one's means of livelihood.

—W. SOMERSET MAUGHAM

PEOPLE who live in the city have no idea how beautiful and soul-satisfying the exurbs can be to him who is year-round resident. Unless you've got off a train after a day's work and driven into the springtime of a long-familiar countryside, you can't know what it does to the spirit. For the ruralite the cycle of the seasons may be a pleasure; for the visiting urbanite evidences of it may be a happy experience; for the exurbanite it is purgatory and bliss in one. In spring, when one leaves the city, the day's work is still hot upon one, and the train ride is likely to be dirty and malodorous. Then the train gets to the station in the exurbs. There is the bustle of the platform: cars jockeying, colorfully dressed wives and children pacing the platform, or tooting the horn if they stay beside the family car. Then home, with its problems: the children to play with, the maid and handy man at the peak of their pressing-for-attention behavior, the wifely anecdotes of the day.

But finally comes the moment of almost rural bliss, the moment at dusk when the exurbanite can walk out on the dew of his own lawn, see stars, smell growth, hear country sounds, sense the season and the fresh earth. This is genuine, needs no exploiting, has no angles, breathes of truth which can't be and needn't be sold and improved upon and duked up. There's Orion, there's the Dipper. Even the privet hedge smells like heaven.

Or in midsummer. From air-conditioned office into the city's fetid heat, onto the air-conditioned train, with its people and its bar car and its noise. Out into at least non-city scenery, out to the suburbs flying by, the neat yards, the row-house backyard gardens, with their mingled chicken wire and used-car-parts and rankly growing vegetables and flowers. Out to the exurbs, and then the too-hot car with the sweating, competing kids and the tired, brave wife. And then, finally, home. Of course it's hot. But it's breathless-and-exciting hot, summer-storm hot, night-blooming-flower hot. And then comes the breeze the city never feels.

Autumn in the exurbs needs no celebration. What a gorgeous Maxfield (ugh!) Parrish season it is, with the fall colors bursting into light on the maples, on the browning oaks, on every hedgerow and vine and bush. There's the haze, and there are the evenings when the smell in the air is all burning leaves and first fall fireplace smoke.

There is winter, often grim; but leaving the steamheated, taxi-scarce, shivering city and getting to one's own place where ice makes branches glow in street lights, where snow is clean and silent —these things the exurbanite knows and feels, as he does the sight of his own home as in a fairy tale, as in a big 4-color ad, with the snow on the roof and the windows lighted and aromatic smoke from birch logs at thirty dollars a cord drifting from the chimney.

These are exurban evenings. Exurban mornings are good, too: in spring the ear-piercing songs of a thousand birds at daylight, in early spring the first fuzz of green, pale as dawn colors, on the branches seen from the window. In summer the cicadas going full tilt when the alarm rings at six or seven; it's already hot and if you don't run out in your pajamas to turn on the sprinkler for an hour or half an hour before traintime, it will be too late and the grass will cook unless you wait until sundown. This is kids-in-sun-suits-for-breakfast time.

Autumn mornings are brisk and brilliant. Hot, hot coffee time. Even the car runs better.

Winter mornings in Exurbia have their own beauty: deep, dead-blue light of pre-dawn on rising, thermometer twenty degrees below city levels, ice and hoar on everything—and during breakfast the sullen and reluctant sun of winter, aged and yellowed with cloud screen, finally, reluctantly rising to make the fields of snow and the ice-coated bushes glisten. A man is up against nature in the raw then, when he gets the car started, dons his outdoor gear, and gravels his driveway preparatory to demonstrating his driving skill on the skidding ride to the station.

Season by season, at morning and evening, when the exurbanite and his exurb are together he feels: this is real, this is being a man in his own right place.

And between these mornings and evenings, like the center of a bad sandwich, is the gross and devouring day in the city. City people may feel that their working hours are hard, are hours of strife and effort. But there is not, for them, the daily wrench, the daily severing of some connection with another self which is never fully realized. It is the exurbanite's fate that, with his vaunted sensitivity and awareness, which render him susceptible to being hurt by the abnormal stresses of communications business life, he must additionally face a daily wrench from that aspect of his life which seems valid and meaningful. But this is not the only painful parting he experiences. He dreads to leave the city behind, to leave it to urban competitors and fellow workers who may be using the time of his absence to plot his downfall.

See him board the train, see him disembark, watch him as he goes from home to work and back again. Surly or gay, he does it. Five days out of seven, typically, he tears his innards to do his job. If the rat race must be run, he'll run it and be in the money at the finish. Does he hurt? Is he killing himself? You'll never know if all you observe is the way he acts in public. It's tougher for the exurbanite. It's tougher for this man who spends two additional waking hours a day traveling, who has so much (happy or miserable) to tear himself from and to return to every day. It's tougher, but he'd be the last to concede it. He crows about his superior lot. He asks, gladly, valiantly, for the daily extra beating. Poor soul, let's see what he's up against every day of his working life.

Time was, not so long ago, when if you had sprinkled with anisette all the exurbanites on any given train coming into Grand Central Station and let loose a pack of hounds on their trail, the dogs could have run their quarry to earth without poking their muzzles outside a small rectangle of Manhattan some fifteen blocks long and four blocks wide. This would have entailed ignoring a few trade editors for the smaller publishing houses that still line Fourth Avenue below Thirty-fourth Street, and a handful of motion picture craftsmen in the film studios and labs on the far West Side, but for all intents and purposes the heartland of the communications industry, over which the exurbanites hold uncontested sway, was bounded by Forty-second Street on the south, Fifty-seventh Street on the north, Lexington Avenue on the east, and the Avenue of the Americas on the west. Once inside this rectangle, the exurbanites from Connecticut and northern Westchester were joined by their fellows who had come via car or Pennsylvania Station from Long Island, Pennsylvania, New Jersey, and Rockland County, all of them merging and becoming apparently indistinguishable from the rest of the symbol-mongers in the world's capital of the words-pictures-and-music business. At lunchtime, they thronged into the same continental restaurants, conferring the favor of their trade on a gradually changing half-dozen or so expensive eating-places; whichever were the momentarily most popular half dozen, they were always centrally located within the same rectangle.

To a considerable extent, this concentration still holds true, but there have been changes. Today, such are the exigencies, for example, of television, that some unhappy exurbanites find themselves relegated to office space in decrepit rookeries on upper Broadway, or padding glumly through the streets of Brooklyn in search of a restaurant where they can buy a decent Gibson with their lunch. The communications industry is bursting at the seams.

Anything new that has been added, however, by this expansion, is less significant than what is still the same. For most of those who manipulate symbols, for most of those who have nothing to lease but their brains, the topic emotion is still uncertainty.

This uncertainty is, despite the presence of a lucky few who have escaped its grip, the principal quality that sets the communications industry and all its subdivisions apart from other American industries. There are other differences, and they have been remarked by a host of writers, both of fiction and of fact: there is more glamor in this industry; there are more graceful, intelligent, charming, and amusing people involved in it or with it; there is more time beguilingly wasted; there is more creativity demanded of its personnel; it pays higher rewards, at least in money; in no other industry are work and play so fetchingly intertwined. It is true that its product is far more ephemeral than that of any other industry, but it is reputed to be much more fun to turn out the product. All these aspects of the communications industry explain its attraction for the more than usually gifted, and they explain, too, why it is that often the industry's craftsmen turn the mirror on themselves, and report its life and glamor and enchantments in the movies or on the radio, in television or on the stage, in books or in the slick-paper magazines. According to such reflected glimpses, there are only two types who work in the industry.

First, there are the creative people who are, despite their artistic natures, capable of achieving first-rate creative work in business surroundings—nor will it be denied here that there are such people. The second type portrayed includes the hucksters, frantically competitive, cynical, and corrupt—and it must be admitted that there are a few of these as well. But there are others: those touched by naïveté or the need for self-deception, those who, on no matter what echelon and in no matter what phase of the industry, must believe utterly in what they are doing—the reader for a publisher who is persuaded that a considerable percentage of the trash he reads is worth publishing, the advertising executive who truly believes that advertising is the backbone of all American industry, and so on. There are those who are eager to sell their souls, eager to be corrupted by money, but can't seem to find Mephistopheles.

There are public relations men who have worked out complicated *mystiques* about their profession and psychologists hipped on the notion that they can scientifically arrive at a definition of the public taste, universally and eternally. Talented and untalented, beautiful and ugly, romantics and beasts—there is room for all in this ideogrammic jungle, and nearly all of them take pride in their technical ability. And for all of them, from the highest to the lowest, almost without exception, there is uncertainty—which is, after all, only a nice-nellyism for insecurity, fear.

This is an unhappy state of affairs for everyone involved, but for the exurbanite, who has not the urbanite's financial mobility (he can't, for instance, move to a smaller apartment if things get tough for a while, or sell the car, or dip into savings—since he has none), it is particularly painful. The insecurity is not experienced everywhere throughout the many branches of the industry at the same level of intensity. In some it is so faint as almost to persuade the beholder it does not exist at all. But it exists, and it is felt.

Physiologists have developed a gadget they call the dolorimeter, designed to measure the intensity of pain; it measures what they have called dols, which range from one to ten, or from what is perceived and registered as unpleasant to what is excruciating and unbearable. In much the same fashion, the dolors of fear and insecurity within the communications industry can be gauged. In what follows, a dol count will be given for the dolors of working in various divisions of communications. To gauge the exurbanite's dol level, add one to the readings.

At one dol would be the people in the book publishing business, and especially those in the smaller, older, more established publishing houses. Here, men who might have been college English instructors read and work in relative quiet. Though underpaid, they are relaxed and, because they feel they have consciously selected an intellectual calling over one more crassly commercial, they have an amused and tolerant condescension toward their exurban friends further uptown. It's true that they may get excited by a thoroughly commercial book, a book with no literary merit which they recognize will, nevertheless, sell high, wide, and handsome; and at moments like this, as they are contemplating the juicier Christmas bonus they may get from a best seller, they may seem like a hypocritical version of the richer, more corrupt exurbanite in, say, the television dodge; but in the next hour they may be eagerly preparing for publication a book which all connected with it know will never sell more than two thousand copies, a meritorious but hopelessly uncommercial book, and yet their pleasure in it will be the greater. This, it is safe to say, is an attitude unthinkable for and incomprehensible to a branch of the communications industry where the dols measure higher.

But it should not be concluded that those who work in the staid book-publishing field do not experience and recognize as unpleasant their one dol. They hear about the rat race from their acquaintances in the advertising field, and they can nod their heads sympathetically: they have a better-graded track, and a lesser speed, but all the same they have their own version of a rat race. Increased costs have outstripped sales and prices, the more commercial book must be sought more assiduously, paper-bound books have whipped up an appreciable turmoil, more than one sedate house has discovered that a considerable share of subsidiary rights in a best-selling novel can work wonders with a profit-and-loss statement, subsidiary rights mean movies, television, radio; and so they are brought spiritually closer to the rest of the industry.

But, even though publishers, alarmed by the spread between costs and prices, occasionally let go some of their people for economy reasons, thus far they have always had to hire others back, to get the work done. It makes for a kind of musical chairs: those in the business can reel off in minutes the names of a dozen or so men and women who have worked for more than three publishers in the last few years. As in musical chairs there is one always left standing, so in the publishing business there are always a few unemployed; but they are so few, relatively speaking, as to keep the dol-intensity down. Still, the larger and more business-minded book publishers have a greater turnover than the smaller ones, so for the biggest, let's allocate to all employees two dols.

Again, we must rate any unemployed exurbanite higher. If he's one of those who has, at one time or another, been left standing, his job hunting is not only costlier, but he can't brood glumly and anonymously on his way to job seeking in a subway, or extravagantly in a cab. He has to ride the commuter trains, with successful, i.e., employed, strangers before whom he must keep up appearances and, worse still, with other exurbanites from the book business who know he's out of work, since there are no secrets in this ingrown branch of communications. He suspects, too, that these colleagues may have known he was on the skids long before he had any idea, since he knows that in communications the man on his way out frequently is, like the cuckolded husband, the last to find out. And when he gets to the city, he hasn't even a base of operation. He must make his calls from a phone booth—long, chatty talks interrupted by the embarrassing voice of the operator periodically asking for another coin. And if he doesn't reach his party, which he usually doesn't, he can't leave a number where he can be called back at local rates. And he can't stay home and make his calls from there: the neighboring wives would see him; worse, the tradesmen would know, and his credit would vanish when he needed it most.

At two dols, also, are those who work for monthly magazines. Parenthetically, it should be remarked that many male exurbanites work on the most feminine of women's magazines, but no stigma attaches. It is quite arbitrary to set these folk at only two dols' intensity, and perhaps an exception should be made in the case of the occasional magazine where the editor, or the publisher, has a penchant for hiring and firing with methodical regularity. Even in such cases, however, it is reckoned as a normal and predictable hazard, and is not calculated to increase insecurity too much. Here at this level, rather as Virgil plucked at Dante's sleeve to call his attention to a soul in particular torment, we must pause to survey an exurbanite in special dolor.

He is the managing editor of a national monthly magazine, a position, it would be assumed, that would insure a certain security. And so it did, until he moved out of town. The trouble is, his boss, the editor-in-chief, is still fanatically urban. The magazine's hours have always been nine-thirty to five-thirty, its tempo has always been relatively relaxed, rarely has there been need for anyone to work later than six, except for a few days a month, just before closing deadlines. The managing editor could with ease catch a six o'clock train to his exurb and did, for the first few weeks. Then his attention was arrested by an apparently idle, aimless remark his editor underhanded him.

"Oh, by the way, Bob," said this editor, "a few of us were sitting around the office last night, talking about the front of the book. You know, some of the young guys around here have a lot of good ideas about how to fix it up."

"Why didn't you call me in?"

"We looked for you, but you'd gone. Don't worry about it, Bob, I can give you all that was said in a memo. That'll cover it."

"Gosh, Joe, if you're thinking of having any more of these editorial meetings, I'd like to know about them. I can always plan to stay late, you know. . . ."

"Sure, sure, forget it. This was just one of those impromptu bull sessions. Valuable, when they, you know, get the spark that some of these youngsters seem to have. I'll send you a memo."

Since then this managing editor has been staying around the office, staring at articles in his slush pile, until he is sure his editor has gone home. Both used to leave by six at the latest. Sometimes, now, the managing editor misses even the 7:08. On the dolorimeter, he would register close to six, maybe seven; and he is having more than his customary recourse to his favorite analgesic.

Add one dol for those who work on weekly magazines, but only because of the added tension that accrues from the more rapid deadline. But add two dols for the weekly magazine exurbanite on the editorial side, who must miss the five-to-seven bull-sessions in the bar downstairs at the end of the working day, or miss his train and thereby subject himself to being tormented by his wife (whom he will torment in return—if not out of pique, then out of guilt). For the urbanite to stay a half hour late, or to be asked if he'll cover a play or a screening or a concert because of the regular reviewer's calendar conflict, entails one ten-cent phone call home, to suggest dinner out and an evening of free entertainment. For the exurbanite, the phone call entails a lengthy explanation—made no more palatable to his wife by the inter-office comments she overhears—which results in his either eating alone, going to the entertainment alone or with a male friend, and getting home after midnight to a frightened and lonely wife, or making an evening of it with a male or female friend, getting too drunk, staying in town, and praying to Santa Claus that it can all be fixed up at home later, thanks to some miracle not yet vouchsafed.

On the next level, at four dols, are the free-lance artists, illustrators, comic-strip artists, public relations employees, and publicity men. All these individuals have more freedom than the

HERE AT THIS LEVEL, WHERE THE
PUBLISHER HAS A PENCHANT FOR
HIRING AND FIRING WITH ME-
THODICAL REGULARITY, WE MUST
PAUSE TO SURVEY AN EXURBANITE
IN SPECIAL DOLOR.

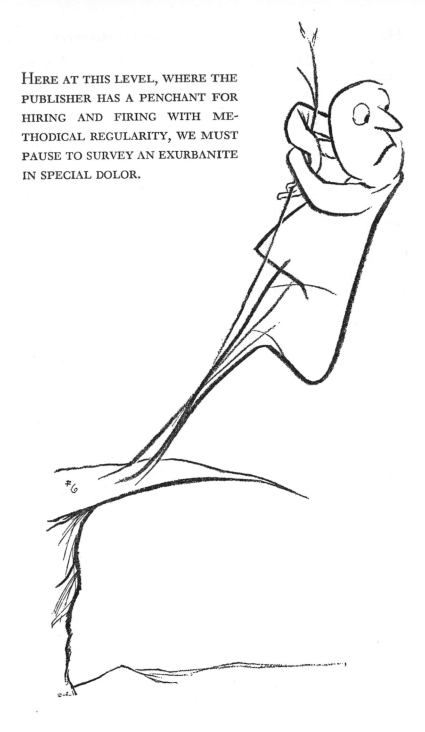

staff men, but they are dependent on managerial whim to a far greater extent, and so their insecurities increase.

At five and a half dols, because of greater unemployment, and also because they are approaching closer to the final, ultimate gogs and magogs whose decrees mean so much to the communications industry, are the musicians, concert artists, song writers, and recording people generally. At six dols, because they are still closer, are the actors, directors, and stage designers. Even some of those whose shoulders are bowed down under the title of producer share this level. Here also are the New York motion picture people.

At seven dols, and now it is beginning really to hurt, are the radio and television executives and those on the loftier reaches of the advertising plateau, those whose income is, let us say, in excess of $50,000 a year. These are the men who joke about ulcers. It should be remarked of them that, while their job mortality is high, here, too, as with the publishing business, the game of musical chairs gets quite a play. A man can have been a vice-president in charge of radio and television for an advertising agency, be fired, catch on with an advertiser, be fired, catch on as program development genius with a talent agency to build shows for the agency's high-priced stars, be fired, catch on with a network as program manager, be fired, and return to an advertising agency as vice-president in charge of new programs, all within the space of two or three years.

What this means to the people under him, in each of his posts, is not pleasant to contemplate. For, however benign his feelings for his fellow man may be, it is incumbent on him to make changes, to do something that shows he's on the job. And for his own protection, he will bring with him his own henchmen, tendering his colleagues words something like these: "I'm not saying this as criticism, mind you, but after all I do have a fresh slant on things here. If I put my foot in it with what I'm going to say, for Pete's sake check me, will you? I don't want to be standing around with egg on my face. But it does seem to me there's a lot of fat here. We've got spear holders that haven't had their tails kicked in years. If we're going to phase in with the chief's great program for new daytime billing, we'll have to get in some new blood. Now, I know several men we could bring in to replace the deadheads. These are real hot guys, young and aggressive. Now, I'm not criticizing and I haven't really got my feet wet here yet, but what about the copy department? What about those three oddballs that take a half-hour coffee break every day to discuss begonias and rose hedges? Do we need them, I mean? I know one man —and please don't think I'm saying this just because I've worked with him before, because it's not that we're friends—but bring him in and he'll get real results out of those guys, or else."

So there will be a period of greater fear for everyone, until things settle down and the dol count levels off for those still left in their jobs. But now, with the shuffling that's taken place, a period of personal realignments occurs. Everyone is familiar with the transitory quality of office friendships, and how, no matter the closeness of a group, the move to another job virtually terminates the mover's connections with his cronies. For, despite their pleasant aspects, these friendships are more like temporary military alliances than lasting human relationships. But when there's been a shake-up in a firm it becomes necessary, for a period, to be wary of too overt displays of friendship toward anyone until one knows who's on his way up and who's on his way down—or out. Bull-session gossip increases, but it's guarded. And the men moving up start an often unconscious but nonetheless systematic ditching of some old friends and seeking out of others.

It will have been noticed that no mention has been made as yet of the executives who earn less than $50,000 a year. They have not been forgotten.

At eight dols are those who free lance in radio and television. Their deadlines are, if they are working, just as frequent as those that confront the staff men of a weekly magazine; they must work much harder; what they do is gone as soon as it is produced, to vanish into a Stygian limbo; they are harassed at every hand by men who know little or nothing of the craft but whose position gives them the right to interfere, even to dictate; and even the demonstrated popularity of what they do for an audience does not confer on them any security. These are the people who are on what Fred Allen aptly describes as a treadmill to oblivion.

When the treadmill has spliced into it a commuter train, as it does for the exurbanite, the dol count fluctuates, adding pangs to the steady throb. This puts some exurbanites who, by occupation, should be in a lower dol group, into the eight-dol category, since the nine- and even ten-dol stabs push up their average.

If it seems stretching a point to claim a higher degree of pain for the exurbanites in this group, consider the case of one magazine man, let's call him Joe, who found it desirable from a business standpoint to spend four late evenings in town within a month. (His story is not unique.) The reasons, in order, were: 1) a last-minute dinner invitation from the boss, whose wife was in Florida and whose mistress was indisposed; 2) an important out-of-town advertiser to entertain; 3) a cocktail party and dinner for a best-selling author; 4) untangling an alliance connected with 2) above.

The first night in town went like this. At five twenty-five the boss appeared and sat down on the edge of Joe's desk, which he'd already neatened (by stuffing a drawer and loading his secretary's desk) preparatory to a dash for the 5:37. When the boss sits on your desk in this office it's generally a sign of a long chat. Joe resigned himself and tried to figure out a tactful way to cut it short enough so that he could call his wife before six to let her know she needn't drive to the station to pick him up as planned that morning. He knew what would happen if he interrupted the boss for this purpose. He'd say, "Excuse me, B. R., but I've got to call Muriel to tell her not to pick me up."

B. R. would say, "Oh, I'm sorry. Don't call her. You run along." And there would be strain in their relationship for weeks afterward. Or, if B. R. had something important on his mind, he'd say, "Sure, go ahead and call, if it's not too inconvenient, of course. You commuters lead such complicated lives." And then he'd hum to himself and drum the desk, mentally registering the toll call at company expense, while Joe tried by inflection and manner to indicate to his wife that he was trapped and being overheard. But no course that was open seemed desirable. Besides, an impromptu after-hours chat with the boss was a priceless boon usually enjoyed only by urbanites for whom working a few minutes later didn't mean an hour's wait for another train. So Joe and B. R. had a nice long chat, during which Joe was able to mend some fences of his own while loosening the strands of those of some of his colleagues. This wasn't all accomplished in the office, though. First they went to a bar, then to dinner at Chambord (more cocktails, Strasbourg paté, lobster in absinthe sauce with an accompanying wine, coffee, three brandies), and then Joe took his by now beamish benefactor home in a cab. It was great for Joe.

He got home after two in the morning, already hungover, exhausted from hours of being careful and sharp while the boss relaxed, dirty and dishevelled from the antique, late-hour local he'd had to ride, and took a cab to his house. He found the door locked. His wife claimed she locked it as a precaution when he was late, but he believed she did it so he'd have to wake her to get in. He lifted and let fall the wrought-iron knocker, and he had his speech ready: "Not tonight, please. Whatever you say is true, you're right, I'm an inconsiderate bastard—but let's not discuss it now, may we? Not tonight."

Later, when Joe was setting the alarm for seven, it crossed his mind that an urbanite who went to bed late could sleep an extra fifteen minutes and be only fifteen minutes late to the office. For Joe, that extra blessed quarter hour in bed meant getting a train an hour later than usual and a slow train at that, so he'd be almost an hour and a half late.

Joe's second night in town that month was pre-planned and his wife knew it was important and that he might be late. She made her plans accordingly and they approached and passed the event in peace. This time, so as not to be dependent on trains, Joe drove in to work in the morning. This meant leaving home a half hour before traintime, fighting traffic, paying a few dollars for the privilege of an open parking lot. The dinner with the important advertiser went very well, but it got so late, what with dropping in to Ruban Bleu, Birdland, the Blue Angel, and the Embers, that Joe was too tight and too tired to go home, and accepted the man's invitation to sleep on the couch in his suite at the Waldorf.

Now, before the dinner Joe had been in a typically exurban situation. He was to call for his guest at seven. This meant working late just for a place to be, or finding someone with whom to pass the time. This was hard because Joe was out of touch with city people and, besides, he had to exclude as possibles all office people, with whom he'd have had to go to a bar for a drink. Even if an office acquaintance had been willing to stay with him until six forty-five, it would only have been to have several drinks, and Joe couldn't show up at the Waldorf stewed, or even mildly stimulated, since he would then be unable to keep his head while taking drink for drink with the advertiser, which the protocol of such meetings requires. So, he did what he had to do: he renewed an acquaintance which it had taken him years to break off.

It was a dreary writing couple Joe went to visit, in a mean and dingy apartment in Chelsea. They were a homely, untalented, aggressive writing team. The man had been in Joe's class in high school and had forced himself on Joe when he learned Joe was working in what this creep insisted on calling the literary game. Joe had let himself be pushed into seeing these people quite often before he realized they'd moved in on his life and were exploiting him. Then the long, sticky process of disentanglement had taken place. And here he was back again in their cheerless, aggressively run-down, pre-first World War, Bohemian, dank apartment. As he left there that night, Joe figured it would take a long time, and at least one gruesome week end having them out to the house come summer (the envious wife driving Joe's wife half out of her mind), before they could be ditched again. But Joe had to have a place to go and somebody to talk to between five-thirty and seven.

He had other problems, that night. He wanted to look his best, but had no clean shirt, no place to bathe and shave. (In the

morning, at the Waldorf, he could use his host's razor, but he'd
have to put on the same rumpled shirt, and stop on his way to
work to buy a toothbrush to use before he died of the morning-
after taste.) But there was a surprise in store for him the next
morning. There, right around the corner from the Waldorf, stood
a muddy and familiar-looking car against the curb. It was splendidly lonely, the only car parked on the wrong side of the street
after eight in the morning. As Joe walked toward it he recalled
that the night before, somewhere between Birdland and the
Embers, it had seemed like a good idea to stop depending on cabs
and get out the car. Who knew—they might have wanted to drive
out to Jones Beach to see the sunrise, or so they'd thought at
the time the decision was made. By the time he saw the ticket
hanging on the car, Joe was suffering the pangs of total recall.

The third night in town went like this: Joe had told his wife
there was an author's publication-date cocktail party he had to
attend, but that he'd catch the 7:47 for sure—or did she want to
come in for it? She explained to him, for the three-hundred-and-
twenty-sixth time, what this would entail: asking another parent
to take the kids from school to dancing class; asking still another
to pick them up and bring them home; asking the maid to stay
late and get the kids' dinner; arranging for someone to drive the
baby-sitter to the house; arranging for the sitter; getting home in
time to take the sitter home. Besides, they couldn't afford it.
Besides, he'd have to take a cab to the station and leave her the
car, or vice versa. Besides, she hadn't been to the hairdresser in
weeks. And she had literally nothing to wear.

So Joe went alone, which he'd wanted to do anyway. He got
careful after his second drink and made the third last a long,
long time—past traintime. He got carefree on the fourth drink,
accepted an invitation to dinner with a select group which included the guest of honor, and decided he'd find a way to pacify
his wife later. He did not.

It was the following week that the nasty writing-team couple
began pressing for a week-end invitation. Joe dodged like an ace
halfback, but they had him hopelessly cornered; after all, he had

an office and office hours, and a secretary can do only so much. On Friday, they nailed him in the reception room as he was on his way home and told him they'd been bequeathed a car for the week end and wasn't that a break because they had a great series to discuss with him and would be glad to drive out to the country the next morning, since he was obviously (judging by the difficulty they'd had reaching him) too busy in his office. Joe didn't want them hanging around in the reception room; he couldn't put them off with vague assurances of a happy week end in the country and then discuss the best way out of it with his wife, because she wasn't speaking to him. So he took them to an unacceptable bar, bought them drinks (the jerks, he thought, as they ordered rye and gingerale), and got drunk enough to tell them the sad story of his neurotic and hateful wife, who refused to entertain his friends, who mistreated his children, who flew into rages at the mere suggestion of company. He told them he didn't really feel brave about sticking it out. She was sick, and the kids needed him. But a pair of perceptive writers would understand—he couldn't see them any more. No week end. Nothing. He was so desperate that he was even going to make a sacrificial gesture which might hurt him in his job: "I hate to say it, but I think I've got to urge you to take your series idea to another shop," he said. "Have another drink."

So, he'd got rid of them, and when he got home he was so relieved, so tired, so depressed, that he ran into the house, grabbed his silent and grim-visaged wife around the waist, kissed her, said, "God, how I love you," and then she cried a little and he got tears in his eyes and they didn't eat dinner but had a few drinks and went to bed. End of Joe's week. End of Joe's month. Eight dols seems a conservative score for him.

It may be argued that Joe is hardly the type that gets ahead; many will think him, rather, a neurotic weakling who multiplies his own problems for his own reasons. Freudian hipsters may even nod significantly at the fantasy he concocted for the writing team about his wife: "Ah! Why make up just that particular story," they'll say. "Is it a secret wish?"

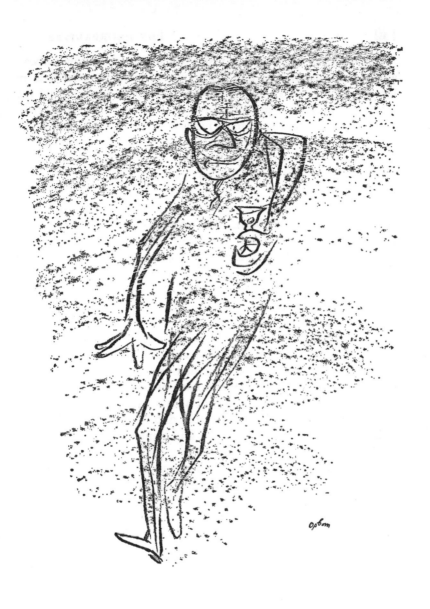

. . . AND MADE THE THIRD LAST A LONG TIME
—PAST TRAINTIME.

And now, at nine dols, or just short of the absolutely unbearable, are the advertising and high-powered publicity executives in the salary range of $10,000-$50,000 a year. Their pressures are the greater because they are still striving to reach the top of their profession, because there are so many of them, because there is so little room on top, and because they are all so shrewd, so intelligent, so imaginative that they have been able to devise marvelous methods of making each other's lives miserable as they compete with each other.

Such competition is taken for granted. People say to them, "Oh, you're in advertising? Gosh, how do you stand it? I understand the competition is terrific." It is, but these people don't realize how intense it is, nor will they ever know until they have worked in the business. What they probably have in mind is the kind of competition that is comparatively healthy, the kind of competition among, say, a copy writer, a commercial artist, and an account executive to do the best possible job on a campaign for a client; or even the often less savory competition that obtains between two agencies for a given account. It is true that such competition exists, but it is obscured and sometimes completely undermined by a more nefarious kind of competition, a ruthless, internecine, cut-throat contest, not always to get ahead, but sometimes just to hang on to the status quo. This competition is a bastard by Fear out of Insecurity, and some of its manifestations are fascinating.

There was once, for example, an agency that boasted the names of three partners on its letterhead. This story concerns the two men whose names came first. The senior of these two, the senior partner of the firm, was, despite his exalted position, on the seven-dol level, and he had reason, for his junior was an adept at a form of attrition which might be called name-dropping in reverse. Junior was skilled at seeming to know a great deal, perhaps everything, of what went on even on Senior's accounts. He had pipe lines. He never mentioned names. Sometimes he never even spoke. But his expression was eloquent. His expression said: "I've been talking to the sales manager, over at the client's office. I hope things aren't as bad as he seemed to think they were." And Senior squirmed.

Senior's principal client was a very large and important client indeed, with offices in Cleveland. Regularly Senior would take a plane to Cleveland, sometimes just for wetnursing, sometimes on important business. Once he went to deliver a big presentation. Much headway was made; the contract seemed assured, for increased billing. While he was on his way back, Junior put in a phone call to Cleveland, and did no more than say hello to a friend at the client's office. Presently Senior walked in, and Junior looked at him, his face wearing that inscrutable expression that seemed to suggest so much. Senior, who had arrived exultant, almost singing, felt his stomach turn over. Did Junior know something?

"Hi," said Junior. "I was just talking to Cleveland. Things don't seem so bad—" tiny pause "—after all."

That was all he said, and it should be pointed out that Junior and Senior were good friends, and that actually Junior had no wish to go poking around in Senior's business. But he couldn't help himself. He had always acted that way, and he always will. For him to say such a thing, for him to add fuel to the fire of Senior's fear as to whether the account was shaky, was not in the nature of a ploy in a game of one-upmanship; it was the way of his life. Had Junior deliberately intended that it should end as it did? We will never know; but today there are only two names on the agency's letterhead, and Junior's is senior.

As for the quality of inter-agency competition which keeps the dols ticking on the dolorimeter like atomic fallout on a Geiger counter, consider this story, told in the New York *Herald Tribune* by its advertising-field columnist, Joseph Kaselow. The subhead under which it ran is "Rough Stuff."

> Never a dull moment in this business. Representative of a well-known New York ad agency tells us that his firm has consulted its attorneys to find out what can be done about a former executive who has been engaged in a personal vendetta to knock the agency down. Clients of

the agency have been getting telephone calls from persons who say they represent trade publications and who ask where the clients are planning to place their accounts "now that the agency is dissolving." One client had his secretary make a stenographic record of the conversation with the "reporter" and when he called the publication he learned—as he had suspected—that there was no such person on the staff. The campaign also has involved planting reports of internal dissension in the agency, imminent resignations and client trouble with various publications. No wonder it's known as Ulcer Gulch.

This sort of phenomenon is everywhere to be seen, in inter- and intra-office competition. An account executive calls together the men who have been working on an account, and tells them he is going to be out of town for a few days. He says, portentously, that he is going to attend a convention where the client will be. What he in fact proposes to do is attend a convention where the client will be, but his manner conveys the impression that he, the client, the president of the National Broadcasting Company, the executive secretary of the American Newspaper Publishers' Association, the chairman of the board of directors of the Curtis Publishing Company, and the President of the United States have set up appointments over a three-day period as a result of which many broad, sweeping decisions are going to be made, all of which will vitally affect the careers, incomes, and future lives of everyone in his hearing. Then he leaves for the convention, and the worrying begins. He will do no more than buy drinks for his clients, but behind him his underlings are wholly persuaded that what he is up to will mean for them either a vice-presidency or the axe.

A caveat belongs here. The reader unfamiliar with this working milieu must not think that all the jockeying for position is a matter of conscious conniving. Ask the average communications man if he's guilty of it and he'll be hurt. Of course not. It doesn't apply in his case. He works hard, is simple and straightforward, is filled with esteem and regard for his fellows and wants nothing but the best for them. He's aware, of course, that bitchery, back stabbing, and assassination by innuendo are prevalent in his business, but he himself is innocent and so are the people with whom he works. "It's true," he'll insist. "In our outfit there's temperament, of course, but conscious throat cutting? No."

The operative word is "conscious." It isn't always consciously intended, but the throat cutting goes on, throughout the communications world.

Everyone does it. Two men can be working on a layout over the same drawing-board, and one will attempt and usually succeed in giving the impression that he is privy to some secrets, some weighty matters, some important decisions about the account, the campaign, the client, whatever. Everyone acts as though he is more important than he is, as though he knows more than the next man about their joint business. The effort is to make the next man feel inferior, and the effect, logically enough, is to destroy working morale and working efficiency. Everyone is back in the Navy again, but there is not a happy ship in the fleet, but only tight ships.

The president of a large and important public relations firm has under him four vice-presidents. They have all been in their jobs for pleasantly lengthy periods, anywhere from seven to fifteen years; they are all well paid. But they are all unnerved: when the president goes with one of them to lunch, the other three worry. "What's going on? What's he telling him? What's going to happen?" And down through the chain of command, each vice-president thereafter, in a formal pecking order, endeavors to do the same to his underlings, and they to theirs.

One of these vice-presidents is a commuter. To try to compensate for the exposed position his train schedule leaves him in every evening, he resorts to elaborate expedients. For example, it had been his custom while he lived in the city to patronize a barbershop near his home, a small but good one where the same man had been ministering to him, in the manner he had taught him, for many years. Recently, however, he learned that his boss (as well as other important contacts) patronized the barbershop of an East Fifties hotel. It took quite some conniving to get on the regular, by-appointment, client list there, but the v.p. figured it was worth it. The day he was admitted to the club, when he could tell his secretary to call and make an appointment for him (having learned this was the boss's day, too) he felt he'd pulled off a major coup. He felt so good about it, in fact, that he wandered down the hall and beamingly reported the fact to a colleague, straight-faced and unashamed. The colleague, with typical communications-business, bitchy cracksmanship said, "Bully for you; maybe some day I can get you into the men's room at the Ritz." The vice-president was quick to laugh—at himself and with the other man—but only after a lightning estimate, casing the situation (What goes on in that men's room? Really worth going to? Get biz? Meet the right people?) and then instantly re-jecting the notion as absurd. It was a good laugh, but it was, just the same, worth one additional momentary dol.

And that night, he had a whole hour on the train of being up one dol as he worried about whether, in the moment of weakness induced by his need to share his good fortune in being admitted to a hotel barbershop, he had not put himself at a terrible dis-advantage with respect to the man to whom he'd confided the good news. Right now, it was all right; they were friends. But a good, juicy story about him, told with tolerant amusement in the right company at the right time, might give his friend of the present too strong an incentive to be resisted. The v.p. knew that in his clique-ridden, tricky, pally business an innocent confidence can be treacherous, can turn (if competition for position suggests it) into a lethal time bomb, so that suddenly, retroactively, you're not a member of the in-group any more and really never were.

When he got home to the peace of his exurb that night, the v.p. canceled the appointment he'd made with a real estate agent to discuss buying an adjoining parcel of land for protection. He felt that, despite his barbershop triumph, he might easily lose all he had, since it was already pretty heavily mortgaged.

If this seems incredible, suspend disbelief until you read the facts reported about one exurbanite's income and expenditures, in the next chapter. Then multiply, for a medium-sized firm in the communications industry, that exurbanite and his problems by a dozen. Remember that each of these dozen men is faced with the harsh necessity of doing well enough that he will receive, via raise, bonus, or promotion, a healthy annual increase, quite apart from the ugly fear that someone will stab him in the back in some fashion and make him lose what present income he has. Inter-office politics, in most industries an annoyance, or an amusing pastime, becomes, in the hands of the symbol-manipulators, Machiavellian. That is one reason for the indulgent, mild response these people accorded Stephen Potter's books on gamesmanship: in a world where you can sink if you're not two up, being merely one up seems like delightful but harmless child's play. For the over-extended exurbanites, Potter's ploys have all the bite and sting of blancmange.

It is interesting to see what happened when the psychiatrists took a look at the advertising fraternity. As reported in *Sponsor*, a trade magazine, most advertising agency executives are driven by fear and insecurity. Dr. Ernest Dichter, president of the Institute for Research in Mass Motivations (a thing called Motivational Research has assumed in some quarters almost the nature of a revealed religion), himself resident in an exurb, after examining two hundred agency executives, concluded: "The average advertiser, be he a company man or an agency man, is bewildered and confused. . . . It is the outcome of insecurity and fear—and fear is bound to leave the marks of its destructive influence."

In the face of these morale-shattering difficulties, the technical excellence of most of the work turned out by the communications industry is nothing short of miraculous.

For the exurbanite, this endemic anxiety works both ways. In the first place, it is largely instrumental in shaping his decision to become exurbanite. He can be subjected to only a certain amount of these constant pressures before he begins to shape his limited dream, and yearn to be able to take time off from the rat race. Unfortunately, it doesn't work that way. As soon as he is ensconced in his exurban home, and has even drawn his first deep sigh of relief, he finds that his worries have climbed on the train with him and, slipping their hot, moist hands into his, have accompanied him right to his fireplace and curled up with him in his favorite armchair. Out in his exurb, he broods. And so he gets on the phone in an effort to find out what's really going on, and this results in a lofty phone bill; or he tries to forget all about it and the hell with it until tomorrow, and this results in a lofty liquor bill.

One way or another, the exurbanite finds that he must commit himself solidly to the expense-account economy. What with his added expenses, it is one of the few ways he has of coming out even at the end of the month. The expense-account economy is not, of course, exploited exclusively by the exurbanites, but it is safe to say that the exurbanites, with their special financial burdens, are its most skilled and persistent devotees.

The expense-account economy functions on three levels. At its simplest, a man goes to lunch with a friend from the same branch of the communications industry but from a different company; each spends perhaps three dollars for his cocktail and lunch; each thereafter repairs to his office and presents to the appropriate fiscal authority (sometimes to a department head) a chit for as much as the traffic will bear. Or a man may, for a wonder, actually be taking someone out to lunch on legitimate business. In this event, he has every right to present the chit to the fiscal authority, and so he does; this time the chit will be for, roughly, twice what he spent out of pocket. This practice is universal, and is counted on to assist in eking out the family income. In addition, it is, for many husbands, their only secret money, that is, the only funds they can lay their hands on that their wives do not know about; money like this can be used for an infinite variety of purposes. Such expense-account practices are regarded with a tolerant eye by most firms in the communications industry, or at any rate the squawks have not yet become anguished.

On the next level, however, things are getting out of hand. This is the use of the expense account by a relative few, but in spectacular fashion. Where, on the primer level, the individual spent money out of his own pocket and was subsequently reimbursed, here on this secondary level, the individual simply says, in a casual way, to his secretary, "Go pick me up a couple of hundred, will you, honey?" He will not have to account for his expenses, he who operates on this level, until the end of the month, and a lot can happen in that much time. There are not too many such individuals in any given company. An estimate of ten percent of the employees might be about right. They are the men who move in relatively rarefied circles; not all of them are vice-presidents, by any means, but in general they are the men who have achieved a stipend of $20,000 a year or so. As they grow more accustomed to the enviable power of gathering in two or three hundred in cash simply by asking for it, they incline to do so more capriciously. And soon they discover that a month's end can go by without their having made a full accounting. Before long, they are perhaps one thousand dollars behind, or ahead if you look at it that way. This figure is an average; there are unquestionably some men who are two or three thousand dollars behind (or ahead). In this way, a man can acquire quite a reputation as a gentleman, generous to a fault: every anniversary is in the tickler file, every ocean-going acquaintance carries away his basket of fruit or wine, every business associate gets his occasional gift, every girl friend her tithe of loot. During a war economy, bosses could afford to wink at this practice. Excess profits were to be taxed heavily in any event, and salaries were frozen. But more and more, these days, the noose is tightening around the neck of the expense-account economy. Accounting is stricter, and there is even agitated word going around that some companies are employing gumshoes to check up, to see if A in fact did have lunch with B and C, as alleged in Requisition D. It is easy to see why this must be so. In a large company, where maybe fifty or even a hundred men may have had free access to the expense account, if they are averaging a thousand dollars apiece in unaccounted expenditures, it can tot up to a tidy sum. Nor can this money be charged off to the client. This all comes out of the fifteen percent.

Furthermore, it often happens that a man on the expense account goes out in a group which includes one of the owners of the business. This owner is on the third level of the expense-account economy, and if he happens to see a second-level account-claim, he may shoot an extremely vexed look at the man who has submitted it. For the owner of the business does not avail himself of the expense account, he doesn't have to, he has enough money so that he can pay out of pocket and never file for reimbursement. As part owner, why should he? He would only be taking out of one pocket to put in another anyway; and besides, it is to his advantage to pay out of his own pocket, in the expectation that he will subsequently make quite proper business deductions on his personal income tax statement, something a second-level man simply can't afford to do. The second-level man is bitter enough about that, but he is even more bitter as he sees what has been, in the past, a lifesaving safety valve for his financial pressures being gradually turned off.

Throughout the communications industry, but especially in its advertising agencies, the search goes on for such safety valves. One of the most threadbare of these (it has been turned so often its threads have been stripped) is office humor. The humor has an arcane, exclusive quality; it is strictly for insiders. Those who are in advertising especially sense (whether accurately or not is unimportant) that they are under constant attack by outsiders. They feel that all over the country there are people sneering at them, calling them hucksters or worse, impugning their ability and their integrity. They have two choices: they can associate only with those who will freely admire their high technical ability, or they can make better fun of their plight than do the outsiders. Examples of this sort of humor abound, and one or two specimens are included here, for the interest of the morbid:

Exhibit A. This is a memorandum of uncertain authorship which was widely circulated around Madison Avenue in 1953, shortly after the publication of J. D. Salinger's Novel, *The Catcher in the Rye.* It is headed:

The Shortstop in the Scotch

I work in one of the biggest goddam advertising agencies in the whole goddam world. Very big deal.

That's what people think. They really do. They think just because your name is on the old receptionist's roll-book, you make a goddam million bucks or something a year. That kills me.

I know guys who've been working here for 90 years and all, and they're still scraping for luxuries like toothpaste and shoe-laces. Not just one guy. Lots of guys.

But people don't believe that. I mean like the lady I met the other day. She says, "Where do you work, dear?" And when I tell her, her eyes light up like a pinball machine and I thought she was going to rape me or something. "Oh, you don't work there!" she howls, acting like "there" was a gold mine in South Africa or something. . . .

I know the guys around here who make a million bucks, though. I mean, I don't actually know them real well and all, but I know who they are. They're the ones who sit behind their big fat desks and buzz for their secretaries all day long. Then when they buzz, I mean, the secretaries run like mad to blow their noses for them or something. That kills me. I wouldn't want those old secretaries touching my nose. I wouldn't mind having a buzzer, but not a secretary.

Those old secretaries are crazy. They really are. They're always taking collections. They take collections for having babies, pole-vaulting six feet, or getting a date with an elevator man. . . .

All these big slobs . . . have a charming slob of a wife and two little kid slobs. They raise chickens and turnips and have a summer place on a lake. What phonies. They all commute with brown satchels.

And you've got to drink Scotch. If you happen not to like Scotch, you don't say anything. You just keep your breath smelling of it all the time.

What makes these guys even worse is that they have to tell you about it all the time. They even tell you, then sell you stuff. I buy asparagus from a slob who makes five million a year. I hate asparagus, honest to God I hate it. But this guy raises it for a hobby and I buy it for real. He always says to me, "Your work isn't so good, boy. You're not eating enough asparagus." I eat more asparagus than any asparagus farmer in the goddam universe.

They earn their money, though. They write memos. Billions of goddam memos and all. I think they get paid by the memo. I really do. They put fancy names on them, headlines like:

Re: The Use of a Semicolon in the Buckwheat Campaign, Small Space Ads. . . .

It's really a hot place, this agency. I mean, it really is.

Exhibit B. A more recent memorandum, attributed to individuals working for NBC Television. It was mimeographed and distributed widely. It is headed:

How To Sell a Second-hand Pencil Which Has Lost Its Eraser

Forget your laundry bills!

This pre-tested chrome-yellow, hard-finish writing instrument positively will not leak, no need to blot—keeps your hands free of ink, your clothes safe and spotless.

Fabricated from the finest second-growth hickory, it is graphite-filled with fine-grained, jet-black carbon which cannot snag or catch on any paper surface.

Oven-baked enamel coating, with die-stamped copper blue markings. Octagonal contours slip easily into any size hand.

Tipped with cold-rolled forged steel collar, machine-stamped in our own factories in two-toned filagree.

Removal of eraser guarantees pencil to be 100% latex-free!

No push-pull, no click-click—the point is always there, ready to write.

Free from unsightly pocket clip, it writes in any weather. Funnel-shaped point handsomely decorated with scalloped edge. Unnecessary to refill—can be discarded when finished. Fits any standard sharpener.

Write for *FREE* photograph today!

In the communications industry, the practical joke is complex and expensive and elaborate. The art department of one agency with a view commanding the offices of International Business Machines is reputed, according to one probably apocryphal tale, to have spent an entire afternoon on a beautifully lettered sign which they are supposed then to have placed in such a way that IBM's executives would see it. It read: "The Hell with Thinking," and is supposed to have resulted in high-level representations from IBM brass to the agency's brass.

The jokes, the self-ribbing, the elaborate memoranda, all are designed to alleviate the tension. They also serve two other purposes. One is to pass the time. For the fact is that creative work, however commercial its purpose, requires too high a degree of concentration and too great an outlay of energy to be conducted at an even pace eight hours a day. Business being business, that's the working-day span that's required by custom, so the gaps between spurts of concentrated effort must be filled while four to five hours of hard work are spaced out over eight.

The other purpose has been briefly alluded to already. It concerns total cynicism about everyone's work but one's own. For one's own work there is an overt attitude of cynicism and a covert real regard, which can only be admitted to a degree to colleagues and not at all to outsiders. While the work is being done one can be completely wrapped up in it, working hard and enjoying the techniques of the profession and the exercise of skills and talents. At such times one can also apply odd measurements to a job's intrinsic worth: if one has spent a week selecting

and endlessly rearranging the six words which will spearhead a
national institutional ad campaign on which a million dollars will
be spent, the words themselves can take on, somehow, a value of
one sixth of a million dollars each.

It is only when the assignment is over and there is a hiatus
before the next job's taken on, that perspective returns and a
man can ask himself whether it's ultimately desirable for a
mature and gifted individual to spend his energies on selling the
crackle in a cereal or the suds of a soap. Or, instead of asking the
question of himself, he can distract himself, relieve tension, and
amuse his friends by abnegating manhood, for a bit, in favor of
sophomoric humor. And there's always tension within, to make
the respite more delightful, to make the humor more elaborate,
to make the laughter when it comes more explosive and prolonged.

The ultimate tension in the industry is reserved for those who
have forged two-thirds of the way to the top. The game of musical
chairs, after all, is most fun when it is in its early stages, when
there are a dozen chairs for the thirteen contestants. The game
loses its fun and acquires its suspense and its tension as the chairs
are subtracted, one by one. There are, in the communications
business, so many who not only want to seize the ultimate chair
but, among the exurbanites, must seize it to survive. But here
we can introduce a cheering note for Exurbia. For a change has
been in progress in recent years, and it can be predicted that it
will grow at an accelerating rate.

Throughout the communications business there are now
pockets where the worms are turning and it is the exurbanite who
has the edge. For, as Exurbia grows, as the exurbanite army in
the business increases, it is the urbanites who are beginning to
feel left out and the exurbanites who start one lap ahead each
day of the rat race—and two laps on Monday. Especially up
where the dol count is high, one hears increasingly, "Well, let's
shelve it now and discuss it on the train." That's music to
exurban ears. One hears, too—and this is hard lines for the
urbanites—"Let's discuss it on the train—oh, I forgot, you live

in town, don't you? Well, don't worry, Fred and I will discuss it and we'll memo you in the morning." Ouch!

Especially in the summer, but increasingly all year round, the exurbanite has a greater and greater opportunity to do his fence mending with his boss, his conniving with his colleagues, and his contact work with potential customers and employers of his talent, right at home in his exurb. But even the encouragement he can derive from this fact is hardly enough to compensate him for the dols with which commuting loads him. And for urbanite and exurbanite alike, the basic facts don't alter: the higher they go, the fewer jobs there are to go to.

And there is not too much time, for they are all getting older, and they all know that the race is to the swift and the young. Many of them feel that they are renting their brains out by the day, with nothing to show for it but money. The harder they work, the higher the rent paid for their brains. But it is not the same as, for example, owning a business somewhere, manufacturing something, building an enterprise which, if they choose, they may later sell and retire. It is still nothing but the leasing of something intangible—and something which, they fear, will go with their youth. It is not only the insecurity that results from the fear that they will lose their jobs, but the insecurity that results from the dread that their mental agility will one day inevitably slow up. And what will they have to show for it?

Only those wholly unacquainted with the financial burden of life in Exurbia will be tempted to shrug off the plight of the exurbanite with the comment, "After all, he is making a lot of money, isn't he? What's wrong with that? I wouldn't mind making—what's he make? Twenty-five grand a year?" Such a comment ignores the fact, long since discovered, that such a sum, in Exurbia, counts for very little. The exurbanite leads a hell of a life to earn that money, but it seems to require of him no effort at all to spend all of it—and then some.

7

MOSTLY ABOUT MONEY:
AN EXURBAN BUDGET

*All progress is based upon a universal innate desire on
the part of every organism to live beyond its income.*
—SAMUEL BUTLER

NEXT to reading somebody else's love letters,
there's nothing quite so delightful as being privy to the facts of
his financial life, especially if they tend toward the disastrous.
That's just what we're going to be now.

Side by side, on a sylvan lane in Westport, sharing a common
stone wall dividing their properties, live a commercial artist and
a TV producer. Across the road, in a new ranch house, lives Fred
Barber, a William Powell type who is ad manager of a trade
magazine. Bill Dahl, the artist, is in his late thirties and has
behind him ten years of pretty steady free-lance work, and a
good reputation in commercial art circles. His wife is several years
his junior and looks great: nice figure, lively face, neat and well
groomed most of the time. Bill himself is casually tweedy and

manages, because of non-commuting, to attain an earlier spring tan than most exurbanites. Their house is a remodeled salt box which they have painted pink and fitted with faded blue shutters. It looks charming and original. Bill drives an MG and they have a Chevrolet station wagon. Two kids under ten, two dogs, and a cat round out the family.

Ted Daniels is the producer. He's heavy-set but rather dashing, wears his hair longish, and has been described by an exurban writer as looking like a pin-stripe Walt Whitman. He commutes, sometimes the darnedest hours. This year he's doing an important Sunday night show. His week works like this: Monday, full-day story conference; Tuesday, production meeting in the morning; Wednesday and Thursday, at rest at home; Friday, afternoon script session; Saturday afternoon, dry rehearsal; Sunday afternoon, dry rehearsal and camera rehearsal, then the show, then late supper with too much to drink and to bed in a hotel. Not a tough week, but plenty of work; yet it appears to some of his office-hour-keeping neighbors that he's home a lot more than they are and can take later morning trains and earlier evening trains on the days he does commute. He, too, has a nice wife, nice kids. They own an English Ford, a Plymouth station wagon, and a fieldstone semi-Colonial house with a modern sunroom added to the back.

Ted and Bill get on well. So do their wives—rare thing. So do their kids. And their pets. It's a pleasant intimacy with enough privacy to insure keeping the peace. Both families know all about each other—almost. Ted did know how much Bill got for painting a *Saturday Evening Post* cover, and he could make a shrewd guess about what he'd been paid by BBD&O for a series of cute line drawings of talking dogs who were the stars of a national ad campaign in which the happy dog told the sad dog, cartoon style, how much better things were at home since the humans had invested in a brand-new unitized-alloy kitchen. But what did he get for that trip of a few weeks back, when he was sent by Benton & Bowles to South Bend, to do sketches for what was to become an artistic oil painting of a steel mill at night? How

much did he make on the side for that trip? And what was he
paid for the painting, which ran as a full-page institutional ad in
Fortune and a half-dozen other top national magazines, and which
was hung in the board room of the steel company's home office?
How much does Bill earn a year? How much unsigned advertising
art is his? Bill Dahl, Ted knows, spends a lot of time in his semi-
detached studio, but is he painting and drawing all the time? Is
it true, as Ted has heard, that Bill never does anything on spec?
Is it true that he illustrated that children's book last year only
for fun—or did he need the extra income?

Bill wonders about Ted, too. He's heard rumors that the big
boys at the network are sore because Ted's contract for that one
Sunday night show has an escalator clause and is now bringing
him more than some vice-presidents earn. But the rating is high
and the sponsor is happy, so Ted is in solid. What could he be
earning, though, for a half-hour show once a week? What about
cancellation clauses; what would happen if the sponsor or the
agency or the network didn't renew? Or maybe it's the other
way round, maybe Ted is so hot he'll be able to renegotiate for
a still higher figure. And what about those one-shots he directs
from time to time? There was also a rumor last summer that Ted
owns a piece of a packaged show. And Ted had once said something about royalties he was still getting for a radio documentary
he'd written and directed ten years ago. How much was that
worth? Bill once heard, too, that Ted is being paid a percentage
of the Sunday show, but is it off the top?

It is not suggested that Ted and Bill spend a lot of time
wondering about each other's incomes. But when they do
wonder, they have no clues to guide them. The families live
about equally well, but in Exurbia that's no clue.

What each does believe firmly about the other is that the
truth of his own financial situation would appall his neighbor.
We, being omniscient, know each man averages $25,000 a year.
Both are barely solvent. Both operate on the necessity to earn
more each year. If they don't, they'll go under, they're sure. And
they are not unique in Exurbia. Nor is it unique for each to

feel about their neighbor across the road that *he's* the really lucky one, that he can't possibly be in trouble, because he's a regular commuter with a regular, staff job and an annual salary which is predictable, and a predictable future with a retirement income at its end. "Good old Freddy," they say of him, amused. "Regular as a clock. Thinks he's better than other wage slaves because he works for a magazine, but he isn't even in the editorial end. A businessman, that's what he is."

But Fred Barber, good old Freddy, has his own troubles. It was promised that an exurban income—and outgo—would be laid bare and the dissection will take place on schedule. But first, let's look into the causes for Exurbia's chronic state of subliminal financial crisis. We can then get to work on poor old Freddy's private, yet typically exurban, money life.

Exurbia is filled with intelligent, witty, amusing, clever people, people who are fun to be with and provocative to talk to. Indeed, they have to be, for in many ways it is their profession: wit, comedy, brains, intelligence, and animal cunning are the commodities they have to sell—to the advertisers, the producers, the publishers, the broadcasters, those whose business, in turn, it is to amuse, entertain, instruct, inform, and con into the purchase and consumption of tangible commodities the rest of the country (and many millions outside the country as well). So it is reasonable to conceive of Exurbia as the brains and the sense of humor of America. We must look elsewhere to find America's heart, America's hands and muscles, or America's conscience, but it can at least be contended that New York City's exurbs are the nation's brain and wit. But they are more than just that, in our body politic and social.

We are all of us consumers, so presumably we must all of us together constitute the national stomach. But the exurbs are such remarkable maws of consumption, exurbanites in general are such heroes of the consumption line, that they must rate acknowledgment, even national primacy, on this score as well. Perhaps, since they are of such importance in guiding the national taste, stimulating the national appetite, and creating the national hunger, we may think of them as being our national taste buds. The taste buds are an oval group of spindle-shaped cells; the exurbanites are an amorphous group of variously shaped individuals who, individually and collectively, perform epic deeds, qualitatively and quantitatively, in terms of our over-all consumption. Not content with spending up to the limit of their considerable ability, exurban consumers indomitably spend each year far more than they can. They are doing their bit to keep the national economy expanding. Say what you will against the exurbanite, you can never accuse him of any meanness, any parsimony, any hoarding. You may chisel on the stone over his early grave (if some one of his several creditors has not beaten you to it): "He spent all his plenty—and then some."

It is not true that all exurbanites live on a standard exceeding their income. An exurban lawyer, himself a counselor to other exurbanites on their tax problems, investments, etc., estimates the break-even point at $60,000—that is, at around the time the average high-spending exurbanite starts making $60,000 a year, he is probably beginning to be able to make all his ends meet. But before he reaches that point, it is murder.

His principal difficulty is that, like Bill, Ted, and poor old Freddy, he must live on the common exurban level, no matter what he may happen at the time to be making. The exurbanite making $10,000 a year (and it is rarely possible for an exurbanite to survive at such a level) tries to look like, act like, and live like the exurbanite who is making $100,000 a year. But while the Federal income tax rate is a great leveler, it is not that great, and, since most exurbanites move in a social scheme where they see each other constantly, visit each other back and forth, run into each other around the same swimming-pools, at the same beaches, on the same tennis courts, at the same cocktail parties, it takes some doing to maintain the illusion that they are making what everyone else is making. The exurbanite's problem is not that it's difficult to do, but that it's difficult to pay for.

It is not difficult to do in the first place because of the factor already mentioned, taxes. The $10,000-a-year man becomes an

$8,000-a-year man after taxes (with luck), but the $100,000-a-year man becomes a $40,000-a-year man, which cuts almost in half the difference. In the second place, these days, the very rich man is not concerned with any of the one-time display spending described by Veblen. He may have three cars, but still drive the jeep, while the $10,000-a-year man may as reasonably have one car, and that one a two-year-old Cadillac convertible picked up on a special second-hand deal.

Even the question of servants is no true test, at least to the casual glance. The $100,000-a-year man may keep a staff of three servants, especially if he is blessed with a tax-exempt trust income, and when you go to his house, you may see all three of them; but the $15,000-a-year man, when he entertains precisely the same people, will have a hired couple for the night, and only those who have hired the same couple themselves may realize what is going on.

The differences between the two, then, are observed in smaller ways. One looks to see if the garage is for three cars or two. If the whisky is served from labeled bottles, rather than from decanters, one notes when it is Imperial Grand or Bellows Reserve, instead of Old Taylor, or James E. Pepper—but even a test like this can be deceptive, for the rich are often stingy. One exurbanite's personal test is to look at the old newspapers pulled out of the woodbox, to assist in lighting a fire. If they are *Wall Street Journals*, he figures the owner is trustworthy, should he ask for a loan.

These subtle differences of degree, and the rather more significant but still less evident distinction between those who buy goods and services with cash, and those who buy them on time or with loosely extended credit, are the most serviceable methods of separating the exurbanite who is just getting by from his neighbor who is truly wealthy. For the rest, each will consider the same things to be vital necessities of life in the race to keep up with each other and ahead of the Joneses.

And now we're ready to get down to cases. Nothing is more instructive than to examine a specimen case at close hand. The case chosen, good old, poor old Freddy Barber, is difficult to describe as typical, for his income is in the top one half of one percent for the country as a whole; nevertheless, for the exurbs, it is by no means atypical. Fred is married, living with his present wife and their two children, and is paid $25,000 a year. He considers that he earns it, too. In reporting herewith his expenses for the past year, all figures will be rounded off to the nearest $25; this is for simplicity's sake, to eliminate (an exurban trait) the need for counting pennies, and in order to mask his true identity from the operatives of the Federal Bureau of Internal Revenue—a hope which is, in any event, hollow, as will be seen from the very first item.

Taxes. On last year's income, he is paying $5,000 in taxes to the Federal government and to the state of New York. He does not live in New York state but that makes no difference; as long as he earns his money there he could commute from Timbuctoo and would still be required to pay the New York state tax. This is, to say the least, a source of concern to him. He resents it bitterly. He cannot, for example, deduct any sums which he may have given to charity in his home state of Connecticut. The method by which he arrived at the gross total of $5,000 for his national and state taxes was somewhat cavalier, involving principally an abstruse formula in which the two principal factors were: 1) the amount of money he could lay his hands on at the moment required, and 2) what he thought he could get away with. He is too realistic to think he will be able to get away with such a paltry sum indefinitely, but he rather hopes he will be able to escape the Feds until next year. By that time, maybe something will have turned up. In the meantime, he clutches at pathetic straws. For example, he has heard that only one out of fifteen returns is actually scrutinized with more than cursory attention, so he crosses his fingers and hopes his luck will hold. Or he has heard an account of how Robert Benchley once sent back his income tax return attached to a check made out to John Wanamaker's. According to this fable, it took the T-men three years to catch up with him. There is also a well-authenticated tale of an exurbanite who never paid the state tax; at least, not for years. When at length the state caught up with him, he made a deal, on the spot, with the agent. He showed him his bankbook, which in turn showed a balance of about $35. The agent, according to the tale, settled for $25. Our man hasn't yet tried this system, but give him time, he well may. You may ask why Fred didn't have his income tax returns prepared for him by a lawyer or an accountant. He did take his problems to one lawyer, but this man, a man of discretion and probity, advised him, as a friend, to plead *nolo contendere* and throw himself on the mercy of whatever court assumed jurisdiction.

Before we leave the subject of taxes, it should be reported that the city of New York has been making ominous gestures in the direction of levying some sort of tax on the commuter. It is the city's contention, denied with anguish by the commuters, that all commuters are free-loaders, and expensive ones at that, and should be made to help swing the expense of paying police salaries, or repaving streets. One civic spokesman, the chairman of the tax and assessment committee of the Real Estate Board of New York, has said: "One of the most pressing problems confronting big cities is that caused by the large number of persons who earn their money in the cities but reside outside their limits. These people receive the full benefits of police, fire, transportation, and sanitation services without making any direct contribution toward maintenance of these services. The larger the commuting population of any city, the greater the need for these services and the greater the burden the city must assume."

Maid. The Barbers' jewel is a sleep-out, but otherwise full-time domestic. They pay her $2,500 a year. She has boy friends who drop in occasionally, and help push the food bill up, and probably the liquor bill as well, although Fred hasn't been able to catch them at it yet. There will be some of his friends who, looking at this figure, will make the mental note that it is too high. Should be, they will say to themselves, around $2,000 a year.

But it happens this maid is a hell of a maid and a hell of a cook, and helps keep the children under wraps by day. He believes she is worth it.

Mortgage, insurance, local taxes, amortization, and interest. The house is a $35,000 job. It costs him around $2,500 a year. He has had to refinance the mortgage once. The local taxes referred to, of course, pay for school, most importantly; both his children are enrolled in the near-by school.

Heating. By oil. Cost $350 a year.

Repairs and improvements. This item relates only to the house. $650.

Commuting. Why, he grumbles, isn't this deductible as a necessary business expense? $300.

WORKING SUB-TOTAL: $11,300

Cars. He owns two. Or rather, he owns one, and is in the process of getting to own the other. One is an old Ford, and this he owns outright. The other, a Buick, he is still paying for. Upkeep and carrying charges: $1,000. Is there any point in his selling the Ford? Not really, for he wouldn't be able to get what he paid for it, and he needs a station car anyway. He might sell the Buick, except that he has hopes, once it's fully paid for, that he will be able to borrow on it. And this is a consideration of some importance.

Charities. Local and national. $100. He likes to keep this down to a minimum, but it is not the easiest thing in the world to do. In his exurb, it is fashionable to support the public school system with an annual "do" of some kind, usually an affair with gambling devices. Last summer, he and a group of pals were charged up when they reached the festivities, and his wife couldn't drag him away before he had contributed $80 to charity in one evening.

The outdoors. This item comprises the lawn and its care, and the garden and its care, and the fruit trees and their care. To pay for a part-time gardener (the local who comes by to pick up the pieces, after Fred has had a whirl at trying to tell the weeds from the perennials), a part-time lawn-cutter (an insolent youth, given to whistling between his teeth), and a part-time handyman: $400. And, as any exurbanite will tell you, he's getting off cheap.

Garden tools, and repair thereof. $150. There is always something, although he is fairly well equipped. He has had the automatic roto-tiller, the power lawn mower, and the electric hedge-clippers for some time. But there is always something new.

Miscellaneous upkeep. Like taking down the storm windows, putting up the screens, taking down the screens, putting up the storm windows, doing a thorough spring cleaning, getting a man for the chimney, rebuilding the driveway where the big rain washed it away, etc. $200.

WORKING SUB-TOTAL: $13,150

Insurance. This item is only his own life insurance. He bought $20,000 worth when he was young, and at various times he has been able to increase it. He now pays $1,000 a year, but gravely doubts whether he is adequately insured.

Floater and liability insurance. Here he knows he is inadequately taken care of. But what's he going to do? $100.

Interest. On a bank loan which he floated to pay the balance of last year's tax after withholding, and to pay his life insurance premiums. $300.

Storm damage. He has never met a girl named Hazel or Carol, but if he ever does, he may strike her in the face. $150.

Regional stigmata. These are the little touches around the house and grounds which (he feels) are required because most of his friends feel they are required. They can also be described as the crucial improvements he never knew how he had been able to live without before he bought them and ignored completely a week after their being put in place. An example is the post-lantern ($120); another is the special light for the terrace, reputed to keep mosquitoes away, or kill them, or whatever

($25); another is the fieldstone barbecue (various). His total for last year: $500. This sum presumably could be reduced by anyone with a grip on sanity, but not by the exurbanite.

It will have been noticed that up till now Fred has spent nothing directly on himself or his family, but nevertheless he has arrived at a

WORKING SUB-TOTAL: $15,200

Food. His wife protests that she budgets carefully, and it is she who levels an accusing finger at the maid's many boy friends. She claims that she reads all the women's magazines for inexpensive recipes, and who screams loudest, she demands, when the dinner consists of canned tuna fish, canned mushroom soup, and canned peas, a perfectly delicious combination? If you insist on roast beef or leg of lamb, and don't forget the kids have got to eat properly, and— All right! All right! $3,500.

Booze. Fred is careful. He is not an alcoholic, and neither is his wife. Some of their friends are, but when really hard drinkers show up unexpectedly of a Sunday afternoon, they lock away the choicer brands of sauce. Nevertheless, $1,000. A very conservative figure.

Medical. It must be explained, about this item, that Fred's younger child is undergoing a fashionable but expensive course of orthodontics. Besides, both Fred and Rita are prey to the Exurban Syndrome. $1,000.

Vacation. Under this heading, besides the trip the Barbers took to Canada, are included two week ends in town. $700, and Fred feels martyred because, in comparison with most of his exurban friends, he is.

Baby-sitters. At fifty cents an hour, or seventy-five cents an hour if equipped with own transportation, baby-sitters cost him $350. What are you going to do, deny a man the chance to see his friends once in a while? By comparison with some exurban families, this sum is regarded as cheap.

Clothes. The problem is not only the two tailor-made suits for the breadwinner; he has also to buy the necessary regimentals for such exurban pastimes as going to a barn dance. He may go to only one barn dance in two years, but he must be prepared for it. His wife chewed the bigger hole in this item: her share included a sheared beaver. Total: $2,150.

Telephone. Mostly long distance, to New York or to friends in other exurbs. $200.

Entertainment. Last year the Barbers were niggardly. Every time they entertained they did it the cheapest possible way, except for the four unavoidable dinner parties arranged for the four men (and their wives) who are most important in terms of Fred's future. This figure will scandalize every true exurbanite, but Fred claims he spent only $500.

Books, magazines, and newspapers. He isn't sure about this item, but it can be deduced from his habits, and those of his wife. He buys the *Herald Tribune* every morning and, in addition, the *Times* on Sunday. He likewise buys both the *World-Telegram* and the *Journal-American* every weekday afternoon. The week does not go by in which he does not buy *Life, The New Yorker,* and *Time;* the month does not go by in which his wife does not buy either *Vogue,* or *Harper's Bazaar,* or both. That much totals about $100, and he (and she, too) insists he buys and reads an occasional book. Say $150.

As far as the children are concerned, there was:

Day camp. For one of them. $200.

Special lessons. Sailing, dancing, tennis. He figures $200 covers it, and thanks God that his girl is not, as are the daughters of some friends, studying ballet, in which case the figure would be doubled.

Toys. There is a general recognition throughout Exurbia that the toys bought for the children are guilt offerings. In a fumbling attempt to compensate for the tensions around the house, out pops an expensive toy. Of course, it is also true that some exurbanites are still in their nonage, and are buying toys for their children which they propose to play with themselves. Our man spent $200 and will be generally regarded as a cheapskate.

Birthday presents. For the children's friends. For some reason, it seems that each child has nine closest friends, who collectively celebrate a birthday at least three times a week. At $1 per capita, $100.

Children's allowances. $75. At which point, he has arrived at a

WORKING SUB-TOTAL: $25,525

Hobby. It happens that Fred is a hi-fi buff, but he could easily be a do-it-yourselfer, with a workshop, or a photographer, with a darkroom, or a day sailor with a Comet or Lightning. In any case, it would have cost more than he spent on hi-fi equipment and records last year. He spent $500, and is seriously considering giving up his hobby next year.

Laundry, dry cleaning. And storage of summer clothes. And storage of winter clothes. $400.

Club dues. This permits Fred to remain a member of his university club (good for business) and to belong to one exurban club (essential for business). $150. This figure could easily be tripled, if Fred were a joiner.

Weekly New York expenses. Into this catchall goes his money for cigarettes, taxis, lunches, and weekday drinking. A considerable amount is, of course, added to this sum, but subtracted by padding expense accounts. Hereunder, also, his fairly regular poker losses, and the gifts he occasionally gives to ladies who have caught his roving eye. $2,000.

Wife's allowance. Fred used to have Rita on a regular weekly allowance, but a man must economize. As it is, what he tells her is to go ahead and have her lunch at the soda fountain of the drugstore, when she gets bored, and he'll include the whole deal under the drugstore bill ($200). She put up a stern squawk, pointing out that quite apart from the vitally necessary trips to the beauty parlor, there was the question of her PTA dues, and what was she going to do, if she had no money in her purse? She settled the matter by spending whatever she had to spend whenever she had to spend it. Last year, $800; and her husband can fetch a huge sigh of relief.

Christmas. The cheeriest time of the year. What with Christmas cards, presents for the family, presents for relatives, presents for business associates, presents for office help, presents for maid, and presents for friends, $500, and dirt cheap.

Domestic romance. This was to square a beef at home. Item: one black lace nighty. Item: one bit of jewelry. $100.

Extramarital romance. On the income tax form, this is covered in quite a different fashion, and perhaps should not be included here, as being an individual case. But so generally does an item of this sort bob up, when an exurbanite settles down, at year's end, to tot up his accounts, that it seems worthy of mention. Paid for two presents and the week end spent in town, $300; and a plurality of exurbanites will chorus: "Why, the cheap son-of-a-bitch!"

WORKING SUB-TOTAL: $30,475

Miscellaneous professional. Legal fees in connection with a secret dream that never materialized. $100.

Alimony. This, again, may seem like an individual aberrant. But in Exurbia, it is most decidedly not. The only thing that is unusual in connection with this item is the ease with which Fred got off. $1,500. Note that he was not stung for support of children by his previous marriage. This was pure dumb luck.

Contingencies. He allows for none, but last year was forced to spend an additional $350 on purchase of new furniture.

Last year he was fortunate in at least two other respects. He did not, as he had the year before, drop $600 on the hot market tip, nor did he have to write off, as he had the year before, $350 in bad debts. His total expenses stopped here:

TOTAL: $32,425

What would Ted and Bill, exurbanites of the semi-genius category, think of Fred's budget if they knew the facts as we do? Their first reaction would be gratification and relief. He's just as badly off as they are and misery's affection for company would be operating strongly. But once the immediate reaction passed, they'd feel contempt, and after that a desire to avoid Fred's company because of his secret difference from other exurbanites. For it is typically exurban to really believe that everyone else is doing better than oneself, or that those who appear not to be are intelligently budgeted, so that they live, if not well, at least in solvency.

"Look around and you'll see I'm right," Ted or Bill—or even Fred—would tell you, if he could be persuaded into a confiding mood about his finances. "Don't try to con me. All these guys on the train aren't in the hole I'm in." And then he'd tell you about how a man down the road goes to the Bahamas every winter, or another man in his office who lives in New Canaan owns a thirty-four-foot cabin cruiser and takes it up to Mount Desert, in Maine, every summer, or about other men he meets at the club who are buying annuities and will retire at "age forty with a guaranteed income for life," as the ads say.

It's probably all true. But each of these lucky fellows could tell you with equal certainty and eloquence about how dreadfully behind they are, and how lucky Bill and Ted—and even Fred— are, if they only knew it, and they obviously do, because they never look worried nor seem to do without everything they want. (Didn't Bill buy himself a new MG just this year? Didn't Ted add a sun porch to his house? Doesn't Fred spend hundreds on hi-fi stuff?) Yet chances are that less than twenty percent of exurbanites in the $15,000 to $40,000 brackets are any better off than Fred, which is to say that they are living sixty percent on money, and forty percent on credit and a belief in a raise— or Santa Claus, or dollars from Heaven. (A goodly percentage of them, being from the comfortable upper middle class, solace themselves with the thought that someday pretty soon, not really soon, though, they really hope, but let's be realistic, the old man or the old lady, or both, will die, God forbid, and then there'll be an inheritance to not only balance the books, but . . . And then they think of all the things they'd buy, things they really need, things they're always sure they'll have some day and isn't it a shame to wait?)

As a matter of fact, the Freds of Exurbia may be thinking to themselves, as they push from their consciousness the truth about their finances: why wait for middle age, or decrepitude, for that trip to Europe? Somehow, the cash can be raised to do it this summer, while the kids are young enough to send to camp, before there's another war and it's too late. And somehow it's done, as any tourist bureau will tell you.

So Ted and Bill say bon voyage to Fred, and know for sure that he must be not only solvent but really in the chips if he and Rita can take off like that for Europe and send the kids away for an expensive summer to boot.

For a man who is not criminally minded to live thirty percent beyond his means is unusual; when, in addition, his means are as high as $25,000 a year, his case takes on the giddy verve that students of Exurbia find so endearing.

Various questions arise, among them: Does Fred approve of such a state of affairs? Can he do anything about it? How does he do it? How long can this sort of thing go on?

The answers, reading from left to right are: No, No, He's not sure himself, and He's scared to think.

His plight may seem to you, depending on the state of your bank account or your morals, deplorable, comical, tragic, or incredible. So far as the exurbanite is concerned, when he thinks about it at all (which he does as little as possible), he thinks of it as frightening but unavoidable. There was a time when he had a speck of savings; no more. There was a time when he had a few stocks, and a sprinkling of quarterly dividend checks; no more; he borrowed to the hilt on them, then had to sell; no more, no more. He has nothing but what he earns, and what he can borrow. The gap between income and outgo cannot be narrowed by cutting down on outgo. With the possible exception of his hobby, he feels that he has cut to the bone already. His family and his wife's family have alike experienced his touch, now lightly, now heavily; there is little more that he can borrow there. His best formula seems to be to borrow to the hilt on everything in sight, and pray for a windfall.

He is worried; naturally he is worried. Depending upon a variety of factors, mostly personal, he may be the sort of exurbanite who finds his predicament absolutely intolerable, and is inclined to feel that the fault may lie somewhere within himself. In this event, he will seek psychiatric assistance. He will spend two sessions with an analyst, interviews of an exploratory character. The upshot of this will, in all likelihood, be that the analyst will tell him he is neurotic, that his financial troubles are psychogenic, that the prognosis is bleak, that the sooner he enters analysis the sooner his financial troubles (and his other, associated problems) will be solved. Additional expense: from $2,500 to $3,000 a year. The hell of it is that the exurbanite will feel the analyst is probably right. (He probably is.)

The alternatives are not pleasant. There is little point in his considering moving back to the city. He could sell his house, and probably at a profit, but in New York any apartment fit for a $25,000-a-year man will cost at least $3,000, or $500 more than what he is presently paying on his house. In addition, he will have to send his children to private schools, another enormous bruise. He must keep a tight grip on himself to keep from ever harder drinking, and there have recently been one or two examples, from among his large circle of nodding acquaintances,

. . . INTERVIEWS OF AN
EXPLORATORY CHARACTER.

of what might happen to him if he lets go and does undertake more serious drinking.

In this dilemma, one thing is certain. He will have white nights, in which the ugly prospect of his losing his job will rise up to stare him out of countenance. He must subsist on hope: the hope that he will be able to get a walloping promotion, perhaps an appointment to a vice-presidency, or a new and bigger contract. If he is to preserve what balance he has left, the hope must offset the fear.

He is truly a remarkable man. For he continues to be witty, amusing, clever, entertaining; a man who is fun to be with and rewarding to talk to. He will, of course, be more relaxed when he arrives at the point where he can fully close the gap, the point arbitrarily set at $60,000 a year. But then, this exurbanite may believe that he need only arrive at the $32,000-a-year level to close the gap completely. Mercifully, he may not realize that at $32,000 there is every likelihood that he will spend $38,000, and so on. But if the pleasant conceit that a $7,000-a-year raise is all that he needs helps to sustain him, by all means let us not disillusion him. God knows he has little else.

8

AT PLAY

*He had told her that everyone was buying farms in
Connecticut, especially in the neighborhood of Westport, and that now the whole country was being filled
with all sorts of people who wanted to get away from
the city. They were just like all the people that they
were trying to get away from, except that in the country
they had allowed their personalities to expand.*

—JOHN P. MARQUAND

*What is it that drives men who have been surrounded
with people and their problems on the day shift to seek
often exactly the same company on the night shift?
Perhaps in part it is the terror of loneliness. . . . But
certainly it makes for strain.*

—DAVID RIESMAN

THE adjuration to "work hard, play hard" has
long been axiomatic for many Americans, but the exurbanite
seems to carry it, typically, to its ultimate extreme. He is so
busy relaxing, so intently absorbed in occupying every moment of
his leisure time, goes to such length in the diligent contriving of
the casual, that the resultant appearance is quite convincing.

But even an exurbanite must sleep some time, and even those
who are most assiduously playful must manage to store up sleep

by getting to bed relatively early, during the week. Unlike the camel, which drinks hugely against the time—it may be days or even weeks—when it will need the sustenance, the exurbanite snatches extra hours of sleep during the desert of the week so that he may splurge in the oasis of Friday-to-Monday. His week-day play will therefore consist of little more than an occasional dinner out, occasional guests in, and perhaps some neighbors dropping by in the evening to watch television, or to play Scrabble, if the minds of all aren't too tired.

This routine is quite different from the life he led before he moved. In New York, depending on his branch of the communi-cations industry and his relative level of importance in it, he averaged from one to five cocktail parties a week, during the season; he often dined out in the city's superior restaurants or in its holes-in-the-wall, and like as not he was a regular theatregoer. He was also a regular patron of the cinema houses that exhibit English, French, or Italian movies. He knew by their first names the captains or maître d's of at least a half-dozen smart, fashion-able nightclubs. Even if he didn't get home till one or two, he could count on seven hours of sleep before his presence would be really demanded on the job. Week ends were reserved for per-haps one big party, and catching up on sleep.

When he moved to the exurb, he took with him many of his Manhattan habits, but with an important difference: where before he could spread his social activities over a whole week, now he had to concentrate them into one sixty-hour period, along with a bushel-basketful of new social chores.

The week-long parlay is clearly out of the question. He simply no longer has the time for weeknight shindigs. Having moved to an exurb he has offered up two or three hours of his weekdays on the altar of country living; it doesn't take a man long to realize, if he is on a regime of rising at six-thirty or seven, that he must hit the sack by eleven-thirty or twelve if he expects to be his usual bright, winsome, companionable self the next day.

What he does with his week ends, how he goes about spending his time, will vary, depending on the exurb he has selected as home. A more accurate way, perhaps, of saying this would be: his selection from among the available exurbs will depend in large part on what kind of social life he prefers over a week end. The playground is large and adaptable: there are sand-piles for drunks, for farmers, for libertines or Don Juans, for intellectuals, for sportsmen, for chronologically adult infants or adolescents, for the lazy or the active, for sailors or fishers or hunters or riders or swimmers. During the week-end recess from the rat race there is no supervisor to blow the whistle and demand that the escapees do one thing instead of another. With remarkably true adaptability, the exurbanite finds his own level, his own part of the forest. Playtime, play manners, play opportunities, play facilities, play techniques, even intensity of play—all vary from one exurb to another, but at the same time there are basic and striking similarities. Just as the residents of each exurb have had to forego (to their general subsequent dissatisfaction) some of the amenities of life in Manhattan when they undertook to escape its tensions, so the residents of each exurb share alike some leisure-time activities.

There is, for example, a heavy traffic in week-end guests from the city. There are three main categories of these transients. First are the people one might normally be content to spend an hour or two at a time with, in the city. In Exurbia, the only way to see them is to have them up for the week end. Since the showing of the house and grounds and the small talk are pretty rapidly used up, the rest of the week end must be devoted to actively entertaining the visitors—against the possibility that they may be bored or become boring. Generally, social life with city friends diminishes with each year's exurban residence, so the first category gets smaller and smaller for the average exurbanite, leaving him finally with only lifelong, close friends (category three), and even some of these are lost by reason of geography and changed living habits.

The second category comprises genuine and pseudo-business acquaintances. A city man can play golf with a business acquaintance who needs leisure-time cultivation to make him bear fruit; an exurbanite must invite the man and his wife for the week end. Active entertainment for these visitors, and plenty of people around, are musts.

Third, as has been said, are the old friends, an important life line for the exurbanites to the Manhattan they have left behind them. Sometimes these old friends come early and often, sometimes they are reluctant dragons, sometimes they sit disconsolately indoors, scowling at the unaccustomed green that surrounds them outside, sometimes they show that they are the stuff exurbanites are made of, and drag their hosts on tours of near-by houses for rent or sale, and sometimes they switch the old chestnut, and maintain that the exurbs are okay for a week end, but they wouldn't live in the place if you, et cetera. But almost invariably, when the guests are settled with their first drink in hand, the questions come, usually from the exurban hostess: What's new in town? Have you seen any plays? Do you see the Smythes any more? The thirst for urban gossip is unquenchable. Nor is it simply a matter of steering the conversation into channels that the guests will find easily negotiable. Urban gossip is an exurban need.

Again, no matter which his exurb, every exurbanite makes a ritual of his Sunday New York newspaper. Some cynics claim that the curling up with the paper that goes on in so many exurban households is merely a measure of the endemic nature of exurban hangovers, but this is not so, for even in the living room of the member of Alcoholics Anonymous (and there are Westport residents who proudly contend that their chapter of A.A. is the largest in the world), the Sunday newspaper is a comfy ceremonial.

Then there is the question of children. In every exurb, parents find their hours of relaxation partially circumscribed by the activities of their young. Most exurban fathers cheerfully undertake a responsibility toward the children over the week end which is borne solo by the mother during the week, and over a summer week end this may entail scouting about for likely prospects to add to a Little League baseball team, or patiently coaching a few rallies of small-fry tennis, or instructing Junior in the function of a Genoa jib, or even going for a walk to get the kids out of the house and away from Mother when all other recourses have failed.

There is, moreover, for the do-it-yourselfer, a similarity of interests from exurb to exurb. Everywhere, beyond the fifty-mile limit from Manhattan, hardware stores are the most important single retail outlets in town, only excepting the liquor stores.

In every exurb booze is the common palliative for stress and strain.

There are other similarities, but these are the most striking. The differences, from exurb to exurb, flow from the varying possibilities for recreation. There are other differences, of course, depending on the season of the year. Nor can there be any precise patterns delineated, even within a single exurb, for these are not primitive folk, but highly complex, highly civilized, extremely articulate, and, in general, at all times attempting to prove that they fit into no pattern. Nevertheless, they do, by and large. In fact, their patterns are recognizable enough to provide material for their favorite weekly magazine, *The New Yorker*, which has gradually undergone a distinct change: its situation jokes and much of its fiction concern the exurban life, and less and less frequently mirror Manhattan. In 1940 a cartoon which had for premise something exurban was rare; these days there seems to be at least one such in every issue. This is not particularly astonishing, especially in view of the fact that so many of *The New Yorker*'s regular contributors and editors are themselves exurbanites par excellence; but it is still a noteworthy fact. These days, Peter Arno and Whitney Darrow are about the only regular cartoonists whose subjects are generally limited to urban situations and urban milieus. Even Hoff and Steig have turned their gaze outward, away from the Bronx, to the country. The fact that the magazine can still accurately be called *The New Yorker* serves to underline what was said about the exurbanite in the introductory chapter: that he is always at heart a New Yorker no matter how long he has been resident in a country place fifty or sixty miles away.

One way to search out the patterns of exurban play is to follow a handful of exurbanites from the time they step off their Friday evening train from New York to the time when, on Monday morning, they appear on the station platform, bright-eyed and bushy-tailed or white-gilled and hungover. For the sake of simplicity and unity of compass, the exurbanites whose course we will follow, as closely as the postal regulations permit, are, we shall imagine, all resident in the environs of Westport, in Fairfield County. At the same time, as we are following some specimen Westport exurbanites on their course of week-end pleasures, we will pause, while the ice-trays are being emptied for the next round, to point out the more obvious differences that obtain between life in Westport and Fairfield County generally, and the other New York exurbs.

Here, as the evening train from New York stops at the Westport station, come a couple of hundred exurbanites, either hurrying for the cars that have been parked in the lot all day or plaintively whistling a familiar signal to attract the wives who have driven to meet them. Our eye is caught by four from this crowd.

One of them is Ben Martell, whom the trade knows quite well as among the first successful radio writers to make the switch to TV. Ben is in his late thirties and looks older, especially tonight. We can judge the reason for it from his erratic gait: he comes from the bar car. He makes it safely to his MG, climbs in, and heads purposefully home toward another martini.

The man greeting his wife at the wheel of a Buick convertible is none other than Gideon J. Philips III, an advertising agency account executive. Note the charcoal-gray suit and the glossy, initial-embossed briefcase. Just beyond him, climbing into a Cadillac and giving his wife a perfunctory peck on the cheek, is Duke Cameron. He's in his late twenties and, although his hair is thinning, he looks fit and full of energy, despite his harrowing day and the unceasing flow of loud talk he exchanged with colleagues, with whom he was playing bridge all the way out on the train, to the considerable annoyance of newspaper-readers, work hogs, and nappers. Duke's sharkskin suit is a little too sharp, his tie knot too small and tight. He knows all this;

he knows, too, that until he's promoted to a better job, this is the correct uniform to wear in his business dealings with the small manufacturers on whom he must call. And what does he do for his living? Duke was captain of his college golf team; the transition was natural and swift to becoming an advertising salesman for a potent, nimble newsweekly. He will contrive to lose enough close matches to potential advertisers in the next few months to become assistant advertising manager, and can then dress according to his taste.

The fourth man we will watch in the next few hours is Armand Santini. He is clothed in ambiguous fashion: a turtleneck sweater under his tweed jacket, and sneakers. While he is getting his Model-A Ford, to drive it round and pick up the couple who are his week-end guests, we can tell that he is a "genius," a commercial artist who is not a regular commuter.

And now let's pause to consider the cars these men drive. Santini is a member of Westport's Model-A car owner's association, whose membership dues are spent in buying up other Model-A's, which thereafter become boneyards for all members, who may strip the purchases for necessary replacement parts. As for the MG owner, Ben Martell, he belongs to the Sports Car Club of America which, it will be remembered, is headquartered here in Fairfield County. If his option is picked up for another cycle or two, he will sell his MG to buy a Jaguar; he knows where he can pick up a hell of a second-hand Jag. (Despite its expense, the Jaguar was for some time the best seller among foreign cars, thanks to its popularity in Exurbia. This sports car has been displaced, however, by the much cheaper, purely utilitarian Volkswagen, perhaps because Jags were becoming so common. In northern Westchester, for example, the Volkswagen sold as many as its five nearest competitors, last year.* But the Volkswagen is usually a second car, while the Jaguar is a first and often an only car.) The Buick driven by Gid Philips is

* In 1954 foreign cars sold in this order: Volkswagen, Jaguar, MG, Austin-Healey, Hillman, Austin, English Ford, Triumph, Morris, and Sunbeam Talbot.

intended to reflect, and does, his comfortably realistic and mature acceptance of the simple need for dependable transportation. Duke Cameron's new Cadillac is an important business expense, and so appears on his tax returns.

Other exurbanites belong to the Classic Car Club; they are impassioned devotees, even fanatics, who urge on you the superiorities of old Cords or Stutzes or Pierce Arrows. Their living-room walls are covered with pictures of antique automotive gems, they have a special intramural publication, and some of them even have a special classic-car watch-charm. It is from listening to the classic-car nuts that some psychiatrically minded exurbanites have become persuaded of the validity of the theory that the car is a phallic symbol, and that much can be posited about a man's sex habits from his attitudes toward the ancient car he loves and shines and polishes and tends so devotedly. It is interesting to note that only some seven percent of Fairfield's exurbanites are Cadillac owners; they are content to seek their status in other ways.

It is not only by their cars that ye shall know them. Let's attend to Armand for a moment. It's not because he is seeking status, but because he genuinely likes wine, that Armand Santini, the artist, has pulled up in his Model-A outside the liquor store which is conveniently situated just across the road from the rail-road station.

While Armand is buying his two bottles of domestic Pinot Noir, we have time to reflect on the problems the exurbanite poses for such an expert taxonomist as Russell Lynes: is the exurbanite highbrow, or middlebrow, or upper-middlebrow? (He surely isn't lowbrow.) It would seem safe to state that he is not middlebrow. He does not belong (nor does his wife) to the Book-of-the-Month Club, or to the Literary Guild. Indeed, if he has any book club membership, it is to one of the smaller specialized groups, like the Science Fiction Book Club, or the Seven Arts Book Club, or the Book Find Club.

He is likely to have bought such highbrows trinkets as Eimer & Amend chemical jars for his kitchen spice shelf ten or twelve years ago; he may even hide them now, as being somehow infra dig, now that everybody knows about them. Armand cannot or will not remember the time when he did not grind his pepper fresh from a small mill. He is likely to have at least three special salad dressings for his, of course, tossed green salad. In everything but the most intellectual aspects of life, he is ahead of the high-brows or he will know the reason why. But in intellectual matters, he is only upper-middlebrow, and this is because of his belated anti-intellectualism, his reverse snobbism, the factor that today drives him to hide his butterfly chairs away or leave them out in the weather, because too many people have copied him by buying them in cheap copies. It is the same reverse snobbism that leads him to buy a domestic Pinot Noir, and when he gets home he will put the bottles in the refrigerator, too, because he knew that red wines are supposed to be served at room temperature so long ago that he feels he not only can but should break the rule. Armand, his wife, and their guests will be dining late, for they are not planning anything special for the evening. Not so with the others.

The others are already busy pouring martinis (in three out of four homes, the cocktail is martini). Gid Philips and his wife have another couple in for dinner. Duke Cameron and his wife are going out for dinner. Ben Martell, the television writer, already fairly well sozzled, is taking his wife to a friend's house after dinner. All have something to do. All must have something to do. Each would feel he would sink to the level of a fifth-class power if the word got out that he wasn't invited out somewhere, or inviting someone in. This compulsion, this fear of being alone, is prevalent in Westport (and Fairfield County generally) to a far greater extent than it is in Bucks and Rockland counties.

It is seven forty-five. Gid is filling martini glasses. Taking advantage of a momentary silence, he clears his throat, catches the attention of his wife and their dinner guests, and tells them a dirty story, fairly new; only one of them has heard it before. The dirty story is common conversational coin in Westport. On this average Friday night it is likely that this particular story will be told some two hundred and ninety times. Gid will, all by himself, tell (if we compute his average output) eight more such stories before the night is over. Here is a significant difference from the conversational formulas that obtain in, say, Rockland County. If you are the sort of person whose idea of amusing talk is to tell stories one after another, and you pick for audience a resident of South Mountain Road or Sneden's Landing, he will stare at you. If he is feeling charitable, he will write you off as depressingly naïve. Because in such matters he is not often charitable, he will more probably cross you off his list without a pang. If he happens to be a writer himself, he will not even be interested in you as a character, for he has met too many of your type before.

The evening goes forward. Between eight-thirty and nine-fifteen there is a flurry of traffic through the winding country roads: this is Operation Baby-sitter being successfully accomplished. Thereafter, the cars once again move purposefully through the darkness: parents, freed temporarily from their children, propose to enjoy adult society for a time. The weather on this early summer night is cool. Later on, when it gets hot, there will be beach parties, moonlight sails; still later, in the fall, the barn-dance cycle will have begun, and the husbands will be breaking out their plaid shirts and the wives their peasant skirts; come winter, there may even be, in the event of snow, a ride in a sleigh. But now, in early summer, things are quieter. It is ten-thirty. Let us look in on our four specimens and see what they are up to.

Armand is sitting quietly at home with his week-end guests and his wife. He is on his fifth highball. In view of the earlier martinis and the wine, he has taken on quite a package, and has reached the point where, a few minutes ago in the bathroom, he was talking to himself in the mirror and making faces at his own answers. Now he is wondering what he ever saw in these people, to make him invite them out for the week end. His wife stifles a yawn.

Ben Martell and Duke Cameron are at the same party. They

exchanged nods when they first came in (they don't know each other particularly well, each is just a train face to the other) and promptly went their separate ways. Duke, ever the salesman, was able to get a poker game started off in the library. He had been miffed, earlier that week, to find that his regular weekly poker game was canceled—one regular had had to fly to the coast, another was in bed with a psychogenic cold, and a third was sitting up with a sick script—and had even thought for a few minutes that Friday night might come and find him with nothing to do. A fourth regular in the poker game had, however, invited him to dinner; together with their wives they had come on to this party. Nothing big or pretentious—no more than two dozen people sitting around, talking, watching television, drinking. Five kindred spirits were soon collared and a poker game set up.

Around Westport, the regular poker games are steep and mixed. Table stakes are usual. Admission to them is only by invitation: when a newcomer is casually approached on the station platform by a real old-timer, i.e., a resident of ten years' standing, with the words, "Why don't you and Jane come over tomorrow night for a little poker?" the newcomer beams and his heart lifts with joy. To find a comparable thrill, one must look across the ocean to pre-war County England, and the familiar scene in which the MFH says off-handedly to the newly knighted jam-merchant, "Why don't you turn up in pinks at the next meeting, old man?" The more dedicated poker players around Westport are inclined to attribute the wildness of the regular games to the presence of the women, yet it is to be noted that many of the men, when they are dealer, are just as prone to suggest games like seven-card high-low with one-eyed jacks wild, and similar nuisances. In Rockland and Bucks, the game is inclined to be more traditional, adhering to five-card stud and draw. Poker does not seem to be particularly popular in northern Westchester, or on the North Shore of Long Island, where bridge and Canasta rate high.

On this Friday evening, because the game was hastily organized, stakes are fifty cents and a dollar, and the dealers have been demanding wild games. Duke's wife, growing bored with spit-in-the-ocean, has picked up her money and left. Duke is ahead. He plays a good, hard game, and his talk bristles with tough slang.

Ben, being a television writer, is as far away from the television set as he can get without actually being outside the house. He was sozzled when he got off the bar car more than three hours ago and nothing he has done in the meantime has repaired the situation, but you have to know him well to perceive how far along he is. His wife can always tell, of course; there is something about his eyes, they begin to look like very slow pinwheels. She said something to him about it earlier and there was a brief, acrimonious exchange, but things seem all right now.

At this moment, Ben's eye has a speculative glint that has nothing to do with pinwheels: he has just seen a young woman for the first time whom he can't remember having seen before; their glances met and did something improper, before she turned away. She is Mrs. Duke Cameron, a fact about which Ben couldn't care less. We may give this pair another thirty minutes to gravitate closer to each other, eye each other again, exchange a few words, and engage in gambit and counter-gambit; no more will be required for them to have gone away somewhere or other, to do something or other. Their liaison at the moment could not be more casual, even more ephemeral; for this reason it is for each of them something that can be legitimately included under the general heading of recreation. It may, of course, develop into something more serious and tenacious: one party or the other (or both) may with time even come to believe that what is involved is a grand passion, perhaps the only true grand passion of a lifetime, in which case it will no longer be recreational but will tug at the seams of two marriages and two families and may well end up in some psychoanalyst's notebook. But for the moment it is more in the nature of a routine, a bit. Such encounters have a deadly sameness throughout Exurbia. If there seems to be more of it in and around Westport than elsewhere it is only because exurbanites are more densely settled there than elsewhere.

Over in Greens Farms, Gid Philips, the account executive, is sitting in his living room with his wife and dinner guests (the husband of this couple is an account executive from another agency). Gid is trying to remember what it was that he wanted to say. Something his friend just said reminded him—of what? He is racking his memory. Shop talk? Real estate talk? What was it? He cannot remember. He sighs, and goes to refill his glass yet again.

It should not have been necessary to comment that an account executive's dinner guest was, in Westport, another account executive. The fact is that most of this exurb is clique-ridden. As by day the toilers in the communications industry consort almost exclusively with those in their own particular branch of the industry, so in Fairfield County the same custom is observed at night and over the week end. In this, Fairfield differs from the other exurbs; but once again, the difference must be ascribed to the fact that the exurban population is sufficiently plentiful to permit it. After all, in Bucks County, for example, if an account executive wished to see socially only other account executives, his circle of acquaintances would be rather limited. Around Westport you will find circles of television people, of people who have clung to radio and still damn and blast television, of agency people, commercial artists, lawyers concerned with straightening out the contracts of all the others, magazine and book people, and so on.

It is, indeed, rather surprising that a television writer found his way to a party of two dozen people that included a space salesman from a newsmagazine. The circumstance can be set down to one of the factors that occasionally nibbles away at the walls erected around a clique: the wives. One wife may have been classmate of another wife at Smith, or may decide at a PTA meeting that here is someone she would like to know better. In consequence, you can sometimes find a sodden light poet sitting among a bunch of talent agency executives, patiently wondering how he got there and how soon he can decently leave.

It is after midnight now, and all these people have worked a long, full day. Moreover, they must be up early on the morrow whether they want to or not; their children will see to that. Besides, for those who are away from home, what of the baby-sitter? Will they not now go home?

In Armand Santini's home, the New Yorkers who are his week-end guests were the first to cave in. They mounted the stairs to their bedroom a few minutes ago, amid a certain amount of re-strained chatter about birdsong in the early morning. (They will whisper to each other about the three-quarter bed, the 25-watt bulb in the light on their night table, and the distance to the bathroom.) The account executives are bidding each other good-night, too, for they must both be up before dawn; they are going fishing, out in the Sound. But Duke is cannily engaged in draw-ing to a flush, and he is good for at least four more hours. His wife, whose sleepy expression is delicately sated, is ready to drive home any time now, and let her husband fend for himself. Out in the darkness, Ben Martell, whose expression would bespeak quiet triumph under other circumstances, has passed out. It happened just a moment ago and his wife isn't aware of it yet; she is still talking to him, if talking is not too mild a word. She is driving the MG toward their home and, she hopes, driving bloody and implacable barbs of fury toward her husband. The lights will be out in their house by one-thirty, and a good thing.

With the early morning, the entire exurb stirs, shakes itself, and is almost immediately transformed into a hive of activity. Saturday throughout Exurbia is children's day. It is the day when the fathers are put to the test of remembering why they said they wanted to move from the city, and it must be stated that in the majority of families, the father rises to this occasion splendidly. Whether the purity of his motives is somewhat sullied by feelings of guilt toward his children is not the point, at least not here; what matters is that from breakfast until the evening cocktail hour he is almost entirely at the disposal of his young.

This is a stern test of paternal mettle, especially if, like Ben Martell, the pater has other things whirling around in his mind or if, like Armand Santini, he is nursing such a considerable hangover that it seems all he can do to distinguish primary colors, count to ten, and essay a few rudimentary steps.

All over the exurb swoop the cars, carrying their loads on their appointed missions. On four hours' sleep, Duke is up for breakfast and presently he is down at the high school tennis court, rallying with his daughter while waiting for the hour of her appointment with the pro. Armand has forced his masculine guest to accompany him and the kids to a near-by boatyard, where there is some necessary painting and caulking to do, against the belated launching of his Comet. As has been said, Gid Philips has gone fishing; he was up before six and out on the Sound before seven, prodded and goaded and harassed into hurrying at every step by his older boy, for whom this is the year's first such trip. And by ten a.m. Ben, although he would never have believed such a thing possible, is busy with the organizational work in a Little League which is scheduled to start its summer schedule of contests in another week. If he has time, he must do some scouting for talent before the lunch-hour, for his son's team badly needs a shortstop without a scatter arm. He has some friends among the Saugapops, the association of fathers who work on behalf of the Saugatuck public school, and he means to put in some purposeful phone calls.

Fortunately the weather is holding up. The sun promises to be hot enough to warrant a trip to Compo Beach by afternoon or maybe even earlier. This boil of activity, which involves nearly every parent in the area, is comparable to what parents have undertaken on behalf of their children from time immemorial, and all over the United States if not the civilized world, but here the fathers seem almost competitive about it, driven; it is more than fun, more than duty. It is, in a large way, the reaction of symbol-manipulators confronted at last with a vibrant, alive reality, a tangible being, which they have (no one can take that from them) produced. A child is a fact. A child is the product of one's being; not only that, one's own offspring are a hope for and a vicarious hold on the future.

There are exceptions, of course, children who are told, on Saturday morning, to, for God's sake, play outside, will you, until Mummy and Daddy are ready to get up? There are, too, more children than one would suppose who are heartbreakingly self-reliant. Gid's wife, Barbara, boasts about their Sue, who, at the age of six, gets up on week-end mornings, sneaks into the bathroom, washes her hands and face quietly, goes back to her room on tiptoe, dresses, and then goes to the kitchen and helps herself to orange juice and milk, to sustain her until the adults' irregular breakfast hour, which is usually about eleven. After she breakfasts alone she goes out to play, and finds some amusement far enough from the house and quiet enough so that she won't disturb the grownups. Sometimes other children call to her, as they pass with their parents on the way to town to buy sneakers, or a new sun suit. She has turned down many offers to go along just for the ride. Not that she wouldn't enjoy it: but Sue has been told that her mummy won't be able to sleep for worry if Sue leaves the grounds before Mummy is up and can be asked.

Down the lane from the Philips house lives an only child, Donnie, with his exurban parents. As frequently happens in Exurbia, he has no playmates within miles—it just happens there are no other boys of five in the immediate neighborhood—and Donnie accordingly plays alone much of the time. Early one Saturday morning, while the rest of the household was asleep, a guest looked out of the guestroom window and saw Donnie busily excavating an earthworm from the lawn. He took the worm to the walk, laid it on a flagstone, and then used a sharp shard of slate to cut it in two. The guest was horrified by this display of the heartless cruelty of children, but his thoughts were interrupted by Donnie speaking to the two segments of worm, which he placed side by side. "There," said Donnie, joyously, magnanimously. "There—now you've got a friend!" And then he put his thumb in his mouth and gazed wistfully at nothing.

The lonely, neglected children are exceptions on exurban Saturdays, however. Sunday morning may be a time of exile for them, but Saturday is largely theirs—and the toy store's too. And the entire day is likely to be scheduled—and crammed. Children notoriously have more physical energy than men in their late twenties to mid-forties, but these exurbanites will never admit it. If it isn't tennis or fishing or sailing or baseball, then it is spear fishing, water skiing, golf, horseback riding. The children, ecstatic, are whisked from here to there. Ahead of them, typically, are children's parties to be supervised by mothers who have in advance agreed to be herdswomen for the late afternoon; there are always birthday parties, but if there happens, by a fluke, to be no birthday, another excuse will be found, something will have been scheduled. On the North Shore, the emphasis is more on sailing and fishing; in Bucks the play relates more closely to the farms on which the exurbanites live; in northern Westchester there will be, in the appropriate season, hunting; there are fewer children in Rockland and the pace is consequently slower; but in Fairfield County and especially around Westport, Saturday is one long romp, interrupted only at midday.

Once again, a largish minority provides the exception. This consists of the fathers who feel, by God, that they've slaved like tartars all week and they're jolly well going to have some fun for themselves on the week end and not be saddled with the kids. These are usually compulsive sportsmen who will beat the daylights out of golf balls, tennis balls, game fish, sports cars, sail boats, or horses as an outlet for the dammed-up aggressive impulses they've choked down and held in leash all week. On the whole, they are very proud of their athletic bent, and feel they are outstandingly wholesome types living amid a group of dissolute weaklings. Sometimes, as in the case of Gideon Philips III on the Saturday in question, they are persuaded to take their offspring along. When this happens, the kids generally come back exhausted and on the verge of tears, having failed to keep pace with the old man despite his deadly serious and veiledly vicious proddings, and having lost interest (they weren't working off frustrations) long before the sporting day's end. These are occasions for one-way "I told you so's" between husband and wife, a point that's rubbed in until the wife concedes that it's no favor to the kids to have them spend the day with dear old Dad. For several week ends thereafter, Dad will take off with his cronies for a day of sport and Mother will have the kids, again. In a way it will be a relief, too—when her husband dutifully stays at home on Saturday he's more childish than the children, either plunging into projects which he not only fails to finish but which leave a mess behind, or sulking like a spoiled martyr.

But throughout Exurbia, whatever the Saturday morning activity may be, at noon, stirred by an inner signal, fathers everywhere stiffen, like a dog on the point. Inside them, a small voice is asking: "What is better than one martini before lunch?" And another small voice makes prompt answer: "Two martinis," wherewith the cars depart from the shores, the tennis courts, the boatyards and the schooling rings, so that Daddy may repair his tissues.

In the afternoon, the hectic round will be resumed, except for the lucky few who can contrive a nap. Duke Cameron is not one of them. Undismayed by lack of sleep and his two sets of tennis, he heads for his country club. He has a date to play golf with an old friend. It has nothing to do with business: he can play for blood and intends to: $50 Nassau. Ben and Armand are shepherding their young to Compo Beach, where the artist's guests will be thoroughly dismayed by the sharp rocks over which they will have to scamper in order to reach the water, which is in any event going out. Low tide will be around four this afternoon. Gid and his son won't be back from fishing till around five, at which point they will join the rest of their family around a friend's pool.

No informed guess as to the number of foot-pounds of energy collectively expended does justice to the manner in which the typical exurbanite family spends its Saturdays. Even in the waning afternoon when, around five o'clock, the first gins-and-tonic are being poured, there will be those who refuse to sit and sip, but instead, drinks in hand, still compete at some physically milder activity like croquet, darts, or archery. (There are some crack croquet players around Weston and Westport, men and women who, after years of contention on crab-grass courses, could match

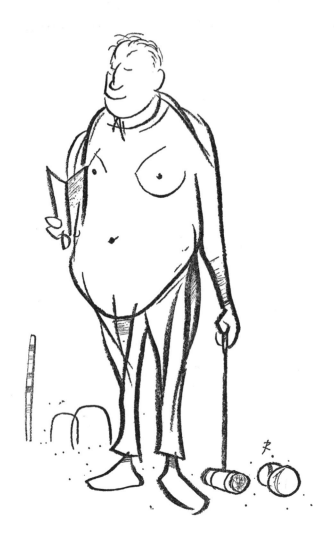

. . . WHO REFUSE TO SIT AND SIP, BUT STILL COMPETE
AT SOME MILDER PHYSICAL ACTIVITY.

and probably whip even the bloodthirsty crew who used to play, years ago, at Sands Point.) Croquet is a ruthless and vengeful game as played in this exurb, but it is nevertheless only a way of marking time. As far as the adults are concerned, their day is about to reach its peak, their week end is approaching its climax. Here comes Saturday night.

Mention was made earlier, in connection with Friday night, that few Westporters care to spend their Friday evenings alone. There is even greater fear of being left out on Saturday night. True, there are a handful of hardy souls—freaks, biological sports —who even around Westport would prefer to stay at home and read a book; and it is likely that there are others, part of the majority, who entertain a sneaking envy for these individualists. But Saturday night's enticements beckon too urgently. All four of our specimens are going out for the evening. The writer, Ben, and his wife are going to a big party in Weston. Ben spent the morning wondering how obvious to everybody his absence last night had been; he remembered that he had been absent—and why—as soon as he became aware of the fact that his wife was not talking to him except in the presence of the children. Come the afternoon sun on the beach, and for the first time he began idly to speculate as to whether the space salesman's wife would be at the same party again tonight. He rather hoped she would not. But after his third pre-dinner martini, he began to hope that she would be there, and to fear that she would not. As it happens, she will not. She and Duke are driving with two other couples to have dinner at Stonehenge, a charming country restaurant on Route 7 near Ridgefield, a place that advertises: "We charge more. We care more. We give more," and that is doggedly cute, featuring a skinker, which is an archaic term for someone who serves booze, and a drink called a Fluid Druid.

The Camerons and their friends will not eat until ten, and when they get back near home they will take dead aim on the party in Weston but will miss it, ending up instead dancing in a darkened room at the Camerons' house. The Armand Santinis and guests are going to a somewhat smaller party. The Philipses are going to a party in Wilton, at the home of an advertiser, big deal. If you ask, But isn't this approximately what they all did just last night? the answer is, Well, yes, and it is also approximately what they all did last week end, and approximately what they will all do next week end. It is evening life in Fairfield County. Some of them will buy tickets to the County Playhouse, in season, but there is a growing dissatisfaction on the part of the highbrows (and therefore on the part of the upper-middlebrows as well) with the County Playhouse, on the grounds that it has grown too commercial, its management seemingly interested less in trying out offbeat playscripts or in experimenting than in booking packages with name performers. There are also occasional concerts in the larger towns of the county, but exurbanites—although when they lived in New York they often boasted to out-of-towners about all the concerts in New York—rarely if ever go to listen to serious music for as much as two hours at a whack.

Parties are their night life, and they are informal about them. Over on the North Shore, across the Sound, there is more disposition to dress, just as there is greater inclination to join a country club. Shops specializing in very feminine and fairly expensive evening dresses do well on the North Shore; but in Westport and in Fairfield County generally the emphasis is on the casual. When the weather gets hotter the men will wear Bermuda shorts or red or rust-colored slacks. If the notion of wearing Bermuda shorts in town, at the office, ever takes serious hold, it will have first to be done by the exurbanites.

The informality of dress carries over from the Friday to the Saturday night parties, even though the Saturday night affairs are considered more important. More care is lavished on them by hostesses. To the bigger ones will come groups of four to six who have dined together ahead of time. Hopes are higher that one will really have fun, this time; the women put a more expensive scent behind their ears and in their cleavage, if any; the pre-party fantasies are more riotous, the search for relaxation from tension more imperious, the chatter higher-pitched, and the smiles more brilliant.

Toward Darien and toward Southport the informality of dress abates, as does the tendency to shun memberships in country clubs. By coincidence, none of our present specimens is spending the evening at a country club, but both Gid and Duke belong, and could go to the Saturday-night dances which are held in these places. In fact, nearly every space salesman and time salesman in Exurbia must belong to a country club; if his income will not hold still for the greens fees or the initiation wallop, his employer will defray it for him. There are many part-time exurbanites, apartment-renters in New York, who nevertheless maintain membership in exurban golf clubs so that they may the more fruitfully pursue their business of landing lucrative advertising accounts and thereby helping to keep the communications industry whee'd up to its present level. The hard core of the memberships of such country clubs are fifty-year-old advertisers and advertising agents, whose children are by now in their early twenties or late teens.

What are our four specimens up to, on this Saturday night? It is getting on toward eleven—we should look in on them. At Stonehenge, Duke and his party are dawdling over coffee. He is talking to the lady on his left (his wife is across from him) but his eyes, as he talks or listens, keep dropping down to a point about six inches below the lady's chin, and his mind is less on what they are talking about than on what may eventuate, should she be the one to sit on his lap on their way home. (They have all six come in one car, although nobody was concerned about saving gas.)

In Wilton, Gid is talking to the advertiser about real estate. This particular advertiser is relatively new to the neighborhood— he has been resident for less than a year—and like so many of the newer exurbanites he is obsessed with stories of sales and resales, of acreage and property, of zoning and building and remodeling. He likes his present house well enough (it cost him $65,000), and will probably never move, but he keeps talking about it, as do a great many others like him. Real estate stories thrive throughout Exurbia, and generally are somewhat enhanced in the retelling.

The Santinis and their house guests are at a party of about twenty people. The party was being given by a middle-aged couple named Mann—Ralph and Eleanor Mann. Their house was quite magnificent, a massive, half-timbered manor which had been built two generations earlier by an honest-to-God country gentleman, since deceased as the result of a heart attack induced by news of Franklin Roosevelt's third-term election. The Manns had bought it at a bargain, a mere $75,000—and had then spent an equal amount modernizing its interior and having it "done" by a pair of Lexington Avenue decorators, very handsome youths who called each other Petey and Bunny, and who had come over from a summer on Fire Island to go screaming with joy through the house, which they later told each other in private, with giggles, was a fright.

And so the Manns had moved in with one strike against them: they had not chosen their own décor. Furthermore, Ralph Mann was not really a member of the communications business—he owned a lithography plant: strike two. Eleanor did back off-Broadway productions, however, which made the Manns acceptable. But both Ralph and Eleanor were a little too eager to get into the Westport exurban social swim. They'd been somewhat lonely when they moved from Central Park West to Scarsdale and they looked forward to sharing their new home in Westport with people they thought of as more sympathetic and interesting. And so, they gave the party—to which the Santinis went this Saturday night—too soon, and invited a too various assortment of guests.

Let's go in with the Santinis. Here's our buxom hostess, already flushed and nervous, talking too fast and too much. And what the hell!—there's Bill Dahl, who took a job right out from under Armand's nose just last week. What is this, a gag, having both of them at the same party?

Bill and Armand greet each other effusively and part company. There, in the corner, with some other magazine people, is Fred Barber. There's his wife, Rita, looking wistfully pretty and overdressed. She's talking children with Jane, which is not odd despite the fact that they spent the whole afternoon sharing supervision of a children's birthday party. There's Ted Daniels, the TV producer, and the only man who hasn't heard the current description of himself as a pin-stripe Walt Whitman. Everybody knows everybody else and they're all on at least their second drinks, except Jack Fuller, the playwright, who's on his third.

But the atmosphere of the party is not relaxed, and everyone senses it. They will, therefore, respond happily to Armand Santini's suggestion that everybody play parlor games.

Parlor games have never really taken hold in the other exurbs. There are men who have lived in Bucks for twenty years who will deny they ever witnessed a parlor game in the entire period. The same tends to be true of Rockland. In northern Westchester, occasionally a houseful of people will find themselves being dragged into The Game, and this happens also, although more rarely, on the North Shore. But in Fairfield County parlor games have a periodic popularity like economic depressions. For years there will be none of it, but somewhere there is an exurbanite who has run across a line in Dylan Thomas that he has never heard of having been used in The Game, and the moment will come when this man will insist on some charades just so he can satisfy himself that his line ("Altarwise by owl-light in the halfway house") is as prickly a proposition as he has hoped it would be. His insistence, at one Saturday night party, will set off a wave of such charades.

Perhaps it is the exurbanite's flamboyant exhibitionism, perhaps it is his spirited sense of competition bursting above the surface again. Not enough that he played two sets of tennis and a bloody game of croquet and then drove his Hillman Minx as competitively as possible from home to party, while his wife nervously braked the floorboards the whole way. Not enough: he must compete some more. Perhaps this is the reason, but most certainly something else is involved too, in other parlor games popular around Westport, and that is aggressive hostility, urbanely masked. These other games (there are at least two that have had a limited run of popularity in the last year or so) are switches on old children's games, and the wonder is that they have not caused more outright violence than they have. Here is how one is played:

One of the group is selected to be It. It is told to leave the room, and that while It is out of the room the others will make up a story of some sort. Then it will be It's task to return and try to discover what the story is about by asking of everyone in turn whatever questions occur to It. The other people are restricted, in their answers, to a Yes, a No, and a Maybe. Once It is out of the room, the others will make up no story whatsoever. They will use up a little time to fill their drinks, tell a joke or two at Its expense, and remind any squares who don't know how the game is played (if indeed there is any square present aside from It) the real rules. The real rules are that when It returns, any question asked that ends with a consonant is answered with a No; any question asked that ends with a vowel is answered with a Yes; a question ending with a "y" permits the answer Maybe. The point of the game is that It will make up his own story, and in the process disclose to the amateur psychoanalysts present, by his free-association, his unconscious fantasies.

Lest the reader think that stories do not in fact come out, herewith, very briefly, are appended two actual stories as invented by unfortunate Its for the delectation of their friends:

1. A girl midget, whose mother is also a midget, marries a boy midget. Goaded on by her mother, the girl midget on her wedding night has sexual intercourse with an elephant, and dies.

2. A sister shoots and kills her brother when she discovers him in her barn, using her milking-machine for the purpose of masturbation.

Once there was a girl from whose unconscious appeared a story about a circus-train which was wrecked and spewed forth freaks who raped all the women living in houses beside the railroad track. When she was told it was her story, that she alone had supplied the details, she burst into tears and fled alone into the night.

Stories like these could never be contrived by a group of people sitting around a room. They can only develop in the course of this malevolent parlor game.

The game as played at the Manns' party illustrates the technique. Fortunately for Ralph Mann and his wife, either of whom would have been good victims, the It chosen was the city guest of the Santinis. When he was called back, this hapless man invented the following story, in the following way.

IT: Is this story about people?
ANSWER: Yes.
IT: Is it about animals?
ANSWER: No.
IT: Then every character is a person?
ANSWER: No.
IT: No? Well . . . supernatural characters?
ANSWER: No.
IT: Is there a monster in the story?
ANSWER: Maybe.
IT: Well, let's see—does a woman give birth to a monstrosity?
ANSWER: Maybe.
IT: Well, does she?
ANSWER: Yes.
IT: Maybe? And Yes? Oh, it's two?
ANSWER: Yes.
IT: Siamese twins! Is there a crime?
ANSWER: Yes.

And so it went. The story unfolded was of a woman who destroyed the Siamese twins she had born out of wedlock by ripping them to pieces with her bare hands. When It was told this was his own story, he reacted in the usual way, with hot denials. It was patiently explained to him, as it has been to every It to date, that the completely mechanical and arbitrary method of answering gave him free choice at every turn, and that, for example, he might have started out by asking questions about time, locale, historical period, motivation, anything. Additionally, it was explained that the question as to whether the story was about people, to which an affirmative answer was given, might have satisfied anyone willing to think about people as distinct from non-people, but that It insisted on having other creatures in his story, even after learning there were no animals.

It took an exurbanite to decide that this game was flawed by the endless post-mortems, and to think up a way to improve it. He felt, too, that it was formless: the person who was It could go on asking questions indefinitely, could spin several stories, and never end until finally, in belated mercy, or out of sadistic impatience for the particular delights of the moment of truth, some player of the game would cut It off and tell him who was responsible for the horrors. But the moment of truth, it seemed to the inventive exurbanite, came too soon. It occurred to him, one night, that at a certain point It should be told that the entire story as contrived by the group had now been successfully wormed out of them, that It was completely the winner. "And now," this exurbanite asked the man who had been It, "what do you think of five people who could make up such a story?" (It was the story of the midgets.) The man was not sure what to say. Like most exurbanites, he was intelligent, and superficially conversant with psychiatry. He shook his head. "If it were only one person," he answered, "who had dreamed it up, I could make a comment. But after all there were five of you had a hand in it." "But what," he was pressed, "what would you think of a person who made up such a story, supposing just for the moment that only one did make it up? In a word, what would you say about such a person?" The many who had been It no longer paused. "If I knew that only one person had made it up," he said, "in one word I would say he was sick, sick, sick."

Then they told him who had made it up.

Another gay parlor game of this type requires, for its success, that its players be high, in order to secure their complete cooperation. The man or woman who is to be It is told, for the purposes of this game, that while out of the room the others will decide that they are going to play the roles of a specific category of personages—kings of medieval Europe, say, or Hollywood stars. The one who is It has the task, by asking the most personal sort of questions (the asking of personal questions is encouraged), of trying to figure out what category of personages is being portrayed. Once It leaves the room, again the real facts of the game come out. Instead of assuming the roles of personages his friends will assume the roles of the actual person sitting at their right hand, and they must tell the truth as best they know it. In a community where extramarital sex relations are not unheard of, such a game, if pursued according to the rules, can wreak a tidy bit of havoc within a half hour. At the Mann party, the playwright was sober enough when he was It to figure out, after a few minutes, the realities of the game, but did not reveal his knowledge. Once that had happened, he was absolute master. There were a number of things he had long wanted to know about relationships between some of his near and dear: he found out, and so did the rest of those present.

Such splendid releases for hostility would seem to be tailor-made for communities where most of the residents are superficially so gay, so pleasant, so charming. The factor inhibiting the greater popularity of these games (and others like them) is of course that a circle of friends very soon runs out of squares. And so their custom declines, for months or perhaps even years, until there are enough new faces in the exurb to justify their revival.

Tonight, the parlor games at the Manns' concluded with a long session of The Game. Wives got fretful with husbands who were too cloddish or too self-conscious to act out their phrases in quick order, husbands got irked with wives for being too goddam bossy, and after an hour interest ran low. Presently the play was abandoned and the talk once again became general. Somebody wandered over to the television set to see if there was a baseball game being broadcast; somebody else told a real estate story, somebody else started to talk shop, and a gag writer began to flirt with a columnist's wife. And so this party became like parties anywhere in the area and was subsequently referred to as a good one.

As with the party over in Weston, where Ben Martell is once again drunk. This party is basically the same. Before the three-dozen guests have left they will have put a severe dent in their host's liquor supply: he estimated that a half case of Scotch, a half case of gin, a half case of rye, and a half case of bourbon would see him through the evening; tomorrow he will be able to count a half-dozen unopened bottles.

Gid Philips, the account executive, and his wife, relatively sober, will be home by one a.m. this time around. After driving the sitter home, they will be in bed by two. Lights will be out at the Santinis' by two-thirty. Ben's wife will experience some difficulty in prying her husband out of his chair, but will get him home by around three. Duke and his friends will keep on dancing in a darkened room, or lounging on convenient couches in the dimness and drinking, until about the same time. They will be reluctant to break it up: the only thing they dislike more than getting up is going to bed, but they will be asleep by three-thirty.

All, because they must now face another day with their children, will be awake by eight, although Duke, who has had only eight hours' sleep in two nights, will petulantly demand another hour in bed. Our four examples have thus averaged, with that extra hour, five and one half hours' sleep a night for the last two nights. They must be counted fortunate.

Sunday, a day of relaxation everywhere, finds the exurbanites relaxing at full speed all over again. It would be too wearisome to list their activities once more; substantially the day is the same as Saturday, with three exceptions.

In the first place, there is the question of religion, which is not a relaxation, but which has, in many exurban homes, especially since the war, brought a merciful letup from the relaxation. Not many exurbanites are particularly religious, at least in any formal sense, and comparatively few are regular churchgoers. But their children go to school with the children of non-exurbanites, and these latter are, as a matter of course, entered in Sunday School by their churchgoing parents. One thing and another, the exurbanites' children want in on the Sunday School, too. This, together with the general postwar revival of interest in organized religion so noticeable all over the country, has made churchgoers of an appreciable number of exurbanites, especially on the North

Shore and in northern Westchester. Here in Fairfield County, too, clergymen have noted increases in their flocks. There are also many exurban parents who gladly send their young trooping off to Sunday School so that they may relax with the Sunday paper and an idle third cup of coffee, perhaps laced with something medicinal, as required. There is a minority of exurbanites who, on intellectual grounds, oppose the idea of their children going to Sunday School; if their children's need to belong to some comparable group is asserted strongly enough, they will impress into service a parent of like sympathies, who undertakes to instruct a group of ten or twelve children in Bible stories on an informal basis.

The second exception, already referred to, is the ritual of the Sunday paper, a period of torpor closely akin to slumber, and consequently important to all whose relaxation has, in the last day or so, been especially exhausting.

The third exception is that, by Sunday, exurban fathers are less thrilled at the notion of consorting with their young than they were before the novelty wore off some time Saturday. It is for this reason that Sunday in some exurban homes sees parents who have grown indignant with popular media of child entertainment, and who have responded strongly and affirmatively to Dr. Frederic Wertham's *Seduction of the Innocent*, urging their small fry to find some diversion of their own. "Daddy is not a toy," Duke says, patiently, "Go find something else to play with. Why don't you read one of those comic books where they kill people on every page? That's very exciting."

But exurban kids are less likely to be fascinated by such fare than most.

Ben Martell, who's proud of the fact that the networks are trying to police the more grisly horrors that appear on TV, says to his own son, "Look, why don't you go into the TV room and watch a show? They've got westerns with people being shot all the time. Right now you can see an old movie where they tie a guy up and drop him off a ship. Wouldn't you like that?"

But Martell Junior says he'd rather stay with the grownups and adds, piously and accusingly, that he knows such stuff isn't good for children, so why should he let himself be conned into looking at it?

On Sunday, again, it is striking to note how all—week-end guest, casual visitor, householder, and wife—as the hour of noon approaches, gradually find that their conversation has brought them to their feet and closer and closer to the bar. At noon, in houses all over the Westport area, you can hear someone say: "Well, I don't know about you bastards, but I think I'll have a martini, for a change," and once again life, which had up till then been almost unicellular, begins to become more complex.

One might surmise that, after the usual Sunday brunch or midday dinner and an afternoon out-of-doors, even an exurbanite would have reached the point where blessedness could consist only in sitting down quietly somewhere and doing nothing. But no: what is working in the exurbanite's mind, pushed down all day Saturday somewhere almost beyond consciousness, is the realization that, tomorrow, he must again become part of the rat race. So as the afternoon sun slides down he once again sets himself the objective of doing something, anything, to push away tomorrow. If he is not himself visited, he now starts to visit.

It would be exaggeration to refer to the gatherings that take place from five Sunday afternoon until around midnight as parties. They are seldom organized, as is a party. It is rather as though every house is considered open, and exurbanites wend their way from one to another house (always within the limits of a given clique) as, in New York, they might have pub-crawled up Third Avenue. Where on Friday or Saturday it was obligatory to have arranged a date before-hand, on Sunday the exurbanite can relapse into his old New York custom of calling a friend without notice. "You doing anything? Come on over," or "You stuck at home with the kids? Rita and I are over at the Santinis', we'll be over. You need any gin?"

In this amiable fashion, a couple will leave their house for that of a friend, pick up another couple and drop in on a second friend, leave the second couple behind and go on to a third friend.

THE SAME SOLUTION IS BEING REACHED,
AT MIDNIGHT, IN A REMARKABLE NUMBER
OF ADMEN'S HOMES, ALL OVER THE EXURB.

Here they will eat a sandwich, there an olive or a peanut; the faces they will see during an evening will in all probability include those of their whole circle of intimate acquaintances, and the circumstances will be, for perhaps the first time in the entire week end, truly relaxed. They are physically tired, so their conversation is more truly casual, pleasanter, more amiable.

And what of our foursome, come Sunday evening? After perhaps three hours of this sort of meandering, the Philipses are home again, having along the way picked up three other advertising men and their wives. It is now ten at night. The admen are talking shop on the Philipses' terrace. Each is persuaded that his agency, for one reason or another, is the best in town. Each explains why he feels that this is so. The others listen, argue, listen. They drink a little more. By eleven o'clock they are coming out under truer colors: each wonders out loud what he can do to get out of his agency and into another, where the grass seems greener. One adman is really serious about this, he insists he really means it, is there any way he could—without losing face—manage to—but the others interrupt him. They are really serious, too. They really mean it, too. Each refills his glass. By midnight they have reached the solution. (The same solution is being reached, at this moment, in a remarkable number of admen's homes, all over the exurb.) Why don't the four of them get together, and set up their own agency? The hell with working for somebody else, clubbing your brains out just to line some bastard's pocket who can't even write a decent line of copy any more, the doddering old meathead.

"Look," says one, "I'm sure I could swing my account to a new firm, fresh blood, fresh outlook."

In the back of each mind is the thought: "It's a way out of the rat race. My own business—and wouldn't it look great, my name up there on the letterhead?"

It is impossible to estimate accurately the number of dream-agencies that have been fantasized in this way, but it is a fact that at least two actual agencies have grown from just such meetings. But not this time. This time, the admen take leave of each other around twelve-thirty or so, the wives protract the departure in characteristic wifely fashion, and the Philipses start to empty ashtrays and collect glassware. They are sufficiently loaded and exhausted to insure a night's sleep.

The Santinis, having seen their week-end guests off on a refreshingly early evening train, could get to bed around eleven, but they sit up two hours, sipping coolers and verbally assassinating their departed friends, who left a ring in the tub, dropped butts on the new lawn, and didn't help with the Friday night dishes.

The Camerons get home from their house-crawling around eleven, and are in bed by twelve. The Martells were home by ten and hoped to get to bed early. Ben's wife is talking to him again and they're happily tired together. But Ben found a message to call the comic he works for in New York, did so, was told that his sketch for next week's show stinks but stinks, and that he'd better have something passing fair ready by noon next day or else, and so he is already involved again in the rat race. He is downstairs in the playroom, walking up and down, drinking some beer out of a can, and thinking, thinking.

Armand Santini is the only one of our four specimens who will not be on the platform of the railroad station in time to catch the 8:12 on Monday morning. He will be in his studio by nine. None of them thinks he has spent an exceptional week end. If you ask Armand, Gid, Duke, or Ben what he does over a week end, he will answer, "Why, what everybody else does, wherever they happen to live. It's no different in the country than anywhere else."

9

WOMEN AND CHILDREN FIRST?

No wedded man so hardy be t'assaille
His wyves pacience, in hope to finde
Grisildes, for in certein he shall faille!
—CHAUCER

The thought of suicide is a great consolation; by means
of it one gets successfully through many a bad night.
—NIETZSCHE

HERE is a message to feminine readers of this chapter: what follows, madam, is not about you, even though you live in the exurbs and even though you be married to an exurbanite; and to male readers—nor, sir, if you have come this far, will these lines concern your wife.

You exurbanites who read on may be described with some ease. You are happily married and completely devoted to your children who, warm and confident in the glow of your high regard, do well in school and are clearly destined for a happy, adjusted life. You live well, but within your means. You share with each other your individual pains and sorrows, triumphs and conflicts. You help each other, and are helped by each other.

218

You love, and are loved. Neither of you can understand why anyone should ever want, need, or indeed even dream of an extramarital adventure. Of course, occasionally you fight with each other: making up leads to such remembered pleasure. So, these lines are not written about you. But they are written about some of your friends, or at any rate your best acquaintances, and perhaps you will be able to recognize them.

We have seen how, for the exurbanite, the train schedules set his daily timetables. In a sense, they also set his wife's. Certainly, whether an exurban marriage is happy, boring, sad, or downright miserable, the morning departure of her spouse starts that part of the day when his wife is on her own. Let's visit a wife, Joan, while Bill's away at the rat race.

Bill and Joan are reasonably happy in their marriage, by exurban standards. When Bill is gone for the day, and the kids are in school, Joan always feels terribly alone. Sometimes this alone-feeling is accompanied by a sense of relief, sometimes she looks forward to the peaceful hours. But far more frequently Joan has to do a daily job on herself of reorientation to sudden solitude and of self-administered morale lecturing. No urban wife is ever so isolated.

Joan has a lot to do, of course. Housekeeping a compact city apartment, with help by the hour and stores and other people immediately within reach, is quite different from housekeeping in the country. The country house is much cleaner. There's no grit on the window-sills every morning, for instance. But it's so much bigger. And even with the modern mechanical conveniences with which her house is equipped, the bulk of Joan's day will be spent on housekeeping chores, including the operation of those so-called conveniences, which are not so automatic as they are touted to be. A dishwasher is a boon, but it has to be loaded, operated, and unloaded. The same holds true for washers, dryers, ironers. Bill has a lawn sprinkler which "walks" itself in a pre-set watering pattern, but Joan's fine new vacuum cleaner has to be perambulated from room to room.

There is also the matter of transport. For Joan, nothing is

within walking distance. Marketing, shopping, schooling, recreation, visiting (except for the immediate neighbors), getting Bill to and from the station, all require driving. Second in Joan's daily time consumption is transport.

Third is the children and their maintenance. City people like to think, especially when they're contemplating a move to the exurbs, that children are pretty much self-tending in the country, where they can play happily and unsupervised out of doors. This, as Joan can tell you, is a fond delusion. It's true that she doesn't have to take them to the park, or let them go by themselves and worry all the time they're gone that they're getting into trouble, or being run over (fantasies which in some cases reflect forbidden and unconscious wishes). But the children themselves, bless their hearts, like Joan's company, and even if they do play outdoors—and exurban children prefer not to—they'll traipse into and through the house frequently to sample her companionship, to say, "There's nothing to do," to require that she adjudicate a disagreement, or just to test the endurance of her good temper.

Fourth is preparation for Bill's return. This not only entails the getting under way of dinner preliminaries, but also a physical and psychic transformation of herself from housewife and mother to sweetheart of Sigma Chi. It's a daily reorientation which contains an element of suspense and anticipation, whether happy or not depends on the current state of the marital climate only in part, and in part on the day's state of Bill's business affairs.

But with all this to do, with all this physical activity (much of it onerous, much of it the sort that Joan grew up believing was ignominious and unfitting to a woman of education and finer feelings) to occupy her, Joan has a lot of time to brood, to think long thoughts, to be face to face with herself. All day long the house is hers. That cup of coffee she has when Bill and the kids are finally gone in the morning is frequently accompanied by resolutions. Today I will start a program of reading good books—again. Today I will spray the nasturtium border with Black Leaf 40. Today I will not spend a half hour in idle telephone chatter with Jane; she's really too stupid. I will organize the housework

today so that I can take an inventory of the Deepfreeze before
it's time to go marketing. Today I will not let myself putter in
the bedroom, getting nothing done, for an hour. Today I must
get through the housework in time to mend the children's off-
season things before putting them away.

These thoughts are constantly encroached on by other thoughts,
less mundane. They sound pitiful and trite when coldly noted,
but we can weep with Joan if we understand their poignancy. It's
a beautiful day and all over the world people are having fun and
doing interesting things, except me. Why? What am I doing
here in this house, alone, hausfrauing and getting older every day
and out of touch with things? What's Bill doing, right now?
Whatever it is, he's meeting people, talking to them, working
with them, active in the world. Is this what I wanted from life?
Why don't I start a small business? What about a shop—with my
taste and judgment it would have to be a success. What about
putting up my onion soup with sherry that everybody always raves
about, and selling it by mail? Why don't I write a children's
book? (Exurban wives have secret dreams, too.)

And then Joan shakes her head, as if to physically clear it of
circular, brooding thoughts. She hums a tune—her voice sounds
loud in the empty house—as she starts busily about her day. Or
she decides to allow herself fifteen minutes with *The New Yorker*,
to change her mood. (She feels about it that it is, in a way, her
magazine.) Or she subsides into romantic reveries—not about Bill.

At any rate, Joan, being thoroughly exurban, will contrive to
set herself impossible goals for the day, thus creating in the
morning the necessary conditions for feeling frustrated and un-
fulfilled by bedtime. She will get through the day's work, well or
haphazardly, but she won't start that program of reading. As a
matter of fact, she seems never to have time for reading what she
thinks of as "really good books." She'd like to know what's in
them, but she not only hasn't the time, she hasn't the attention.
Unfortunately for Joan, it is as E. M. Forster says: "Books have
to be read (worse luck, for it takes a long time); it is the only
way of discovering what they contain. A few savage tribes eat

them, but reading is the only method of assimilation revealed to
the west."

There are those who will feel about Joan that she is unusually
moody and introspective, that she is maladjusted and lacks ma-
turity and emotional tone. She can't be typical, they are sure. Let's
leave Joan, then, and see whether we can make some acceptable
generalizations about exurban wives as a whole.

If we limit our discussion of the exurban wives to those who
have moved to the exurb in the last six or seven years, there are
a few generalizations which it will be safe to make. They are
made in the face of a recognition of the usual dangers that inhere
in any lumping of obviously disparate individuals. What here will
be approximated is a community profile, with no attempt at even
a cursory acknowledgment of the inner varieties that exist within
the group, and none at all of individuals except in so far as they
may happen to illustrate a generality. The writer is a man, and
too many men have already written about women; all that can
be said on this point is that here is one more, and to offer apologies
in advance for omissions or insensitivities. An example of one
such is the heading on this chapter: to include women and children under one roof is to suggest that the women are to be
equated with the children, although their fathers are not. This
apparent insensitivity was, however, quite deliberate, and results
from an attempt, which will be made again every now and then
in this chapter, to reveal the rampant male chauvinism of the
masculine exurbanite. He does too often fail to make any distinction between wife and children; it is the more ironical, since in
many cases he is the one who should be categorized with the children, the proof of this statement being the petulant and childish
fashion in which so many exurbanites compete with their children in clamoring for mother's attention.

As for the generalizations, the wife who moved to the exurbs
at some time since 1948, is in her thirties or early forties, and
looks younger. She has, usually, two children, although there are
many families with three or more.

She may have come here from anywhere in the country; there

was, when she arrived, at least, no regional stamp on her. There may be a trace of Boston in her speech, or of Iowa, or of California, or of Alabama. The likelihood, however, is that in her home town she was well above the average in taste and intelligence; socially, and perhaps in other ways as well, she was a rebel. She was a kind of latter-day Carol Kennicott. She was destined to make her move, away from home, and to New York.

She may have married before the war; she may have married during the war; she may have married twice. In any case, the probability is that she experienced the dislocations of the war. She has had her share of living out of suitcases and trunks, of following a husband around the country, of trying to make a home out of a pre-fab bungalow designed as some officer's quarters, of hotels and trains. She may even have been more directly involved in the war as a government employee, or an officer in the WAVES or the WAC.

At some point before her marriage, she had a job. She may have come to her job from any of several milieus: she may be a Smith graduate and familiar with the uniform cashmere sweater and single string of pearls, or she may have been part of the dirndl-and-dirty-neck set in Greenwich Village. If so, she is almost certain to have had an affair with an unsuccessful artist who, as she puts it, "opened my eyes to a whole new world." But for a time she was launched on a career, either as researcher, actress, editor, artist, fashion model, secretary, or whatever. She knows the inside of many New York offices, and she knows, as well, the manners and customs of New York working people.

She cheerfully, even gratefully, exchanged her career for marriage, and eagerly undertook the job of both making a home and being a fit intellectual companion for her husband (or, more usually, of maintaining rather more intellectual interests than her husband). After her first-hand experiences at trying to make a home in wartime, or struggling with New York apartments, she was delighted with the idea of moving to the country. She probably had one child before she and her husband moved. She was probably not wholly aware of the fact that, for her husband, this move to the exurbs represented only his limited dream. For her, in any event, the move came far closer to an unlimited dream: here, at last, was the opportunity to make a permanent home. Typically, she plunged into the job with zest, and did a great deal of painting, paperhanging, remodeling, and outside work in the garden. Subject to the limitations that will be discussed presently, she still keeps enormously busy at this sort of work. If her husband is on the way up the ladder of income, there is always more of it to do, even to planning and then supervising the building of the new $35,000 or $50,000 house.

The servant problem is one she has not been (and probably never will be) able to lick. Usually, she does a great deal of the work involved in keeping a house running smoothly all by herself, occasionally relying on a cleaning-woman (one day a week) or a laundress (one day a week).

After the move, she has had more children. Her attitude to the problems created by a growing tribe of children differs according to her personality. For some, the difference between one child and none is enormous, the difference between one and two very great, but thereafter the difference is hardly noticeable. These mothers know how to curl up a little tighter to make room for one more, and have organized their lives around the children already, so that three, four, or five seem to cause no appreciable concern. For other mothers, however, the difference is that of a geometric progression: the second is twice as difficult as the first, the third four times as difficult as before, and so on.

In all these things, the exurban wife does not materially differ from her sisters who have stayed in New York, or indeed who live anywhere. But from here on, the unique and characteristic exurban problems begin to make their presence felt, sometimes intolerably.

There is, in the first place, the simple, practical matter of the distance that separates her from her husband. The suburban wife also faces this, but not nearly to the same extent. The exurban wife early learns that she and she alone will cope with emergencies confronting her, the house, the car, or the children. She early

grows familiar with the answer that she will be given on the
phone, should she call New York. (The answer is: "Look, honey,
don't bother me now, will you? I'm busy.") The result is that
when Penny falls out of a tree and fractures her skull, the
exurban mother has the car out and Penny in it, has driven to the
hospital sixteen miles away, and made sure that everything is
under control and Penny out of danger before she will call New
York and tell Penny's father what has happened. In an exurb,
where houses are usually widely separated from each other, the
mother is strictly on her own.

In the second place, there is the fact that she is married to an
exurbanite, with all his special and extraordinary conflicts, anxieties, and problems. His fears and insecurities are easily trans-
mitted to her, although she pours a great deal of emotional energy
into concealing the fact. This transmission occurs in two ways.
First, she can usually tell on first sight of her husband in the
evening, by his bearing, his walk, his connubial peck, whether
things have gone well or ill that day. Second, he's going to tell her.

He may tell her by sullen silence all evening, or by isolating
himself from her by watching wrestling on TV. She wonders,
then, if she has anything about which to feel guilty, but she can
pretty generally determine when the cause of his silence is not
annoyance with her, but concern brought with him from the city.
Or he may tell her by bickering with her in a way which can only
result in a bitter quarrel, out of which he will derive at least a
temporary discharge of the hostile tensions he has been sup-
pressing and building up all day. This kind of attrition she
recognizes, too. Or he may be preternaturally gay and insist on
abandoning dinner at home and eating out, seeing people, drinking, doing something, being somebody.

For the exurban man and wife, he typically with no tangible
product against which to measure his day's achievement, she with
a day of solitude behind her, this necessity to have the ego re-
assembled and bolstered by recourse to friendly company is
powerfully compelling.

But more likely the transmission of her husband's fears and

insecurity is accomplished by the husbandly monologue after dinner, or in the prolonged unwinding of his day's tensions during cocktails while the dinner spoils and the children are exiled to watch television. Typically, she must interpret his account, for while it sounds straightforward and candid, it is edited and it tends to go by opposites. That is, if the monologue is a recital of a day of triumph, in which our caveman hero slew one saber-toothed tiger after another ("So I said to the boss, 'Look, B. R., if you don't like it, why don't you try to find somebody else who can do it better?' Boy, did he back down fast!") his wife can be reasonably certain that he took a lot of pushing around that day. As for the editing, she can, if she allows herself, fill in the gaps. She knows her husband well enough to sense the almost imperceptible pause, the eyes momentarily seeming to look at her too directly, the crossing of the legs, all of which indicate that something's being left out. It may be just bad news, which he thinks he's sparing her out of regard for her feelings, but which in fact he's hiding to spare his own feelings of shame and inadequacy. It may be something worse.

She knows enough about the communications world to hazard that her husband may humorously refer to the couch in his office as "my casting couch," a trade cliché; she knows how easy it is in his business to grant ego-building interviews to eager young things. She knows that when he has lunch in the Barberry Room or Villa Camillo with a person from the office, to talk business, naturally, the person may well be a very personable person who is the focus of every roving eye in the office. (There was a time when she was taken to expensive luncheons by married men from her office.) Perhaps, she consoles herself, he felt so low he needed to get set up again by being seen with a beautiful girl—it could be as innocent as that. Perhaps not, of course.

At any rate, no matter how she interprets his monologue (and despite her own accompanying inner soliloquy) she is as keenly aware as he is that tomorrow the account may be canceled, or the option dropped, or the illustrations rejected, or the show closed down, or the line of books discontinued. And she is probably more conscious than he of the fact that they are living beyond their means. She is a good wife, as has been said, and all this she generally conceals. She listens. Every now and then her attention wanders to her own day and its problems. Sometimes she can't contain herself and takes the conversation away from her spouse by force, or, countering each of his anecdotes with one of her own, pours out the unheroic story of her only human contacts: the butcher, the man she got to fix the TV antenna, the man who came to spray the trees, one of the children's teachers, a brief meeting with Jane when she stopped by to return one of the children's galoshes she'd found in her driveway, and what Jane said.

She knows it's boring to her spouse; God knows, it bores her, too. But often she can't stop on those occasions when she gets started. Her husband gets restless and she talks faster. And if it's really a bad evening for her, she'll bring up the urgent matter of money. The next day, during her morning period of thinking things over, she may realize that her behavior the night before was one more step in the process of driving her husband to seek relief from his tensions, worries, and boredom with home, in the city.

Her husband may, of course, react in many ways, depending on his temperament. But he is an exurbanite, and is, therefore, likely to react fashionably; that is to say, he will take heed of what his fellows are doing, and do likewise. His fellows, he knows, seek relief from the worries of city and home by drinking a little too much, and by following their roving eye and their rollicking impulse.

His wife, as her months in the exurb multiply, will begin to sense, from many revealing little things, what is happening. If he is so typical as to relapse into an occasional infidelity, she may not elect to face up to and recognize these clues for what they portend, but she will probably understand them on some level of her consciousness whether she wants to or not. Those little signs —his absence from the office "for lunch" when she calls at three-fifteen, the increased frequency of his having to work late, and so on—are, for many exurban wives, supported by quite unmistakable evidence of a negative sort at home. Their husbands seem always to be tired.

Exurban physicians whose general practice brings them often in contact with exurban wives report that a most frequent complaint they make is that their husbands are sexually inadequate. They may talk of chronic fatigue, or of backaches, or of sleeplessness, or of nerves, but sooner or later their ailment comes down to sex, or rather to its absence. One doctor may inject such patients with vitamin B, another may have prepared some tonic with a generous dash of alcohol in it, but these are no better than any placebo, and the wives know it. One, who suffered from severe menstrual cramps, at length admitted to her doctor that she knew they were entirely emotional, for she had learned she could alleviate them by going to a movie, any movie that would make her temporarily forget her emotional problems. More tragically, one exurban doctor reports a high incidence of psychogenic abortions in the fashionable exurb where he practices, of women who lose their babies in the fifth or sixth month of pregnancy for no apparent physiological cause; once again, he attributes this to the unhappiness which is at the core of their lives.

The boredom and impatience grow. For many exurban wives, the greatest envy is reserved for the relatively few of their number who still work. ("At least they get to see a different face, once in a while.") When such a commuting wife is invited out to dinner, she can often cut the hostility with a knife. She will note that the social pleasantries are barbed, and she will recognize, if she is wise, that there is little she can do to make it otherwise.

For the case seems to be that many exurban wives fall into the category described by such specialists as Helene Deutsch as the "active-masculine" women. The term probably does not originate with Deutsch, and it smacks, in any event, of psychiatric jargon, but as a term it has its connotative usefulness. The implications are, for this type of exurban women, accurate: they are competitive, inclined to jealousy and suspicion (very often with reason), and aggressive. Thus, some will swear like a man, use four-letter words, want to be treated on the ordinary social level like "one of the boys." Others will insist, when their husbands come home from the office, on discussing "important," "serious" things—politics, trade gossip, the latest books; this flows from their determination not to become a vegetable. But the kind of man these women marry would vastly prefer to leave this kind of talk behind them in the city. They want their wives to relax, and give them instead a little domestic chatter, in consonance with their limited dream.

At this point, both caution and the demands of accuracy dictate some reservations. There are on every hand, in every exurb, women who belong in Deutsch's category of the "feminine" woman, lovely, luscious, womanly creatures to whom envy is alien, whose competitive flame burns no higher than a pilot-light, whose circle of friends is large and warmly regarded, who rarely if ever seek aggressively to assume a shell of masculinity. But in most exurbs they are in the minority. Nor is there solid evidence that they are to any appreciable extent happier than their more competitive sisters. For as Simone de Beauvoir (among others) has pointed out, "Woman's sexuality is conditioned by the total situation," and a total situation which may include fear, insecurity, living beyond one's means, drinking too much, and all the other trying aspects of life in Exurbia, does not admit of much promise.

So boredom and impatience continue to grow until, in the nature of such growth, they are transformed into something else.

The something else may be merely a slow-burning dissatisfaction or, if there is sufficient cause, it may be anger, humiliation, and a reactive withdrawal to any of several other spheres of activity and interest, but in any case away from a happy marriage. It is more rarely divorce. Of course there are divorces in the exurbs as elsewhere but the rate is lower than the national average, for several reasons. Many of these marriages are already second marriages, and the awareness grows, among these intelligent folk, that divorce can supply no solution to a relationship which is seen as one of a pattern, a continuing repetitive pattern. Besides, there are the children, there is the family, there is the home. Once again, it must be urged that these people have insight, they are intelligent, they know what divorce can mean to children, an appreciable number of them being themselves the offspring of divorced parents. And there is the remembered romantic love, which might be saved. So, while the cause is often cause for divorce, the effect is not so often divorce, but a physical withdrawal and coldness which conceal inner emotional anguish.

It is in such circumstances that an exurban wife will select (according to the individual facet of her personality) a sphere of activity, an outlet for emotional energy. The choice is rarely exclusive and discrete, but rather a matter of emphasis. The five principal areas are: the home, the children, drink, outside interests, and sexual dalliance of her own.

Before we examine an example of each of these designs for living, an important distinction must be made. Our examples (and much of what has already been said) concern women who are, themselves, exurbanites, as opposed to women who, though resident in the exurbs and married to exurbanites, are only of the exurban persuasion by capture, as it were. Typically, the latter are from the upper strata of urban life, or pre-exurban county life, and have gone from college or finishing school into courtship and then marriage with no pre-conditioning stop-over in the rat race. They are not really part of the exurban big deal —they're just going along for the ride, and a bewildering ride it is. Their great virtue as wives, and their great good fortune as women, is that they more readily adapt to domesticity. The worst (and most frequent) charge their husbands can make against them is that they tend to be extravagant.

And now, let's reacquaint ourselves with Muriel, an exurban wife we glimpsed only briefly in an earlier chapter, when her husband, Joe, came home to find her glowering and kissed her back into good spirits again.

Muriel is almost compulsively devoted to her home. She won't have a servant, although she can afford one. She does not know how to do anything about the house the easy way. Every job is a production number. She is not inefficient, she's thorough. On a summer week end, when the family and the guests would be content with a picnic dinner, or cold cuts, Muriel decides on a roast with Yorkshire pudding and homemade pie for dessert. She's a wonderful cook and Joe is envied by many of his friends, but she never has time for play. In winter, Muriel fights a constant battle with mud and winter clothing. Her spring cleaning involves removing everything from every closet, the scouring of the bare wood, and several days of moth-proofing, cleaning, mending, re-sorting, tieing up in bundles, stowing away in boxes, exhuming from winter bundles and boxes, brushing and airing, etc., of every item of clothing in the house. That's only a small part of it; the summer slip-cover bit, for example, is heroic.

Muriel will never, no matter what the pressures, spread up a bed that's been slept in. It must be stripped every day. She will never make a one-dish meal. She'll never use paper napkins. She says she'd be glad to send out the laundry and glad to have a good servant, but you can't get laundry done decently any more (they ruin everything) and the only servants around have to be cleaned up after, and never do a good job anyway, so they're more trouble than they're worth.

Muriel's excursions from home are either marketing expeditions, or (happy times for her) shopping trips to antique stores, or the home-furnishings departments of Lewis & Conger or Hammacher Schlemmer. When she can do these with a like-minded neighbor, it's a real ball for both.

Muriel is an extreme case, but she is a case in point. Her husband can't quite understand how so much time can be efficiently devoted to housekeeping or why he feels that the home he works so hard for comes between him and his wife. He, like quite a few other exurbanites who have dedicated themselves to the advertising campaigns that sell the labor-saving devices with which their homes are equipped, is persuaded that, these days, a woman doesn't need to spend much time running a house.

Of course, it is not only the Muriels of Exurbia who must

consign so much of their waking life to housework. A few years
ago a Bryn Mawr report demonstrated that housekeeping activities ate up 78.35 to 80.57 hours a week in the average urban
household. Exurban households, with their added burdens, require
more.

For exurban women must live graciously, as the women's magazines say. They must run a house that can compete with its
neighbors on exurban terms, and they must seem to do it easily.
It is quite a trick, especially as it involves, among other things,
the uncertainty of the exurban master's hours, and his not infrequently showing up fifty-five minutes late with two city friends
in tow who, he is determined, will see his limited dream in
operation, and this must include urban envy at how pleasant it
is to live in the exurbs. The exurban husband rarely notices how,
after preparing a four-course dinner for six people, complete with
crystal, damask, and silver, all on two hours' notice, his wife
takes her seat white-faced and trembling. He may, if he's something of a boor, wish she looked more attractive; if he's not, he
may still take it as a matter of course. She was home all day,
wasn't she? What else was she doing?

There are compulsive housewives in every stratum of our society,
but the compulsive exurban housewife has it tougher. For just
as her husband has the problem of keeping ahead of the Joneses
in his job of guiding and controlling the Joneses' taste, so she
must seem to set the style in the disposition of her house's
interior effects. And where the suburban matron has no qualm
about the presence of *House Beautiful* on her coffee table, the
exurban matron prides herself on never taking her lead from anywhere but her own pretty head.

The dreadful tedium of household chores, the thrice-daily cleaning of dishes only to see them dirtied again, the once-daily
making of beds against their being unmade all over again, those
things especially gravel the woman who has sniffed the excitement of a career, and more than often been singularly successful
at it. The fact that, in the case of the Muriels, much of each
day's tasks is purposely made more punishing does not mitigate

the dullness; all it does is keep them too busy to be constantly aware of it, or provide a focus for their unhappiness which cloaks their marital dissatisfactions and frustrations.

This does not mean that these women are constantly overworked and disgruntled. They do love their homes and often derive a kind of spartan satisfaction from running them, and a real joy in living in them and displaying them. But there is one thing about housework that makes their days often less easy to bear than those of their husbands in the rat race. A man with a hangover may dawdle over his copy or his artwork or his score or his script; he may be able to tell his producer or his copy chief or his director that he just isn't up to snuff on this given day, realizing that his producer or copy chief or whatever has often experienced days like this himself. He works against deadlines, and can either shirk today and redouble his efforts tomorrow, or, if the deadline is upon him (as it usually is), he is pressured by other people who will drive him if flesh and spirit are unwilling and weak. But for his wife at home, there is the daily, dogged plugging which, no matter how much she is willing to skimp, must be done, and nothing to bolster sagging morale, no directive from someone else to rally her forces, no finally finished product which can be submitted for approval and then forgotten while a new project is undertaken.

And to make it additionally tough for the Muriels, remember that these women were the exceptional girls in their home towns, wherever they were, the girls who dreamed of being stars on Broadway, or by-line special correspondents, or top-flight fashion models. The girls have grown up to become superior drudges for $20,000-a-year husbands, and there must be something they find unforgivable about that.

Observation tells us that perhaps one in five exurban wives has channeled her energies in this direction.

A somewhat larger group, faced with the chilly prospect of a marriage that is not all they had hoped it would be, devote themselves to their children. This is not to suggest for an instant that most exurban wives are not good mothers. Nearly all of them find that their lives center around their children. But here again it is a question of emphasis. Some exurban mothers, giving up the unequal struggle to keep their marriages exciting and trustful, become almost exclusively maternal. These mothers may have five children or only one, their absorption is equally complete. They brood and they hover, they pore over their Gesell, they engage in earnest conversations with teachers and school psychologists. Their concern spills over to embrace not only their own children but their children's friends, and their friends' children.

Every exurban mother will sigh when she thinks of the enormous amount of transport she must undertake in a single day or over a single week. Here again, the exurban woman whose emotional energies are focused on her children will be seen to take over. It is she who does far more than her share of picking up and dropping children at their respective homes—and coping, on the floors of closets and in hallways, with snowsuits, rubbers, galoshes, and mittens. In every circle of intimate friends there is one woman who seems to be supremely masochistic in permitting additional children-chores to be loaded on her shoulders, one woman who is regularly the patsy in taking charge of picnics, small-fry barbecues, birthday parties, beach excursions, and whatnot. It is not so much that she is the managerial or the magisterial type. It is just that she is there, she is available, she steps in, she asks for it.

Some of her friends refer to her, if she has more than three children, as a brood mare, but it seems more likely that she is the exurban woman who has decided the hell with it, she'll be a vegetable. She makes little effort to participate in bright, smart, sophisticated, intelligent, hip talk. The acid has gone out of her, except for one thing. She reserves a special venom for the nonvegetable wife. It is a thoroughly moral, chip-on-shoulder disapproval, and some of these determinedly maternal women manage to let a little of their hostility toward the gayer, more irresponsible mothers seep out, as it were, so that all the children in the neighborhood will be conscious of it.

The maternal mother is the one who runs a party for children "from four to six," and, when at six-thirty, the phone-call comes from a parent imploring, "Can you manage somehow for another half hour?" will purse her lips and shake her head—but agree. An hour later, and here will come a somewhat tipsy father to gather up his double armful and drive them home. The maternal mother knows what will happen. He will drive too fast, and once he gets them home he will hurry them through the living room full of cocktail drinkers and jam them down the backstairs to the playroom and sit them down in front of the television and command them to enjoy themselves for still another hour. The maternal mother is right to purse her lips and shake her head. She contrives to make her disapproval as public a manifestation as she politely can, and perhaps she is right about that, too. But it doesn't send her popularity rating soaring.

Once again, it must be emphasized that these comments by no means are meant to apply to all exurban devoted mothers. A majority of them have a healthy maternity and a healthy brood of average size. Being mature women, they do not practice on their children the over-protectiveness or over-permissiveness which can spoil the lives of those whose mothers are of the dedicated variety we've been discussing.

There are even some perfectly normal exurban mothers who have had three children in the last four years, to make a present total of five or six, with the end not particularly in sight. These mothers (and fathers, too, presumably) simply don't know how it is possible to have too much of a good thing. What waspish cynics have referred to as a postwar fad, the sudden upsurge of babies all over the place, is something to which these parents seem to have an indefinite commitment, not caring that the same cynics say it is now considered démodé in better circles.

These mothers, then, are not to be included with those who have retreated from the challenge of a difficult marriage to concentrate on being fussily maternal during their every waking moment. At any rate, they do not concern us here.

What does concern us is the compulsive motherliness which

serves as assuagement for marital unhappiness. Typically, it puts a terrible burden on the children and their fathers. The children's burden is that they will be asked to fulfill vicariously their mother's abandoned hopes and aspirations, while being frustrated in attempting to do so by their ensnarement in the silver cord she will not let them break.

Typically, the husband's burden is that his wife so contrives to arrange the hours when he's at home that she will neglect him in the interests of the children. This is easily accomplished. If he returns from the rat race with the appearance of a man who has a problem to share, it will automatically leap to this woman's mind that the children must have a shampoo before dinner so that their hair will be dry by bedtime. Away she goes to the bathroom with the kids, and to hear the shouting and laughter you'd think this was the happiest family in all Exurbia. Except that the nominal head of the house is brooding alone downstairs.

Or, if things have been going unusually happily for the entire family from seven (when Dad returned home) to nine (the children's bedtime), the compulsive mother may—out of unconscious fear of resuming an intimacy which has proved it can end in misery—recall that she hasn't read aloud to the children as much as she might and she will keep them awake by reading not one chapter of an Oz book, or *Mary Poppins*, but two or three. By the time she returns to her spouse he has cooled and found something else to do.

These maternal activities impose an additional burden, perhaps a crueler one, on father and children in their interrelationship, and this, too, is an unconscious achievement of the compulsive mother's marital hostility. There comes a point when her husband is goaded into making some observation about what seems to be going on. It may be as simple as "Can't you do these things before I get home?" or "Can't that wait until tomorrow?" or even, "For Pete's sake—can't they do anything for themselves?" Such a remark is immediately attributed by the wife (usually, thanks to her unwitting conniving, correctly) to hidden resentment of the children by their father. Now she flares up, she is the mother primeval protecting her helpless brood. The children do not remain unaware of these exchanges and undercurrents, no matter how careful the parents think they are, and so we find a household in which the father is a necessary but unwelcome stranger. Father and children are enemies, and he feels helpless guilt. This is the covert story. Overtly, the woman in question may seem the most warm-hearted, devoted, whole-souled woman in her exurb.

It shouldn't be necessary to point out again that we have been discussing an extreme manifestation. It may be worth mentioning, though, that it is rare in Exurbia for a wife to start her career as mother in the compulsive manner described. Usually, her disillusion with her marriage postdates motherhood and this behavior is adopted later.

Now for the third emotional outlet chosen by exurban women. They may turn to drink. They will have ample precedent. The exurban wives who are on the sauce are of two (some say three) kinds. There are the baleful souses, the progressive nippers, and (perhaps a separate category) the competitive drinkers.

Isobel, who lives in Rockland, is a baleful souse. It's a nasty, shocking phrase to apply to any woman, but when you see Isobel during the day, see what a pleasant and sensitive person she is, it sounds grotesque to apply it to her. She was quite pretty, once, and is still possessed of a look of fineness. In midsummer, when she's been working in the garden, she looks radiant and quite lovely. Come the cocktail hour, though, and she undergoes a transformation. The period of convivial gaiety is short for her: she undergoes a metamorphosis from nice woman to baleful souse in half an hour. The lines in her face deepen and the puffiness is accentuated. One eyelid droops more than the other. Her hair gets stringy.

Isobel knows all this, dimly, and it makes her all the more baleful. And it's hell for her husband. She becomes quarrelsome in the extreme. The next morning, while he's still angry and baffled, she is hurt by his attitude. It's not that she's forgotten how she behaved: she never knew. She is an alcoholic Jekyll and Hyde personality who goes through the schizoid cycle every day in the week, and sometimes twice on Saturdays and Sundays. It's hard to pin down the trigger event that starts her off. The simplest explanation is the clock—cocktail time comes every day. But her husband comes home every day at that time, too. Could it have something to do with him? It could; in fact, it does.

Isobel's husband goes in for protégées. Sometimes they are his secretaries, who are brought home so he can get some important work done over a week end. Sometimes they are feminine business associates he's befriended to help them find themselves in new and difficult jobs. Once, he invited home for the week end a male friend who is a commercial photographer and who brought two models with him; the story was that pictures would be taken beside the brook under the apple trees, to be submitted for a magazine cover. The pictures were duly taken on Sunday morning, in a couple of hours, but Isobel was hostess to the models from Friday before sundown to Monday morning.

On such enforced social occasions, Isobel isn't quarrelsome as she is, after a few drinks, when she's alone with her husband. On social occasions she is self-effacing, to the point of drinking herself out of consciousness.

This is not the place to apportion blame. Isobel, who would hotly protest if one suggested she was alcoholic, might admit that she ought to drink less, and might even become so confiding as to assert that she would drink less, without trying, if her husband didn't humiliate her so. For his part, he knows his wife is a problem drinker and believes that if she weren't, if she'd do something about her fading looks, he wouldn't have recourse to other feminine companionship. He even went on the wagon himself, once, although drinking was not a problem for him, thinking it might lead Isobel to do the same. It did not: she accused him of doing it as a piece of calculated aggression. Whoever or whatever is at fault, this couple is plainly miserable.

Typically, among the circle in which the baleful souse moves, a pretense is made by all that she's perfectly normal, maybe drinks too much, but don't we all, now and then? She is, fortunately for the wells of compassion in all of us, which might otherwise be drained dry, not encountered too often in Exurbia; just often enough, perhaps, so that we may recognize the type.

On the other hand, the progressive nippers are increasing in number almost as swiftly as each individual progressive nipper is increasing her dosage. Typically, progressive nipping takes the form of small doses—tiny around eleven in the morning and getting larger as the day wears on—of whisky, or gin-and-tonic. It helps one over the rough spots. Nippers are in the main good holders of their liquor and seldom are noticeably fried before their husbands have got home and caught up with them.

There are, too, progressive nippers who know their loved ones will get off the bar car already fairly lubricated. For these, there is the excuse that they want to be in the same state of insouciance as their husbands when the day's work is done. Among them, the nipping starts later in the day, at first just before traintime, but by and by at four and then at three, and finally they have joined those who started their progressive nipping by having a quick pick-me-up just before lunch. For these drinkers the problem is less often infidelity, more often sheer strain, tension, and boredom.

Not long ago, an exurbanite ran onto something he thought was excruciatingly funny. It amused him so much that we must suppose there was some bitterness in his readiness to guffaw at a thing which was seriously intended. It was a suburban wife's set of rules, which she'd lovingly inscribed in the back pages of her cookbook, where room had been left for recipes. The exurbanite couldn't resist showing this priceless piece of naïveté to his own wife, so he had his secretary transcribe it from the copy of the original which another exurbanite had lent him. (This is how a lot of exurban humor gets circulated.) The rules the suburban woman had composed were to govern her behavior in the trying thirty-to-sixty minutes between her husband's arrival at home and the time the first hot plate was put on the dinner table.

"1. You can be a harridan all day if you wish, but melt into something sweet and compassionate for just thirty minutes when your husband gets home at night.

"2. No matter how many troubles of your own, ask him about his problems first. Remember he is counting on your sympathy to right all the wrongs, real and imaginary, that he feels he has suffered at the hands of his employer, his train, and a host of other adversaries, human and inanimate, actual or fancied.

"3. Greet him with a cocktail. The timing is more important than the stimulation. One martini placed before your husband at this critical juncture will do wonders for his mood, no matter how late his train or difficult his day. Psychologically, it is the nearest you can come to acknowledge that he deserves at least the Congressional Medal of Honor for his hard day on the city battleground.

"4. Remember he is also hungry—the later the train the hungrier. If dinner isn't quite ready, have some potato chips or crackers-with-cheese on hand to keep him at bay until you are ready to serve.

"These simple instructions, if followed by wives with commuting husbands, could go a long way towards establishing domestic bliss in Suburbia."

The exurban wife who was shown this didn't find it so funny as her husband did. She didn't get around to reading it until the next afternoon while she was awaiting his arrival on the 6:57. On this day, in addition to her normal ten hours of incessant fetching, shopping, carrying, cooking, washing, tidying, feeding, tending, cleaning, scrubbing, dusting, polishing, ironing, bending, walking, and climbing, she had had to get a plumber for the septic tank, butter up a man from the bank who called about an overdrawn account, spend her weekly two hours at the second-hand clothing store run to raise money for the school, and stop a fight between her spaniel and a neighbor's boxer. By six-thirty she had crammed an early supper down the gullets of her young, fed the spaniel and dressed his wounds, set the table, stuffed a fowl and put it in the oven, prepared a coffee mousse, put water on to boil for wild rice and a green vegetable, and gotten ice out for a cocktail.

Now she sat down, for the first time in hours, and read Rule 1. Her expression was stony. "Sweet and compassionate, is it?" she muttered, and turned irritably to Rule 2. As she read about how she should sympathize with his wrongs, real and imaginary, she thought how earlier that day, as she was cleaning out the pockets of his brown tweed suit so that she could take it to the drycleaners, she had found in a hip pocket a handkerchief smeared with lipstick of the shade known as Bachelor's Carnation (her own being Snow Rose). It was now six thirty-two, and she dropped five ice-cubes into her glass martini pitcher, added three ounces of gin and a half ounce of Noilly Prat, stirred, and moodily read Rule 3. "The timing is more important than the stimulation," she read, nodded her head in agreement, and drained her glass. "One martini will do wonders."

At this point she got up, walked into the study, rolled the set of rules into her own typewriter, and dashed off the following: "It is doubtful that any wife will ever finish reading Rule 3. Certainly she will never get as far as Rule 4. Try as you will, you cannot imagine a scene in which the average wife will be able to follow these rules and act on them faithfully. All they will make her do is drink five martinis between six thirty-two and six fifty-seven. By the time her husband gets home he will be lucky if there is any gin left in the house, and as for the potato chips, he may get the whole bowl, flung."

Progressive nipping isn't very funny, though. Drinking as a regular thing seldom is, and the fact that the nippers of Exurbia generally manage not to make spectacles of themselves doesn't mitigate much. It's too easy for these women to discover self-deceiving subterfuges to conceal the increasing size of the hourly slugs, and to disguise the indubitable fact that with the help of a little alcohol, problems which seem solved are merely being shelved. One progressive nipper, reprimanded by a compulsive mother for not knowing, at four in the afternoon, where her

children were, replied, "Well, after all, the reason we moved out
to the country was so that the kids could learn a little self-
reliance, wasn't it? And if the kids can't run around outside in
a lovely, peaceful place like this, then what do we pay taxes for?"

Our last entry (a subclass) in the catalogue of the lady lushes
of Exurbia is Lucy, whom we have not met before in these
pages. She is a strikingly handsome woman, an excellent tennis
player and swimmer, and has about her a forthright charm. She
is also, sadly, a competitive drinker. Competitive drinkers are
those who insist on going drink for drink with their husbands.
This would be harmless enough, except that it does not stop
there. When the husband decides no more highballs after dinner
(something quite a few exurbanites decide, for a week or so at
a time), the wife thereafter competes with her guest or her host,
depending. It is impossible to estimate the number of exurban
wives who have selected this particular form of narcosis to assist
them in forgetting that their marriages are not destined for the
ages, but it is certain that their tribe is numerous.

Lucy is, as you will have guessed, not only competitive about
her drinking. She is a frustrated writer, poet, artist, linguist—a
lot of things, anything, in fact, at which the men of her acquaintance are successful. It would be glib and characteristically exurban
to dismiss her as a victim of penis envy and, having given her
problem a name, to dismiss her. The fact about Lucy is, however,
that her career dreams are an outgrowth of her marital frustra-
tion. The creative stirrings which disturb her are an expression of
her need to find a fulfillment in some other sphere to compensate for the sterility of her marriage. Her rejection of femi-
ninity is retaliatory. She competes with her husband and with
other men in the only way she has been able to find, one which
assures that she won't fail, and that she won't be smacked down
for succeeding in. She drinks competitively, and thus smacks herself down.

Let us now leave the drinkers, an unhappy crew at best, and
turn to those exurban women who have channeled their dissatisfactions into outside activities. However, taboo are all outside

activities which smack of a Helen Hokinson drawing. Taboo, in other words, are the outside activities generally considered suburban. This is not to say that there are no garden clubs in the exurbs; there are, and they flourish, but they flourish without the assistance of the exurban wife looking for an outlet for her emotional energies. If the exurban wife feels that her marriage is on the rocks, it is difficult for her to comfort her wounded ego by taking a course in flower arrangement. Possibly it has been done, but the precedents are not numerous. On the other hand, she may play cards, but if she does it will be at a game where the stakes are high, if not for blood. A Hokinson cardplayer would be cut to ribbons in an exurban bridge game.

On the positive side, there are such activities as the school system, the community, local politics, welfare work, and sports.

The school system, because it is exurban, is in process of growth and change at all times. This means there is always something for an unhappy exurban wife to do. Husbands are infrequently involved in PTA meetings, but the wives find them a fine outlet. If, occasionally, they can involve a husband or two in committee work, so much the better, but with or without husbands the wives can spend an heroic number of woman-hours in one phase or another of school life. There are charity bazaars, there are surveys to be taken of new schools, there are battles to be waged against the township's politicians, there are psychologists to be interviewed and hired, there are schools to be planned and built, and so on and on. Husbands with special talents are often impressed into service in these various campaigns, but it is the wives who do the day-to-day work. (When they can, they see to it that their own husbands are not shanghaied. It saves recrimination and arguments, and it's an opportunity for a new face or two.)

And the community has problems, as well. Sometimes these wives don't understand how an ancient village has been able to struggle along with its inadequate sanitation or sewage system. It seems to them that it has required their particular public-spirited efforts to rid the river of the rats that infest it, or to

solve whatever the problem may be. There are free libraries to
build in New City, there are plots of land to be surveyed for
new schools in Chappaqua, there are town meetings to attend at
Westport, where tax rates are to be discussed; and these women
will see that the jobs are done.

Once again, a disclaimer must be entered. There is no question
but that many of the wives who are eager to rid the Saugatuck
of rats, or to build free libraries in Rockland County, or to elect
their candidates as a result of Jamborees in Greens Farms, or to
organize new schools in Chappaqua, or hire full-time psychologists for the public school in Pleasantville, are quite happy and
happily mated.

Welfare work offers the exurban wife with altruistic motives
and time on her hands a fine opportunity to do good among the
community's unfortunates. Being a Grey Lady for hospital aid,
doing social service and counseling work (even to merely manning
the mimeograph or licking stamps), can be very satisfying. In
Chappaqua, the problem of juvenile delinquency in Westchester
has been courageously approached from a long-term and novel
direction: a sensible and systematized—and adequately financed—
adoption service has been launched, which will find children for
the childless and homes for those children who might otherwise
be brought up under undesirable conditions. This is an almost
exclusively exurban enterprise.

But welfare work is not restricted to the altruistic. Here is a
rich field for the unhappy and socially insecure woman who
wants an outlet. For it not only provides her with something
above reproach to do, it also gives her an opportunity to witness
the distress of others and to derive therefrom a certain degree
of comfort. Added icing is the envy and admiration she is accorded by those materially less fortunate.

Of course, the major outside activity open to unhappy exurban
women is the social whirl. Social whirlers are of two kinds, the
ones who concentrate on doing a lot of entertaining at home,
and the ones who are gadabouts. Of both, it may be said that
the unhappier ones preponderantly go in for daytime formalized

socializing, especially with other women. These are more prevalent on the North Shore and in northern Westchester. In these exurbs, too, we find the formal party givers. In other exurbs, the whirlers tend to prefer big and frequent parties which are informal in atmosphere but for which a lot of preparation is required. But for the unhappy women of Exurbia, the point of all the whirling, of every variety, is, of course, not to think, not to brood, not to be lonely.

We have glanced briefly at the kinds of outside activity available in Exurbia for the frustrated and unhappy homemaker. If she does not find surcease in these, or in her home, her children, her bottle of firewater, she still has an alternative.

Exurban wives who feel their marriages are meaningless and empty, or sense that their husbands are unfaithful, can always seek solace in the same fashion. And if at first they do not find it thus, they can try again.

There are an astonishing number of exurbanites who are prey to the prurient suspicion that exurban wives languish, after their husbands have departed for the city, in the arms of other men. The viper most typically suspected is the non-commuting exurbanite, the "genius," the literary chap or artist who can transform an entire exurb into his personal seraglio. (This notion will cause a bitter smile to curve the lips of some wives.) This being a prevalent male notion in Exurbia, let's see how it squares with what has been determined from the wives themselves, both those who have not resorted to infidelity and those who have.

To discuss the exurban practices of sexual dalliance with one of the wives who for reason of temperament has chosen any one of the other available emotional outlets is an illuminating experience. Most of them flatly do not believe such dalliance is a practicable matter. (They may add that they wish it were; they may disingenuously inquire as to possible methods.) They point to the problems posed by gossiping servants, by children with inconveniently timed entrances, by cars parked overtime in driveways, and they insist in consequence that there simply cannot be much infidelity.

But, of course, there is.

It is not the intention here to blueprint a lot of techniques for hurdling the obvious difficulties that confront the exurban wife bent on dalliance. The suspicion exists that she is sufficiently resourceful and undaunted to contrive her own schemes. But perhaps, in view of the stubborn insistence of so many exurban wives that the thing simply cannot be arranged, a scene might be suggested. The four principal characters are Victor and Margot, an exurban couple, and their week-end guests, Fitzroy and Betty, an urban couple. It is a Sunday morning. Margot wishes to be alone with Fitzroy and in fact has been planning for this moment since approximately two weeks ago, when the week-end invitation was first extended. After permitting her husband to dawdle over his second cup of breakfast coffee, for she is anxious that he be in no particular hurry, she says:

"Say, Vic . . ."

"Mnn?"

"Be a woolly lamb. Drive down and get the Sunday paper."

"Ah, the hell with the Sunday paper, we can pick it up when we go to the beach."

"Vic. I want to read it, and I'm sure Fitz and Betty started missing it as soon as they got up. Didn't you, Fitz?"

"Hmmm? Oh, sure."

"Margot, look, it'll take me at least twenty minutes to drive all the way to Westport" (or Pound Ridge, or Syosset, or New City, or New Hope) "—closer to half an hour, and I'm not sure how much gas we have anyway—"

"That's something else you can do. Buy gas. Go on, dear, don't argue all morning over a simple thing like the Sunday paper. Take Betty with you. The countryside is beautiful this time of year, Betty. . . ."

"Okay, okay, okay. You want to come too, Fitz? Come on."

"No, let Fitz stay with me. We'll talk about you, and you can talk about us."

Say twenty-five minutes to drive to town, and twenty-five min-

utes to drive back. Add five minutes more to get the gas. Almost an
hour for Margot and Fitz, and who said that the inconveniences
of living so far from a newsstand don't have their compensations?

It may be argued that Margot is living dangerously, that the
other exurban ladies of her kidney who dally in such spots as play-
rooms, beach cabañas, and what not are likewise simply asking to
be caught in flagrante delicto (as, indeed, are also the men involved), and the answer to this is that quite possibly they are
seeking the painfully pleasurable sort of attention, the hullabaloo,
the dramatics that would follow on their being caught. Then too,
if a wife is so caught by a husband who she has good reason
to believe has been equally guilty on one or more prior occasions,
what better way for her to retaliate?

One generalized comment seems warranted. While her partner
may be, and probably is, engaged in something quite casual to
him, accompanied of course by verbal blandishments designed to
persuade her of just the opposite, she is often genuinely caught
up in what she conceives to be the real love of her life. Dis-
mayed by the inadequacies of her marriage, confused and unhappy, angry and often humiliated by the behavior of her husband, she is psychologically prepared for the man who will
skillfully and judiciously apply charm, wit, and seductive behavior.
And, by definition, there are any number of such men in the
exurbs. So, at the beach parties, at the Saturday night parties, on
the long car rides from place to place—on all of which occasions
the couples naturally split up—the first words can be spoken, the
ground first prepared, the first fantasies conjured up, the first
meaningful glance exchanged, the first desperate kiss snatched.
And often, later, when the woman realizes that what was important to her was casual to him, she can cry and then she can
dry her tears and look around again.

But no matter how unhappy the exurban woman may contrive to make herself, no matter how unhappy her husband may
make her, she is not forced to contemplate her plight all the
time, or to spend all her time in trying to escape it. The most

miserable of these wives can count compensatory blessings. She lives, in the first place, amid pleasant surroundings. Her friends are likely to be as companionable as can be found. She is, despite the fact that outgo may consistently exceed income, well off, comfortably well off. And, probably most important, she is usually a busy and able mother.

The exurbs and all exurban life are primarily centered around the children. A couple may have had all sorts of bemused reasons for moving so far from the city, but the wife had one compelling one: her children are out of the city in the country, away from expensive private schools or inferior public schools, with plenty of children just like themselves for companionship. It is for these pleasant surroundings and for the children that the exurban wife will endure the very real discomforts of her life. She will abide the most irrational behavior, the most painful and unsavory burden, the most intolerable husband; stability is her goal. In the pursuit of this goal she has become a remarkably effective mother. Submerged, as much as possible, are her guilts and anxieties. Both she and her husband, being intelligent beyond the average, are acutely sensitive to the pressures and tensions of their life together, and they strive in every way to keep their children apart from them. More of their leisure time is devoted to the children than to anything else. The tennis lesson, the sailing lesson, the dancing school, the dramatic school, the special party, the Little League, in every way their efforts are centered on making for their children a time charged with happiness.

It is as if what they do is a way of saying: Things may have soured for us; we have experienced the pain of remembered wrong and present fear; but we will shield them from all that; they shall escape the white night and the black moment of despair. And so, especially on week ends, especially in the summertime, the parents, in the main, live for their children. So many of them have children by earlier as well as present marriages you can tell by the set of their jaws that they propose to draw the line here. They know that their children will pick up such things as their speech habits and intonations; they hope against hope that their children will not also absorb their tensions and hostilities. They are doing everything within their powers to avoid such an eventuality.

And how do the children fare? It's especially difficult to generalize about them, because they have not so completely submerged their individualities in conforming to a stereotype, despite childhood fads in garb, slang, and TV heroes. Some conclusions can be drawn, however.

Exurban children are children in a limbo world. They are not country kids and they are not city kids. Knowledge of this is usually drawn to their attention in the public schools, where they encounter the children of locals. These "native" children are from a totally different environment. Frequently, they are the children of the host of technicians and tradespeople who service the exurbanites. There is a degree of class tension implicit in this, and it is not eased by the fact that precocious local kids know from grown-up talk which exurban families owe their parents money. Nor is the complete lack of fraternization among the adult exurbanites and locals calculated to endear the children to each other.

The city plays a tenuous but important role in the exurban children's lives. Frequently, they know it as a place where they were born, where Daddy goes to work, where relatives live whom they visit, where they are taken to see the Radio City Christmas tree, the circus, *Peter Pan*, and the Zoo. The city is also where Mummy and Daddy go when they get all dressed up and some other adult comes to spend the night while the parents stay in a hotel. The city is where week-end guests come from. It's where the family money comes from. It's where TV comes from. As they grow older, they will understand that they are irrevocably connected to this place where they do not live.

Exurban children see less of their fathers than native children or city children. This is because most exurban fathers commute, and in consequence frequently leave the house in the morning before the children go to school, and inevitably return home an hour or more later than they would in the city. Conversely, they generally enjoy more of their mothers' company than do city kids, which makes for rather greater dependence on her, and in extreme cases leads to estrangement from him.

The other extreme exists, too: there are children whose life is cycled around the week end, when Dad is suddenly, wonderfully, at home all the time, spoils them, takes them to the toy store on Saturday and spends five times their allowance buying them gifts more suitable to Christmas or birthdays, and plays with them endlessly.

Exurban children, especially the younger ones, are no healthier than city kids of comparable class and background. Their noses run all winter and in summer the exurbs are not so wholesome a place as the summer camps to which the city kids are sent, or the real-country homes some city people rent or own. But it is more than the physical environment which affects their health. The tensions of exurban life and marriage penetrate the child's world in uncountable ways. For some, the end-result is anxious overprotectiveness in their mothers, for others it is distracted neglect, punctuated by oral assurances that "Mummy loves you very, very much, dearest—come give Mummy a big kiss." But a child needs more evidence than this that Mummy hasn't her own concerns uppermost in mind most of the time. Perhaps the most common parental attitude which adversely affects the exurban child is permissiveness. The exurban mother is frequently so permissive that her children have no structured home life to which they can adjust themselves. With no framework on which to lean, or to fight, or to accept, the children often display socially unserviceable modes of behavior, in part out of knowledge that it will, at least, elicit some definite response from mother.

With all this, however, it would be incorrect to assume that exurban children are not happy and generally mentally and physically healthy. No environment has everything; given the conditions of a family life which is financially dependent on the vicissitudes of the rat race as run in the communications world, childhood in Exurbia can be presumed to be the best that is possible in the circumstances; certainly, as exurban parents insist, it is far preferable to what they could provide for their children in the city.

Whether or not the same can be said for the mothers remains an open question. The evidence would suggest a negative answer for a great many of them. These lines have been written about exurban wives and mothers who are, generally speaking, in their thirties and early forties. Their children are, generally speaking, all going to secondary school. What will happen to them when their children have sufficiently grown to attend prep school or college, what will happen to them when this major focus of interest is removed, is sobering to contemplate. There is not much evidence to go on, but what there is of it suggests three principal courses.

Indubitably, a great many exurbanites find, as they mature in years, what urbanites and ruralites do, too: the internal storms abate as the internal fire wanes; the secret dream is wistfully regarded as a youthful fantasy; the limited dream is accepted as being the best possible in this best of all possible worlds. The husband has, by now, found his level on the totem pole, one which is, if he is lucky, comparatively secure. His wife, mightily tired after raising a brood in Exurbia, finds the simplified household chores almost a delight by comparison with the merry-go-round she knew. She gardens more, she cooks delicacies, she finally gets around to the reading she's been promising herself. The couple have achieved that state of mutual dependence and regard which ensues on weathering the hard years together. For the wife, there is a muted contentment.

The second course is less pleasant. It is the one chosen by some women whose marriages have been held together by circumstances rather than through some solid core in the relationship. They try to go back to work. But it is too late: they haven't the recent experience necessary, they're out of touch, they've lost their looks, the youngsters to whom they apply for work are embarrassed by résumés which refer to events long dead. And if they do land a job, they usually find it impossible to integrate themselves. They

are too used to displaying individualities of character and behavior, the pace is too fast, the problems too intricate. It seldom
works.

The last course is, simultaneously, the most cheering and the
saddest. This is the attempt of the wives alone, or with their
husbands, finally to seek a secret dream, whether it be his, hers,
or one long shared. It sometimes works. . . .

10

THE LIMITED DREAM

(A) *All human beings are aware of being perceived and evaluated by others;* (b) *they form an idea of how they are viewed by others;* (c) *they are preoccupied with being viewed favorably;* (d) *they keep checking on their fluctuating value on the interactional "stock market";* (e) *their own image of their selves is thus largely a socially produced and internalized conception.*
— JOSEPH BRAM: *Language and Society*

So far, we've concerned ourselves with an examination of the exurbs and the exurban way of life. The attempt has been to present a composite portrait of the subspecies *in situ,* and some attention has been paid to the motives and emotions which are both cause and effect of the exurban phenomenon.

But if this is to be a portrait in depth, we must probe and analyze the wellsprings of exurban behavior, we must get inside our specimen and rummage through his psyche, looking for those manifestations which distinguish him from his urban, rural, and suburban fellows.

Let's visit him at home in Exurbia on a weekday morning not

long ago. He was alone and in bed. His wife had gone shopping, his kids were at school, and he was not at work because he'd been physically unable to get up when the alarm went off at six forty-five. He was stiffened straight by back trouble, which had been plaguing him increasingly in recent weeks.

His ailment might, he knew, have any of several names, ranging from sciatica and arthritis to slipped disc, but he rather suspected, knowing himself fairly well, that it was psychosomatic. (There had been rumors, in his agency, that the client was going to slash appropriations on the account to which he was indentured.) This realization had not, however, lessened his discomfort, so, after a fruitless best-out-of-three falls with a chiropractor, he'd taken his troubles to his physician. This man x-rayed him but, as in the celebrated case of Dizzy Dean's head, found nothing. He was not privy to the status of his patient's advertising account, but he did know enough about his exurban patients in general to decide that nothing he would be able to do would cure the aching back. He was able to prescribe only a palliative.

On the day in question, our man finally struggled out of bed and, pursuant to his doctor's instructions, called a local mattress company. He was put through to a woman whose voice on the telephone seemed to him warm and sympathetic. It summoned up, for him, a picture of a woman with a broad, comfortable, maternal bosom, a woman in whom he might confide. As she spoke, she seemed almost to lean toward him on the phone. The conversation ran something like this:

HE: I'm calling, er—would you happen to make such a thing at your factory as a two-inch hair mattress?

SHE: Oh, you're from Westport, aren't you?

HE (startled): What's that?

SHE: Why, bless you, I can always tell. We get *all* kinds of calls for hair mattresses from Westport. Or Weston. But no one stays on 'em for more'n three or four days. They get bedsores from 'em. I'll *sell* you one, if you insist, but you'll be far better off on a one-inch foam rubber. *With* a bed-board, of course.

HE: You mean this sort of request is—usual?

SHE: You've no idea! Now then, you just tell me how you want it. You sleep single or double?

HE *(growing fascinated)*: Well, as a matter of fact, that's one of my problems. *(Hastily)* How to get, I mean, this kind of a mattress for a double bed. But this is all old stuff to you?

SHE *(seemingly to lean even closer, on the phone)*: Well, now. If you're planning to *live* with a foam mattress for a while, then what you do is, you buy a double bed with a divided mattress. We sell dozens like that.

The exurbanite told her, after hearing the price of a double bed with divided mattress, that he would think it over. He was still thinking it over when, as it happened, his client came through with a handsome appropriation, and the ache in his back cleared up appreciably. But he was still astonished by his experience, by what he had learned on the phone; astonished, and a trifle displeased, too. In the first place, it puzzled him to learn there were so many calls from the Westport-Weston area for such items. Dozens! How could it be? He knew that *he* was inclined to take out on himself his emotional anxieties, but he had always rather supposed that his fellows in the advertising and communications industries were a lot of unfeeling, cynical slobs, who made jokes about ulcers, for example, but in fact rarely experienced them. So he was displeased, because he had always imagined himself to be more sensitive than the run-of-the-mill, more—well, not artistic, exactly, but—well, he knew more. Felt things more. Took them more seriously. He saw himself as an introvert among extroverts. (This is an exurban trait.) To find that he was one of many disturbed him. He took to eyeing his companions on the 8:12 sharply. They seemed as jocular, as affable, as easygoing and full of jokes as ever. But were they?

The Exurban Belt is, in all probability, not, despite the attitude of the woman at the mattress company, also the Psychosomatic Belt. These ailments obtain among us all, respecting neither economic status, geographical residence, or walk of life. Nor is there

available any body of statistics that would inform as to the percentage incidence of these ailments, so it can't be contended
that exurbanites as a group are more often victimized by them
than are the rest of us.

Moreover, it can't be denied that there are some exurbanites
who are as emotionally adjusted as anybody living during this
Age of Anxiety can be. Without presuming to lift a moral eyebrow or sniff an intellectually snobbish nostril at him, let's pre-
sume the existence of a man the summit of whose youthful ambitions was to go to Yale and, in his senior year, assist modestly
at trouncing Harvard in football. Let us imagine that, thereafter,
the limits of his achievement horizon widened to include nothing
further than a job selling advertising for a national magazine, the
ability to play golf in the low eighties, a wife, two children, and
a $40,000 home approximately fifty miles from New York City,
together with all the perquisites. This much, and absolutely
nothing more. Human beings are various, if they are nothing else,
so it does not seem to require total suspension of belief to
imagine the existence of such a man. This man, if such there be,
is tolerably happy. His chances of remaining so are excellent,
unless his adjustment is so splendid as to attract the notice of the
board of directors of his publication, and lead them to promote
him beyond the limits of his aspiration; make him publisher, perhaps, and thereupon plunge him into the depths of gloom and
despair. Success, in Exurbia, has a nasty habit of betraying even
those who do not venerate her as bitch-goddess.

Other emotionally adjusted exurbanites are occasionally encountered. For instance, there are editors of magazines who do
their very considerable best to maintain high standards of prose
and veracity in the publications for which they work, and who
(often correctly) consider that such work is important, significant, difficult, and moreover justifies their efforts. If you spy such
a man and detect extreme internal tension, you may not be
justified in assuming that secretly he may consider he is a better
writer than any of those whose work he edits so brilliantly. It
may derive from some other conflict, or merely from overwork.

There are, in addition, a rollicking few who have so successfully forgotten their juvenile aspirations, so admirably reconciled themselves to excelling in their limited fields of achievement as to warrant their inclusion in any category of the emotionally healthy. And there are those supremely healthy exurban paragons whose aspirations and achievements are in perfect harmony. Not many, perhaps, but a significant few: a man over here whose photographic work is so superb as to require inclusion in *Camera 1955* even though his subject matter is a commercial glass of beer; a man over there whose facility for writing comedy lines and concocting comedy situations has brought him to the attention of the best television comics, despite the fact that he never aspired any higher than he-she jokes for the Stanford *Chaparral;* here a first-rate cartoonist, there a book publisher wedded to the notion that his firm is pandering to no book club.

But if it cannot be said that the exurbanites have a lock on psychosomatic ailments, if it is admitted that a few exurbanites are reasonably well adjusted, it must still be insisted that for the majority things are not good. Their emotional condition suggests that they have been at special, unique pains to snarl themselves up. Some attain spectacular heights of maladjustment. And most have gone about entrapping themselves in characteristically exurban ways.

A physician with many exurban patients states that he has noticed, among a remarkably high percentage of those who are commuters, what he terms "extreme rigidity" and a notable head of steam built up and (mostly) kept under pressure which he defines as repressed hostility. He does not claim to be able to say why they are rigid, or against whom their hostilities are directed. But because he is aware of the tensions and insecurities of the advertising and communications world, it is not difficult for him to arrive, at least, at an informed guess.

As to the somatic ills that these psychic conflicts engender, he has observed, most often: hay fever, hives, bursitis, sinusitis, vasomotor rhinitis, hypertension, low back pain, and chronic fatigue.

The broad areas of vexation, unique and characteristic of the

exurbanite, that will in time erupt in these or more serious ailments, sometimes foreshadow their existence even before the
individual has made the move from town by which he becomes
an exurbanite.

To see what this means in concrete terms, let's consider the
case history of the boss for whom the man with the back ache
works. The boss is an older man who for years resisted with tolerant cynicism the attempts of exurbanites in his office to proselytize
him into moving out of the city. But in 1949, to his own and his
colleagues' surprise, he made the metamorphosis so speedily that
it had about it the explosive quality of the bursting of an egg
by the chick within; so quickly, in fact, that his story presents
a dramatic example in brief of the hidden foreshadowings mentioned above.

This man is a copy chief in a top agency. In the course of
routine, he had been engrossed in the supervision of plans for four
national campaigns. The products involved were various, but the
theme of each was similar, and rang changes on an American
way-of-life deemed ideal and typical (on Madison Avenue these
adjectives are not frequently regarded as contradictory). One layout showed a man, pleasingly grizzled about the temples, his
teeth clenching a pipe, crouched down near a flower-border, his
gloved hands doing something with a trowel. In the picture, the
hour was just before twilight, and the scene shouted of serenity
and peace. Another showed an attractive woman in her kitchen.
Sunlight streamed in through a window, lighting up a window-
box full of kitchen herbs. She was obviously humming, as she
put up some preserves; and a smile dimpled her cheeks as, looking
out the window, she could see her young disporting among some
fruit trees in the middle distance. A third had been peopled with
attractive youngsters gathered around a gleaming convertible,
watching a tennis-match in a country club atmosphere. The copy
chief, as he had okayed each of these layouts, had felt a sharp
pang of—what? Envy? Impossible. Nostalgia? To be sure, some
exurbanites have a highly developed talent for remembering events
that have never occurred, but this man, soon to be an exurbanite,

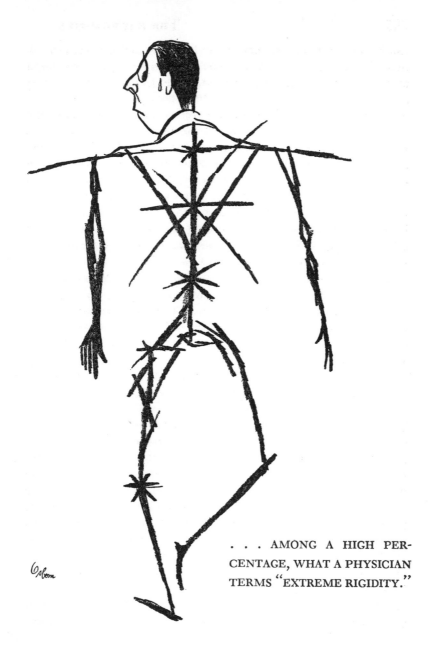

. . . AMONG A HIGH PER-
CENTAGE, WHAT A PHYSICIAN
TERMS "EXTREME RIGIDITY."

would have hotly denied that his youth had been spent attractively draped over a convertible. Still, the pictures worked in his mind, as he rode in a cab to his apartment in the East Seventies.

It was a pleasant apartment, spacious, tastefully decorated, comfortable, and he and his wife had been happy there, perhaps even happier since the kids had gone away to boarding-school. But that night at dinner he sat morose, discouraging conversation, nursing his discontent, drinking highballs that mingled uncertainly with his earlier martinis. After dinner he prowled about, restively. His wife, heedful, decided not to put aside her *Vogue* and sat, her eyes blank on the page and her attention focused on her husband. She could hear him slamming doors and drawers in the kitchen. Presently he came back, his fourth highball in his hand. He had arrived at the moment of alcoholically induced, clearsighted depression in which he was at his most tangential.

"There're no herbs in the window-box," he said.

She might have pointed out that, in the absence of a windowbox, this was pardonable, but instead she hooded her eyes. "The Bakers asked us over, if we weren't doing anything," she said. "To play some bridge."

"They have no roots either," he snarled. "We haven't any of us got any goddam' roots! No wonder our kids are never at home!"

In recapitulating the scene later, the wife admitted to a friend that she had been worried. She knew that he had had a lot to drink, but was not satisfied that this was the whole answer for his behavior. She had begun to fear that his work had got him at last. Even while she was gently reminding him that he could scarcely expect their children to be anywhere but in boarding-school, her mind was busily at work, as in a game of jackstraws, trying to grasp the trivial and unconnected, hoping the whole structure would not collapse. "Well," she said, nervously, perceptively, "if it's roots you want, we can go look for some tomorrow. In the country, maybe. Is that what you want to do? Move to the country?"

Now, as a matter of fact, this man's mind had been so filled with media requirements, full-color bleeds, and display type-faces that he hadn't been able to crystallize his discontent nor had he tried to imagine a simple formula for alleviating it. Only when his wife spoke did he realize how beautifully simple a solution existed—and it was not until several years had passed that he understood that at that fateful moment he had finally completed the tortuous process of selling himself a bill of dubious goods by means of his own advertisements. At the time, however, he and his wife spent the rest of the evening examining real estate ads in the tonier magazines; the next week end they drove out to inspect some properties in various parts of Exurbia; within the month they were settled in Chappaqua; and they have not been happy since.

This case history is illustrative of how a man's self-concept begins to warp. One's self-concept is the total of one's beliefs and impressions concerning oneself. The degree to which the self-concept coincides with reality is one measure of normal adjustment and sanity. As long as this man realized that he was an urban creature who often delighted in the rush and bustle and sense of excitement and power and importance that come with being a busy, successful metropolitan executive, he could be comparatively happy. His days were adequately fruitful and his nights were New York nights. Neither noise nor heat could bother him; he moved from one air-conditioned, soundproofed place to another. He went to fashionable plays, read most fashionable books, appeared at many fashionable cocktail parties, worked reasonably hard, and usually slept soundly. His wife enjoyed the New York shops and had a small circle of good friends who, like herself, took pleasure in lunching in the fashionable restaurants, had servants who did for them, and considered the country was a place like Easthampton, where summer months were spent, or Bent Flower, Iowa, whence (they only occasionally recall) they fled to the city as soon after childhood as they could. Self-fact and self-fancy for both man and wife meshed like a well-behaved set of gears. To change their way of life into the kind portrayed on the covers of the *Saturday Evening Post* was, on the face of it, ridiculous, but it was foreordained from the moment when the man's self-concept began to shift, conjuring up bemused pictures of his wife putting up preserves made from home-grown fruit, and of himself, green-thumbed, whistling cheerily as he pruned hydrangeas or whatever. The poor man has even taken up smoking a pipe.

And yet, comparatively miserable though he now is, there was a dismaying logic that led to the eventual collision of his self-fact and his self-fancy, the kind of logic that ever lies in wait to ensnare the exurbanite. For the fact is, he *had* no roots, in the city. It is debatable, at best, whether he will ever put down roots in his exurb, but certainly he had none in New York. And he was bound to feel this the more keenly, working as he was in a profession which is itself so rootless, so insecure, so transitory.

Such a sense of rootlessness seems to be a hallmark of those who deal only in symbols, rather than in tangible things, and whose yearning to be like, or even of, the audience, the great population of thing-manipulators, carries them inevitably to the exurbanite ambivalence: they attempt to live like normal, everyday (but well-heeled) thing-manipulators. This is behind their move to the country, and it is behind one aspect of the way they live when they get there. It helps to explain some of the regional stigmata: they may have no herd of milk-cattle, but that does not keep them from building the split-rail fence; if one can put down roots by buying the physical accoutrements of traditional country life, then open a charge account at the accoutrement store, at once.

Once in the country, they plunge compulsively into country life, and as actively as their age permits. One exurbanite will buy a jeep and a tractor and address himself to Project Firewood: clearing a considerable acreage of stubborn second-growth scrub, and amassing for himself, in the process, enough low-grade firewood to last three lifetimes.

The do-it-yourself movement owes much to the exurbanites. They may be, and often are, on the lowest level of competence when it comes to hammering or sawing or even changing a typewriter ribbon; but they are in there trying, after buying toolshops

"THEY HAVE NO ROOTS EITHER
. . . WE HAVEN'T ANY OF US
ANY GODDAM' ROOTS! NO
WONDER OUR KIDS ARE NEVER
AT HOME!"

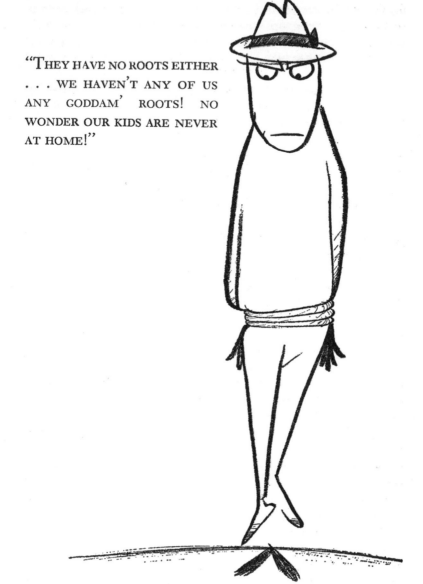

full of electric hedge-trimmers, power saws, and roto-tillers. In some cases, their wives have bought looms, and do-it-themselves to make ragged-hem homespun curtains.

The exurbanites—and especially the younger ones—cheerfully accept the imposing physical challenges of this self-contrived conflict for an important reason: it is a kind of calculated risk in the attainment of the limited dream. And there is no doubt about the fact that preparing the limited dream, setting the stage for the living out of it, is for many exurbanites a very happy time indeed. The buying, the planning with spouse for the new addition, the new bathroom, the turning of attic into kids' playroom, the making of a lawn into a cutting garden, even the frantic budgeting are fun of a kind. They are fun, and they are delightfully, cozily diversionary, providing better than a game of bridge such a potent focus for attention and such incentive for partnership in action that no time or thought is open for the onslaughts of the outside world. This is playing house for real. This is Christmas Eve and Christmas morning all the time, with new lists to make, new goodies to buy and then unwrap and try out—and show off to the other kids in the neighborhood. It's an autoerotic kind of Christmas in which one gifts oneself.

If you've ever seen little girls at work on a rainy Sunday afternoon, setting up a doll house, if you've observed the concentrated attention with which they labor, you'll have some idea of the absorption which grips new exurbanites caught up in the creation of the scene for the limited dream. However, a better and less happy analogy is to be found in two boys at play. Watch them while they open a box of electric trains. They set up an intricate track pattern. That's fun! They connect the transformer, they set up the train itself, they dispose the accessories, a bridge here, a tunnel there, a Dinky Toy convoy of trucks waiting at the crossing, a model village. Then comes the time when it's all set up, when the train has run the course a dozen times, when there's nothing new to do. Or isn't there? What about that truck convoy at the crossing? Maybe stage an accident? Maybe arrange a collision? A derailment? A fire in one of the houses? An enemy attack (that's it!) using pencils shot from popguns!

There are exurbanites who play house all their lives. There are those who can afford to keep adding new toys to their hoard. Some mature—if that's the word—into a quiet acceptance of the limited dream. Others keep it hazy and beckoning with liberal applications of alcohol. Most, however—for exurbanites are pretty perceptive on the whole—ruefully accept it for what it is, and when they do that you may be sure the secret dream is coming into its own.

The secret dream is so widespread that it may be considered symptomatic. It is treasured, cherished, and comes out only in moments of greatest confidence. Typically, at a Saturday or Sunday night party, when one group of males is watching a fight on television, another group of males is exchanging feelers about shifts in agency jobs, a third is listening to a dirty joke, and the members of a fourth are cautiously stalking extra-marital prey, there may be two men, both in their cups, sitting, withdrawn, talking quietly. Chances are they are exchanging secret dreams.

The secret dream has for its invariable keystone some sort of financial independence. One exurbanite will tell you of an inn up in Maine that he happens to know about. Not too big, his wife and he could run it themselves, easily. There's a school near by, for their kids; there's a ski-jump, within an easy drive, for the winter's paying guests; it's near the seashore, and right on a lake. Perfect deal. Doesn't cost too much, either. You ask him when he's going to snap it up.

"I could have had it a couple of years ago."

"Why didn't you take it?"

"Well, I got this offer of a job"—he was recently made assistant advertising director for a snob monthly magazine—"and it was too attractive to turn down."

"But, meantime, you're keeping the dough all ready, hmm?"

"Well, as a matter of fact—"

And it turns out he had to use *that* money to buy a bigger place, to go with the job. But his eye is still on the dream. He married well, and his wife's father won't live forever. And then, and then . . .

Another exurbanite, who has specialized in making documentary films, cherishes the scheme of opening up a health farm. He doesn't believe it will be hard to find the capital to get started: his relations with industrial clients have convinced him there are a slew of companies with money they are reluctant to pay the government in taxes who will back him in order to have available a Shangri-la for their tired executives. He refers to this as "preventive medicine," and is looking for a doctor to act as titular head ("It'll look better that way"). Prospective fee: $100 a day per tired executive.

Another, this one a man who already has his own documentary film studio, says he would sell the whole thing tomorrow, pile his equipment into a seaworthy schooner, and just sail around the world, making films about interesting people and places. "None of your Burton Holmes or Fitzpatrick 'and-now-as-we-sail-off-into-the-sunset-we-take-leave-of-beautiful-Hawaii' stuff," this man insisted, in holding out his dream, in his cupped hands, for inspection. "This would be real honest-to-God anthropological stuff. You know. How people live. What they think. How they go to bed, how often, and with whom. Scientific. There's just this one thing." (There usually is.) "I need an expert linguist. You know some guy can speak about twelve different languages, wants to go around the world for three or four years?"

The secret dream was described as symptomatic, and this is why: the dream is almost never realized, largely because *it is designed only to be a dream*. It is a means to an end but not an end in itself. And the end is not its attainment. The end, the thing which is desired, is a safety valve for the head of steam described by the exurban doctor as "repressed hostility." All the dreamers are hostile toward, harbor aggressive, even murderous, thoughts about whoever it is on whom they depend (the boss, the client, the copy chief, the casting director, the star of the show, the comic, the advertising manager, whoever). The dream is a way to spite the man. ("Then I'll tell him off! And when I'm gone, he'll see how much he needed me!")

For the exurbanite who is in the business end of the communications industry, the secret dream is usually one of owning his own business; for the exurbanite who is in the creative end, the dream is more complicated, and will be discussed in greater detail below. But among both groups are men who have discovered or are in process of discovering that for them the limited dream is a delusion, that, far from helping them escape the rat race, it has merely plunged them deeper into it, and into a mire of petty frustrations which are cumulative in their effect, and wreak havoc with the psychic apparatus. If the disillusioned exurbanite is a humorist, like Perelman or Kaufman-and-Hart, he can sometimes turn his miseries to good account, but not many exurbanites are conscious humorists.

Most of them just worry, God knows they worry, and quite often, to keep from crying, they make nervous jokes about what is wrong with them. Because they are conversant with the jargon, they borrow psychiatric terms, bending them to their own uses. You can hear the knowledgeable talk (on commuters' trains, or more especially at cocktail parties throughout Exurbia) about how the exurbanite is victimized by traumatic ruralism, or urban *Abklingen* (the fading out of the memory of the city), or cultural acroanesthesia (decreased sensitivity to cultural or intellectual pursuits), or coenotropism (a form of behavior common to a species or group). It is clear that some exurbanites have more than a touch of abulia (inability to make up their minds), and alloeroticism (erotic tendencies directed toward others), and perhaps especially contrectation (the impulse to touch members of the opposite sex indiscriminately); just as it is evident that more than a few suffer from aphanisis (fear of loss of power of experiencing sexual pleasure).

Meantime, they joke with each other, obedient to the group precept that one must take his troubles lightly; and one may remind another of Thurber's "varieties of obliquity," in turn quoted from David Seabury, the list comprising Cursory Enumeration, Distortion of Focus, Nervous Hesitation (superinduced by Ambivalence), Pseudo-practicality, Divergency, Retardation, Emotionalized Compilation, Negative Dramatization, Rigidism, Secondary Adaptation, False Externalization, Non-validation, Closure, and Circular Brooding.

But joking of this kind only provides a rather apprehensive compensation. An increasing number of exurbanites, to judge from many conversations, experience anger and fear, in that order, at what they recognize to be the failure of their limited dream, at what some even consider its betrayal of them.

Can they do anything to escape from its trap? After all, most of them are married (at least once); most of them are fathers (at least once). To these responsibilities they must add, as exurbanites, other obligations: notably a mortgaged house, and, perhaps even more important, the increased consumption of luxury items in response to the constant challenge of their peer-group (the group, as David Riesman defines it, of one's associates of the same age and class*).

There can be no overestimating the importance to most exurbanites of the judgment of their peers. Such judgment is in fact a tyrant. But the New York exurbanite's class analogue in, say, Evanston or Santa Barbara or Sewickley is let off relatively easily by the tyranny of his peer-group, which demands of him little more than that he should keep up with the Joneses in the traditional spirit. For the New York exurbanite, the demand is that he shall keep in step with his peers by staying ahead of the Joneses. Such a task imposes something of a financial burden, and something more of a social burden. Mr. Riesman, in writing of the function of the peer-group as regulator of habits of consumption, pictures it as standing "midway between the individual and the messages which flow from the mass media. The mass

---

* In *The Lonely Crowd*. Some of Mr. Riesman's observations, especially as he is concerned with the type he describes as *other-directed* ("a social character whose conformity is insured by [its] tendency to be sensitized to the expectations and preferences of others") seem apposite to the exurbanite.

media are the wholesalers; the peer-groups, the retailers of the communications industry . . ."

But, as has been shown, in the case of the exurbanite's peer-group, it is, so to say, a Wholesalers' Malevolent Association, and to maintain membership and good standing in the association is of paramount importance. This in turn entails fighting to preserve the status quo; in short, hanging on for dear life to one's ersatz roots in the exurbs, at no matter what expense to bank account and psychic needs. A few hardy souls have sold out, and returned to the city, but these are deemed eccentrics. One such found the limited dream so intolerable that in shucking it off he divested himself of his wife—whom he'd married in the city and immured in the exurbs, and then proceeded to make a surrogate target for the hostilities he felt toward all people and things in the limited dream he'd created—as well as of the other impedimenta he'd acquired in its building. Currently, though he's unaware of it and would deny it hotly, he's searching for another urban bride so that he can repeat the experience in the fondly foolish expectation that this time it will be different. Chances are it won't; for him, as for the majority of exurbanites, the limited dream is a booby trap with a built-in fuse set to go off the moment it's firmly embraced.

In the average exurbanite's personal equation there is one constant: his insecurity; one steadily growing value: his obligations; one steadily diminishing factor: time.

Mention of the habit time has of running out calls to mind those exurbanites who toil in the creative wing of the communications factory, and whose secret dream, as was suggested, warrants special scrutiny. (The word "creative," as used here, is intended to connote the radio or television or movie writer, occasionally the advertising copy writer, and, sinking lower in the social scale, the writer of comic strips; the commercial artist and illustrator, the commercial photographer, the decorator of Fifth Avenue windows for the smart specialty shops; the editorial employees of national magazines; some few radio and television directors; and some few composers of musical bridges for the entertainments on those media. For simplicity's sake, the creative exurbanite will be here-after referred to as a writer, but there is no reason to believe the same statements could not be, with equal accuracy, applied to the directors, the musicians, the artists.)

The creative exurbanite, in the likely instance, differs from his confrere on the business side of the industry by having had, as a youngster, vaulting ambition. He was going to set not only the Thames but the Hudson River and Long Island Sound on fire. He was going to write the Great American Novel. His more com-mercially minded confrere on the business side had only the am-bition of making a more than comfortable living; having achieved it, if he is still unhappy, his misery is conceivably not so great as that of the creative exurbanite, whose aspiration was so much higher. For such a man, the secret dream is essentially one of a return to honesty, artistic discipline, and artistic dedication. It is symbolized by the novel-in-the-drawer (or symphony, or painting).

There is no counting the number of these novels-in-the-drawer, but they surely mount up into the dozens, perhaps into the hun-dreds. It is, of course, quite possible that, by virtue of their re-maining in the drawer, we are all being spared the tedious task of scanning much bad writing (or painting, or composing), al-though it should be stressed that the competence of exurban commercial work is high. But, here, that is not the point. Here we are considering the plight of the creative exurbanite.

You will hear an exurban radio or television writer tell you that he is a good writer, even that he is a very good writer; most writers need to believe, in order to keep at their work, that they are (at least potentially) among the greatest writers in the world today, perhaps of all time. Sometimes, wryly, he will self-dep-recate, and cut his superlative down to some such comment as: "I'm the best goddam' eclectic writer in America," or "I'm the best second-rate writer in America." But whether or not he denigrates himself, in his heart of hearts he believes that, given only the time and the release from pressure, he could take the novel out of the drawer, finish it, and make it great. This is his secret dream.

But he is, usually, intelligent, perceptive, and knowledgeable. He is conversant with Freudian writings, to the point where he has at least limited insight into himself. And the tragic thing is that he is aware of his self-betrayal, which is a more forthright way of saying his betrayal by the limited dream he created. He knows that he has been seduced ("I may be a whore, but goddam' it, I'm a $100-a-night call girl, not just some Eighth Avenue hooker") by money, and that if he is lucky, if his back remains strong, if he is not blacklisted, the money will get bigger. He hopes it will get bigger, for most assuredly his living standard is getting more exacting. If he is honest with himself, at some point, however, and this is a black moment in his life, he arrives at the realization that he will never finish the novel-in-the-drawer, that by imperceptible stages which he blames on unavoidable circumstance, his own lack of planning and foresight (or bad luck, or youthful ignorance), he is now in the position of renting his brains out by the day, using up his creativity on the installment plan, and being so engulfed by the demands of keeping his limited dream going that there's no turning back. It is our task, though, to look deeper than he himself can or will.

A hypothesis which bears up nicely under some fairly searching scrutiny is that there was a significant degree of design in the steps which led him to his present plight, that in some layer of his psyche, hidden from his consciousness, a goodly jolt of creative energy went into shaping his path and into selecting which of alternative paths to follow when they presented themselves, as they no longer seem to do. Rightly or wrongly, according to this hypothesis, he hadn't the faith it takes to be a serious writer (assuming he had everything else) or the courage to face the test of his ability; or, possibly—and this is not so far-fetched as it may sound—some ancient guilt rooted in childhood, or some ancient failure or punishment or fear of punishment, made him flee from the danger of creative fulfillment.

But psychological explanations aside, and quite simply, the central fact one can report about him is that, whatever the reason, our creative exurbanite is not now nor will he ever be a serious writer. For one infallible test of a serious writer is this: he does everything in his power to avoid beginning his work, fights it, hides it away from him, tries to forget it—but in the end, to throw the incubus off his back, he invariably finishes it. With the creative exurbanite, the case is quite different. He experiences little difficulty in beginning his novel. He will talk freely about it. He also daydreams about it, turning over in his mind the various shapely phrases he will use in it. But, just as invariably, he never finishes it.

Here is a splendid case in point of the subtle way in which the self concept can deviate from reality while seeming to coincide with it. Our man most assuredly wants to be a writer. His fantasies include every step in the process: he's seated at his typewriter, feverishly, brilliantly, pounding away. It's almost dawn and he's been at it since the previous noon. His wife worries but knows better than to interrupt while the creative river flows strong. Another picture: he's sitting on the terrace, going over galley proofs. Neighbors stop by to ask him to play tennis, but he refuses and they understand. Old Jim—he's not really so old, just seems so because he's an agency wage slave—shakes his head with rueful admiration. "How do you do it, boy? Wish I had your drive (or talent, or ambition)." We dissolve now to a long shot of a book-and-author luncheon; the camera dollies in to a medium shot of the speakers' table and we discover our author seated on the dais. Cut to a three-shot, Albert Schweitzer left, author center, Irita Van Doren right. The dialogue writes itself, doesn't it?—but be sure to keep the author's lines modest. And, fellers, milk this scene for all its worth, it's one of the best—although the autographing party is pretty good, too.

Yes, our creative exurbanite wants to be a writer—but he doesn't want to write. You couldn't get a man who looked and acted and lived the part of writer better if you spent the rest of your life going through the files of Central Casting, but, of course, creative writers aren't listed there. The self concept, thus, makes the starting of a novel an easy matter for the creative exurbanite; then, along come the realities and the abortive start goes into the desk drawer.

The moment of his awareness that he will never finish it, the moment of recognition that he is kidding himself, that his time has run out, that he is corrupt and corrupting, varies according to the individual, and there are quite possibly some for whom this moment, mercifully, never arrives. Similarly, there are various compensatory reactions, depending on the individual. The most important of these reactions number three. Before reviewing them, a legitimate question is: What makes the creative exurbanite who has become corrupt any different from, say, the same sort of man still living in Manhattan or, for that matter, in Hohokus, N. J.? The answer lies in a matter of degree. A radio or television writer, an advertising copy writer, or any other of the various creative toilers in the communications industry, who lives in Greenwich Village has, by definition, a more reasonable living standard, and more time on his hands. The creative exurbanite has his dilemma thrust more sharply upon him: the appearances he must maintain load on him a constant financial onus: having decided to sell his wares on the commercial side of the street, he must continue to do so, and the pressure on him will be to increase, rather than decrease, his commitment to commercialism.

This consideration is of importance, in surveying the three principal reactions to his growing awareness of his self-betrayal.

Those in the first group so contrive their lives as to hide from themselves, as thoroughly as possible. These exurbanites are the ones who drink too much, or who have recourse to compulsive physical exercise. They garden, they play tennis, they ride, they sail, they swim: they are outside doing something physical at every opportunity, so that they may exhaust themselves to the point where they cannot think about their plight. Parenthetically, they also exhaust themselves so that they cannot be fit sexual partners for their wives, and the psychoanalyst does not live who has not been at pains to point out the similarity between the creative sexual urge and the creative artistic urge. The exurban woods are full of examples of this type; one that occurs out-of-hand is the copy writer whose individual technique of hiding from himself is his refusal to read any novel written by a man (or woman) who was, according to the book jacket, born more recently than himself.

Those in the second group become cynical. Not only do they admit their corruption, they glory in it, they wallow in it. They claim any other attitude is juvenile, and to be equated with youthful political radicalism. They demand of you: "What's the matter? What do you want of a guy? Haven't I got what I want? I've got a home, haven't I? It's a good home, isn't it? Home! It's a fornicating manor! Are you making my kind of dough? Get wise, doll baby! I do what I do, and I like what I do, and if you had any sense, you'd try and do the same. Listen to me a minute. Don't get the idea I'm unhappy, or frustrated. I know what I want, I've got it, and I'm going to keep on getting it. It's got nothing to do with truth, or beauty, or any of that crap. It's entertainment, by God, and nothing I touch has a rating of less than thirty. Three-oh. Beat that, Jack!" Some of the members of this group can be extremely convincing; they can persuade the listener of their sincerity and their own low estimate of themselves. The results are not in yet, as to the accuracy of their judgments.

It might be argued that the use of words like "corrupt," "corrupting," or "corrupted" to describe the creative exurbanite is too harsh. To listen to the members of this group is to be convinced otherwise. They use it of themselves. It reflects a tendency to overdramatize, to exaggerate, even when it is at one's own expense. It suggests that these exurbanites, when as boys they first heard Franck's D-Minor Symphony, probably stood in front of a mirror, and went through an exaggerated pantomime of conducting the orchestra.

The exurbanites in the third group seek analysis. The success of analysis depends, obviously, on many factors, and any estimate of its effect on the members of this group is purely speculative. It conceivably could come about that, as a result, the creative exurbanite reconciles himself to mediocrity, and resumes, more cheerfully, his appointed post-position in the rat race. It is even possible, if his other commitments are not too onerous, that analysis will lead (or has led) to his opening the drawer, taking the novel out, and getting to work on it. There are, after all, isolated cases of individuals who quit successful commercial jobs, even without such medical assistance, and launched themselves on careers dedicated to art.

One young woman, a $16,000-a-year advertising executive in 1950, left for Europe and returned four years later for a one-man show of the oils she had painted in Italy. It is doubtful that she realized anything close to $16,000 on the sale of her paintings, but she is sure she is a happier person. Psychoanalysis helped her make her move. But there are not many like her. The likelihood is that most of the members of this third group will join those in the other two by assuming the jejune posture of anti-intellectualism.

There is, finally, a tiny splinter group (not necessarily anti-intellectuals) whose members seek help by joining the Catholic faith and praying to Almighty God to aid them, or the Unitarian church and praying To Whom It May Concern, as one atheistic exurbanite put it. But the sand traps and beaches of Exurbia don't tend to send their inhabitants to organized religion in droves, as the slit trenches and beachheads of the fighting front are said to do. More commonly, the urge is to anti-intellectualism.

The rise of the anti-intellectual intellectuals in the exurbs is striking and symptomatic. It is the line of least resistance, the easiest recourse for those who have even partially recognized that the novel is in the drawer to stay. They cannot deny that they are intellectuals, trained to be intellectuals, with intellectual equipment and habits and turn of mind. And yet, for many of them, the term is almost a dirty word. It is as though they had recognized that, while they have the capacity for the higher forms of thought and creativity, they have permitted their gifts to tarnish, or turned them to ends too mean for scrutiny. In addition, in contemporary America, the intellectual is likely to travel a lonely road, but the exurbanite, even if he is creative, has no taste for being alone. He must have the approval of his peers, the approval and even, if possible, the restrained envy. The memory of the shining talent and the recollection of the vaulting youthful ambition must be stored away in a part of the mind's attic where they will never be seen.

In the meantime, his anti-intellectualism forges a bond between the creative exurbanite and his neighbor, the salesman of space or time for the communications business. Together they can scoff at the egghead, as some sort of case of arrested development. Significantly, throughout Exurbia a similar derisive term is used to describe the non-commuting, creative individual who faces his artistic endeavors with some seriousness and sense of discipline. He is called a "genius," and the sneer is usually unmistakable. Sometimes this term, by extension, is used to describe any non-commuting exurbanite, but if your ear is sharply tuned to the fine distinctions, you can identify the gibe when it is directed at the seriously intentioned artist.

We have seen how, for the exurbanite on the business side, the secret dream operates as a safety valve for his repressed hostility. What, then, of the creative exurbanite who is honest enough with himself to have realized that *his* secret dream is a phony? That it will never be attained? In the first place, he seems, by common consent, to be permitted a wider latitude of irrational behavior. His dress may be more eccentric, his drinking harder, his extra-marital sexuality more adventurous. For safety valve he must rely more on the bitter, often savage, humor directed at his own plight. Certainly much of his tension and anxiety and inner malaise will be channeled against those nearest to him, that is to say his immediate family. Stable marriages are difficult enough to maintain, in Exurbia, under the best of circumstances; for the unhappy creative exurbanite who has penetrated to the sham of the limited dream and the unattainability of the secret dream, there is often a desperate search for equivalent values in the attempt to develop and establish a new familial relationship.

But even if there is no divorce, even if the marriage is stable, even if the adjustment is fairly tolerable, even if, in short, the exurbanite appears to be merry and jocular, easygoing and affable, his life has undergone a change. He moved to the exurb to escape the rat race; now, as like as not, he looks forward to the morning train to New York as an escape from the trap which he perceives his limited dream has become. Hide in the exurb from the insecurities of the rat race, hide in New York from the frustrations of the trap; maintain in the city the bravest front possible, as nimble, potent executive, or able, adept creative force; become in the country the relaxed squire or the manorial seigneur. It is difficult to perform both roles, within the space of twenty-four hours. Can he do both well? Can he do either well? He must be quick-change artist. He must be protean. He must be as adaptable as a chameleon.

To return to the exurban physician whose findings were reported at the beginning of this chapter, he has suggested that the only emotionally successful commuters are stable, submarginal schizoids, having to foster a dual personality in order to survive. A second exurban physician, apprised of this judgment, was inclined only to suggest that the more correct term might be that the exurbanite must assume a kind of schizothymia, that is to say, to take on schizoid characteristics within the limits of normality.

These are strong words, and the temptation is to insert a caveat to the effect that they apply not to the generality of exurbanites, but merely to a spectacular handful. And certainly it is true that, maladjusted though many of them may be, they seem to thrive on it, if—for example—income is any test. Perhaps in no other society, in no other social grouping, could success attend so handsomely the efforts of those who are emotionally dislocated.

The typical would seem to be those who lead lives not of quiet desperation but of wilfully frenetic gaiety. They play harder, they plunge themselves into ritualized social rounds of pleasure, they drink, they joke, they do anything and everything to keep from thinking about the dream that is fading and may never be recaptured. They turn to their children with guilt and anxiety, hopeful that at least these hostages to fortune will never have to go through the same.

And not only do they do the best they can at the difficult and exciting job of living, but the job they do is, under the circumstances, often remarkably good.